0252078

KU-793-419

BONGARD, MIKHAIL
PATTERN RECOGNITION
000252078

612.816 B71

WITHDRAWN FROM STOCK

29 JUN 2000

PATTERN RECOGNITION

PATTERN RECOGNITION

M. Bongard

Edited by Joseph K. Hawkins
Robot Research, Inc.
La Jolla, California

Translated by Theodore Cheron
Aeronutronic Division
Philco-Ford Corporation
Newport Beach, California

SPARTAN BOOKS

NEW YORK • WASHINGTON

Copyright © 1970 by Spartan Books

All rights reserved. This book or parts thereof may not be reproduced without
permission from the publisher.

Originally published under the title Problema Uznavaniya
by Nauka Press, Moscow, 1967.

Library of Congress Catalog Card Number 76-80435
ISBN 0-87671-118-2

Printed in the United States of America.

Sole Distributors in Great Britain, the British Commonwealth, and the Continent
of Europe:

Macmillan & Co. Ltd.
4 Little Essex Street
London, W.C. 2

282371

PREFACE

SCIENTIFIC RESEARCHERS HAVE BEEN trying for some time to design devices that could duplicate the ability of man to solve a large variety of problems. The principal difficulty encountered in achieving this aim is the fact that many interesting problems are not presented in a formalized manner. Rather, they are presented by means of examples, or by indicating analogous cases, or by referring to similar problems, etc.

Different names are attached to these devices, such as "recognizing," "undertaking heuristic search," etc. This book is neither a textbook nor a review of other works in this field. It contains primarily the ideas originated among a group of scientists, including M. N. Vaintsvaig, V. V. Maksimov, M. S. Smirnov, and the author.

Making a selection of unformalized recognition problems, whose solution is to serve as the main objective of the investigation, presents many difficulties, only one of which is the design of devices capable of solving recognition problems. Difficulties are also encountered in attempting to determine, even theoretically, whether such devices can be created. Mathematics (to which pattern recognition probably belongs) is in a peculiar situation when experiments provide the only means of proving theorems. This situation is, hopefully, temporary. However, all attempts undertaken so far to formalize the presentation of the pattern recognition problem lead either to substituting for this problem another more primitive problem, or to definitions that are fruitless because of our inability to see clearly certain significant limitations.

A question may arise here: Is it worthwhile to write a book about such an unarranged and undefined subject? The authors think so for two reasons. First, the fact is that general approaches to this problem are appearing more clearly. Second, a great variety of people are now engaged in various aspects of the pattern recognition field. Engineers and psychologists, physicists and doctors, mathematicians and physiologists are finding it necessary to understand and model such brain functions as the ability to "find similarity," "create abstract ideas," "act by intuition," etc. As these investigators become more familiar with the existing background

v

in the field, their efforts will become increasingly valuable and less prone to false starts.

Many ideas in this book are presented more on the level of intuition than on the level of mathematical formalism. In principle, this approach could lead to misunderstanding. To minimize this as much as possible, the reader and author should share approximately the same amount of factual material (on which intuition is based to a great extent). For this purpose, several pattern recognition procedures are given in this book in the form of actual computer programs. Since the point of view of the author on the pattern recognition problem was formulated while dealing with these programs, the reader may be able to share some of the same experiences. Special attention is paid to unsuccessful recognition procedures, represented by specific program blocks, because progress is best made by analyzing the causes of such failures.

In order to give the reader actual material to think about, the author has included a description of a computer program called *Arithmetic*, which embodies his ideas about pattern characteristics, transformations on the receptor field, etc. This program is described in Chapter 3, before presenting a more abstract idea about the imitation of one automaton by another automaton, in Chapter 4, even though the notion of automata imitation is the intuitive basis for the program, in accordance with the logical scheme adopted in this book.

Thus, the order of the chapters does not always reflect the internal structure of the material (if it could be linearly ordered at all at this stage). However, the text contains many references to previous material, facts, and ideas. Therefore, it is better to start reading this book in the order in which it is presented. The exception probably is Chapter 7 regarding useful information which, although it follows Chapters 5 and 6, does not necessarily need to precede Chapter 8. It may be omitted during the reading of the book without prejudice to the understanding of material presented in the following chapters.

It may be of some benefit for readers to familiarize themselves with Appendix 3 after reading Chapter 2. This will give some understanding of the difficulties encountered in pattern recognition problems.

One of the basic aims of the author is to attract the attention of readers to the interrelationships among various aspects of the pattern recognition problem, and to the analogy between the pattern recognition problem and other related subjects. A multitude of such "contact points" arises when various aspects of one and the same question are discussed in several chapters.

L. Dunaevskii, G. M. Zenkin, and A. P. Petrov took part in the preparation of the programs, the experiments with these programs, and also in the psychophysiological tests.

The author is grateful to E. M. Braverman, R. S. Guter, and N. D. Nyuberg for helpful criticism after the reading of the manuscript.

The author was fortunate to be able to discuss the pattern recognition problem with the well-known scientist, M. L. Tsetlin, who always was aware of new trends in science. Just a few days before his untimely death he read the manuscript of this book, and gave many excellent suggestions. Remembrance of this outstanding man will be always associated with original problems regarding complex behavior, which includes the pattern recognition problem.

—M. BONGARD

June 25, 1966

CONTENTS

INTRODUCTION

DURING THE LAST DECADE many science fiction stories about "robots," "cybers," and other devices equipped with an "electronic brain" have been published. These devices presumably converse with man on any topic, their behavior is purposeful as well as complex, and the conditions to which they adapt are manifold to such an extent that it is impossible not to call them "intelligence machines." Depending on the plot, robots may be good or evil, insidious, self-sacrificing, funny, narrow-minded, or wise. In all cases, the writer seems to relate to them more as a human being than as a machine.

In a real-life situation such robots are not available. By comparison, recall that all the prototypes used by Jules Verne definitely were in existence during his era. Consequently, the question arises: What is "scientific" in the stories about "the life of robots" and what is "pure fantasy?" Is it possible that writers have invented something that could not exist in reality? The invention of a perpetual-motion machine could have been an excellent topic for a science fiction story, but because all readers were "spoiled by the knowledge" of the energy preservation law, this type of story has not been written.

Is the answer that the creation of robots capable of imitating the behavior of man does not contradict any presently known laws of nature? Or perhaps writers have not grasped the idea of the great possibilities of such an imitation. This idea has been borrowed from the scientists (see A. T'yuring, "Could a Machine Think?" Moscow, Fizmatgiz, 1960).

Why then have scientists, who have known design principles of a "thinking machine" for many decades, not developed such a machine?

After the invention of universal computers with programmed control, some enthusiastic scientists adopted the role of omnipotent programmers. Thus, if the programmer wishes, he can make the machine solve any system of equations, play chess, or translate from English into Russian, etc. The universal machine can duplicate any activity of man if an appropriate program is prepared. A complex activity, of course, would require more elaborate programming and entail more work for the machine. In essence, it sounds as though programmers are saying, "Give us a greater memory box and a higher performance speed, and we will create a 'thinking' machine."

It might be said that the field of cybernetics has issued a large promissory note that as yet has not been paid. This has happened not because of small machine memory and slow machine performance, but because of a shortage of ideas; i.e., ideas regarding methods of machine programming needed for the accurate imitation of the behavior of a man under varying circumstances. Wherein then lies the main difficulty?

It is quite simple to write a program if a machine performs one and the same sequence of operations under all circumstances encountered. For example, in order to solve $a^2 + b - ab + b^2$ the machine should be able (under any a and b) to square a, add to the obtained result b, etc.

However, it is another matter if a different sequence of actions is required under other circumstances. The complexity is not very great, however, if it is possible to formulate beforehand the principle by which the choice of the next operation is governed. For example, if the machine is required to calculate a^n at any a (n is the whole positive number), it must compare the number of already accomplished multiplications with n every time prior to the multiplication of the earlier result obtained by a. Depending on the result of this comparison, the machine decides either to undertake the next multiplication (if their number is insufficient), or to type the answer and stop. It is clear that the program for such an operation is relatively simple.

The serious difficulties begin when it is impossible to decide beforehand by which factor the choice of the sequence of operations in the machine is governed. In many cases this choice depends on the circumstances, and thus the nature of dependence cannot be indicated beforehand, but will be determined only in the course of solving the problem. Furthermore, the basis for choice will not in general be the same for all instances during the computer's life. The method should be chosen by the machine in accordance with the peculiarities of the specific problem, and the selection process may need to be iterated.

Precisely such a complex program will be necessary if the ability of man to solve many problems and to adapt himself to various environments is to be imitated. It should be noted, in addition, that the behavior of a machine controlled by such multistaged programs does not appear to be "machine-like" in manner. The actions of such a machine would have such complex dependence on such a varying number of circumstances (including those far removed with respect to time) that a complete illusion would be created regarding the free will and judgment of the machine (as is the illusion of "free will" in man).

A reader may think that if a complex programming is needed, why not start to write one command after another? Even if one hour per command is spent, then after five years it may be possible to arrive at something interesting.

Unfortunately, such a frontal attack on the problem is not acceptable for many reasons. Basically, the programmer who attempts to write a program for a thinking machine step-by-step would soon notice that he himself is unable to determine which of the circumstances influence what, and according to what laws these influences might work. The programmer cannot work without knowledge of these fundamentals, and it is almost impossible for the programmer to know complex systems in detail.

To illustrate this statement, assume that the development of science on Mars is different from that on Earth. Martians already know the inter-action laws of elementary particles, but they do not know either chemistry or the mechanics of large bodies. The only means of travel they possess is by horseback, as the wheel has not yet been discovered. Suddenly a great Martian scientist discovers that it is possible to travel using the internal energy of matter, and that this property does not belong to animals alone. It is decided, therefore, to design an automobile. So far this problem (automobile) has a purely functional meaning for the Martians for the future design of some apparatus for "self-propulsion."

The requirement presented to the designers is to find an arrangement of atoms in space so that a particular combination of these atoms is able to transport a man on a good road with speed not less than that of a horse.

The designers are stimulated by the fact that such an arrangement of atoms in space is possible (the horse also consists of atoms). However, with all their experimental technique they cannot figure out how atoms are arranged in a horse. Therefore, it is decided to proceed step-by-step (atom after atom) until the complex structure begins to move.

It is obvious that this undertaking of the Martians will fail, because it is impossible to understand the operation of an automobile (loom, radio receiver, etc.) while thinking about it in terms of elementary particles and their interaction.

In order to understand and to be able to create a machine, a brief description of larger groups of particles is required, as well as combinations of these various groups. In the case of the automobile, an idea about materials must first be developed as this will make it possible to describe (and to retain the information about) very large groups of atoms. For example, instead of indicating the position and relation of $3 \cdot 10^{27}$ atoms inside the gasoline tank, it is sufficient to say it contains 40 liters of gasoline with a definite heat capacity, specific weight, octane number, etc.

Because of short descriptions of the properties of gasoline, of brass, of steel, etc., the designer may proceed with his task although he does not know either chemistry or quantum mechanics.

Finally, the designer sees in the automobile, as a whole, an engine with certain parameters, weight, power, etc., and therefore does not need to decide whether to install the motor in the front, or in the back, nor to recall every time, nor in what sequence, the valves operate.

It is precisely the ability to think, not in terms of "atoms," but in terms of "large blocks" that makes it possible to create complex devices. The inability of the Martians to think in terms of "large blocks" deprives them of success in this field. Until fundamental basics for "large-block reasoning" are created (mechanics, chemistry, material technology, etc.), Martians will have to be satisfied with the idea that the automobile, in principle, is possible to design, but that only the heroes of science fiction stories will ride in them.

In relation to "thinking machines," mankind resembles Martians with their ideas about "self-propelling machines." A program may be created from individual commands to the universal computer, in the same way as an automobile may be built from atoms. However, like the Martians, modern scientists are still unable to determine which large blocks are needed for design of "the reasoning," and which and how many blocks are contained in "large blocks."

Therefore, to transpose science fiction stories into reality, it is necessary to look for much simpler blocks than the "reasoning" ones in general, but ones much higher in complexity than are individual commands. Furthermore, the description of blocks, which are essential for imitating reasoning, should be briefer than the listing of all the commands that they contain. It would be possible then to design still larger blocks from the simpler.

Recognition, evidently, is one of such blocks needed to imitate the reasoning process. In this book recognition is studied precisely from this point of view. Such an approach will predetermine the points of greater and of lesser interest in the problem of recognition. For example, nontaught recognition systems are only mentioned briefly because they cannot duplicate the ability of the brain to adapt to different circumstances in a flexible manner. In general, when the interesting and noninteresting aspects of the recognition problem are considered in this book, keep in mind that the problem of recognition is part of the problem of reasoning. It is quite natural that the division of problems into interesting and noninteresting fields will change in time. The aspects that are of great interest today could become boring and trivial tomorrow. This book represents simply the present point of view of the authors.

When a chemist wants to synthesize a new compound, he does not begin by the construction of a plant for this purpose, but by experimenting with small amounts of reagents and by using the same test tubes and flasks in the various experiments. Only after the development of a proven method is a special plant built that produces the particular product, for example, fiber.

Presently work on recognition systems is at a beginning stage and, therefore, there is no need to design special machinery for the initial experiments. However, the writing of programs for universal computers is of great benefit. This method of approach emphasizes the fact that the main difficulty in designing recognition systems is not finding elements for its construction, but finding logic for making the greatest number of elements compatible. It is of no importance for the programmer whether a computer is designed of tubes, transistors, or cryogenic neuristors; for him it is sufficient to know which command should be sent to the machine in order that it perform some action or step. Therefore, a programmer concentrates his attention on preliminary operations to which the initial material should be subjected in order to obtain the desired result. Each program, of course, considers the nature of the machine performing the work. However, each program could be adapted to any universal machine with insignificant changes. The peculiarities of the recognizing system are determined, in general, by the program features and not by the machine. The program, or algorithm, in this book, therefore, is identified very often with recognizing systems, and such expressions as "the program learns," "the program answers," etc., are encountered frequently. The latter expression, for example, means that the machine, guided by a program, printed an answer.

The term *recognition* is understood to mean the combination of all processes in the system including the learning process. In order to eliminate confusion, the application of information learned during the learning stage is called *test*, and thus recognition consists (1) of the learning and (2) of the test.

In the literature, there are such expressions as *image recognition* or *discrimination of images*. Different authors each attach a different meaning to the word *image*. Some think that *image* is an individual object, others that it is a class of objects, and still others that it is a class of objects but only those that satisfy some given condition (quite rigid). According to this terminology, there could be classes that are images, and classes that are not images.

In order to eliminate this confusion, the word *image* is not used in this book. Instead, *objects* and a *class of objects* are used. In some cases, when a specific limitation needs to be applied to a method of classification, these limitations (they are different for different cases) are defined and explained.

CHAPTER 1

Location of Recognition Centers in the Brain

1. Behavior and conditioned reflexes

AS STATED IN THE INTRODUCTION, in order to design a thinking machine it is necessary to know how to divide the operations performed by a brain into sufficiently large functional units or blocks. At the same time, the properties of each block must be briefly described or specified. This description should at least include some indication of the ways in which blocks are interrelated.

Is it a good idea to start with this type of analysis of brain performance? We know that physiologists study in detail the behavior of animals. Can the same approach and principles be applied to the design of artificial systems?

For some time it seemed that the performance of the brain was known in general terms. Especially after the studies by I. P. Pavlov of conditioned reflexes, it was thought that by combining a large number of conditioned reflexes of different orders, behavior of any complexity could be created. Many physiologists, even as late as fifteen years ago, could risk saying, "Give us a sufficient number of blocks capable of producing conditioned reflexes, and we will build a system that will adapt to external conditions in the course of training. This system will behave expediently under conditions that vary within a wide range." Can it be that conditioned reflexes are the required basic building blocks for constructing thinking machines? The physiologists, regrettably, have not supplied us with a precise definition of conditioned reflexes, and without this definition it is impossible to answer the above question. Therefore, we will attempt on our part to

1

define conditioned reflexes in such a way that physiologists will agree with us.

Let the rectangular block shown with broken lines in Fig. 1 represent a conditioned reflex. This block has two inputs, A and B, and one output, C.

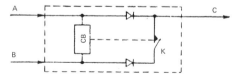

Figure 1. Scheme for a conditioned reflex.

The input A is an "unconditional stimulus." A signal from this block is passed to the output regardless of training. The input B represents a conditional stimulus. At the beginning the contact K is disengaged, and the signal coming from B cannot reach C. However, if signals from A and B come at the same time, the coincidence block (CB) closes the contact K. Now the signal B will cause a reaction at C even without the signal A. This situation continues until signal B arrives several times in a row without the simultaneous occurrence of signal A (without reinforcement). At this time the coincidence block disengages the contact K (the conditioned reflex disappears). Valves in channels A and B prevent the signal from channel A entering channel B, and vice versa, and protect the coincidence block from "self-strengthening" after disengagement of the contact K. This is a very simple description of the performance of a coincidence block. In reality, other details of great importance include such factors as the time of arrival of A and B signals, interruptions in their arrival, times lapses in the "strengthening" of the signal B, etc. Study of the coincidence block was the primary aim of many works devoted to conditioned reflexes. For example, some of the classical experiments by I. P. Pavlov were carried out under conditions such that the signal A represented a food taste signal, B was a visual light signal, and C was the signal stimulating the secretion of saliva.

It is easy to design a "reflex of the second order" from the above conditioned reflex. A physiological example of a secondary reflex is the situation in which food is first combined with light, then light without food is combined with sound, after which sound alone, without food and light, causes secretion of saliva. In order to do this, it is sufficient to connect the output of one block of conditioned reflex to the input of a second block, as shown in Fig. 2. It is possible, probably, to obtain reflexes of the third, fourth, and higher orders by similarly connecting a great number of individual conditioned reflexes of this type.

Can any form of behavior be obtained by suitable combinations of such conditioned reflex blocks? At this point, given that we understand by "conditioned reflex" a specific tangible thing, namely, the block illustrated in Fig. 1, we can answer this question negatively. The reason is that a system consisting of an arbitrary number of conditioned reflexes can only perform actions for which there exist unconditional stimuli from the beginning. In fact, "training" such a system (presenting combinations of different stimuli) can only lead to substitution by the conditioned stimulus

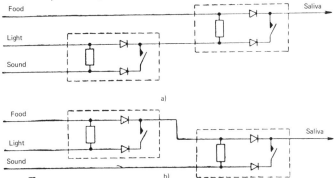

Figure 2. Schemes for reflexes of the second order. The scheme (*a*) makes it possible to devise a reflex of the second order by combining a sound with light prior to and after the development of a conditioned reflex for light. The scheme (*b*) works only in the case when sound is combined with light after the development of the conditioned reflex for light. (At the same time it is possible to develop a reflex for sound alone by combining it with the food.)

for the unconditional stimulus. If there is no unconditional (inborn) stimulus, then we have nothing to substitute. For example, secretion of saliva after training with light and sound in the schemes of Fig. 2*a* and *b* is possible only because there is an unconditional stimulus (food) for the secretion of saliva.

Animals can be trained to perform many actions for which there are no unconditional reflexes. There is no combination of sounds, food tastes, or light effects that will make an untrained dog walk on its hind legs five meters without losing balance. In the course of such training an entirely new reaction develops, but not the substitution of one stimulus for another one.

It is important to note that the failure to develop new actions by means of combinations of conditioned reflexes is due to the basic *structure* of the particular block of Fig. 1, and is not due to the particular choice of learning algorithm for the coincidence block. This statement applies regardless of the rules for the "development of reflexes" or "abolition of reflexes."

Consider now only the reactions for which there are unconditional stimuli. In this case, can all possible (for animals) forms of behavior be obtained by means of conditioned reflexes?

If a dog is given food after the simultaneous occurrence of light and sound, but is not given food after the occurrence of light alone, then the dog will secrete saliva only upon simultaneous light and sound signals, and will not react when each stimulus is engaged separately. Even such a simple reaction for "complex stimuli" is impossible to reduce to any number of conditioned reflex units of the type of Fig. 1.

[In this and the preceding paragraphs, the author is essentially asserting the lack of logical completeness of the particular function implemented in Fig. 1. The function can be written in Boolean form as $C = A + BK$, in which $K = 1$ if AB has previously occurred, and $K = O$ either if AB has failed to occur or if AB has occurred "several times in a row" to suppress the conditioned stimulus. This function lacks completeness such as that possessed by, for example, the Sheffer stroke function, combinations of which can be used to build up any logic function whatever. In particular, the function implemented by Fig. 1 fails to exhibit the crucial negation or complement operation on its inputs, and is therefore seriously constrained as to the possible behavior that its networks could produce.

—Editor.]

At this point, the reader may agree that the conditioned reflex unit is not the universal block from which all activity of the brain can be generated. But if several types of blocks can be added to the one shown in Fig. 1, then it may be possible to devise a universal set of blocks. In other words, is it possible that the conditioned reflex is one of the principal blocks into which the process of thinking can be divided?

This is partially true. In fact, only a few types of blocks are needed to achieve behavior of any complexity. For example, if "unconditional inhibition" (one signal disengages the chain of another signal) and "spontaneous stimulation" (an internal signal source) are added to the conditioned reflex unit, then a universal system is obtained.

However, it should not be concluded here that thinking machines should be based on conditional reflexes, unconditional inhibitions, and spontaneous stimulations. There are many other universal blocks. For example, from blocks carrying out the logic operations AND and NOT, and with delay lines, it is also possible to design a machine capable of realizing any behavior.

Finally, a system of stored commands for any universal machine makes it possible to design any program. Remember that we approached large blocks as a form of universal command system from which complex behavior could be generated. We discussed conditioned reflexes precisely because we were searching for such blocks. In principle, however, we are interested in designing functions which can represent much larger blocks than conditioned reflexes.

From this point of view, conditioned reflexes are not units upon which to base an understanding of the thinking process, because they perform only very primitive functions, namely, the coincidence of certain events with respect to time. They have not progressed far enough from elementary commands, and even with other blocks are very complex for designing major units. Therefore, in the next section we continue to search for larger blocks upon which to base the thinking process.

2. *Multiplicity of situations and multiplicity of reactions*

Imagine the complexity of signals for the brain, both input and output. From the eyes, ears, and other sense organs comes information into the brain about the external world. A whole series of internal receptors sends information into the brain about the conditions of different parts of the body, blood composition, etc. All these signals are input signals for the brain. On the basis of these inputs, the brain makes decisions expressed in the form of signals to control skeletal muscles, glands, and other internal organs.

Every signal sent by each receptor can be expressed by some number. The signals from all receptors at a given time can be represented by a set of numbers corresponding to the number of receptors (about 10^9 in man). Each sequence of such input signals during a given time interval must be transformed by the brain into a set of output commands.

There exist an extreme multiplicity of situations with which the nervous system of man must deal. Even if we assume that each receptor can signal only two states, stimulated and nonstimulated, there can be in principle 2^{10^9} different instantaneous situations.

Suppose that the brain reacted individually to each input situation, not to their sequence, as in reality. If all situations that differed by the state of only one receptor required different reactions, it would be extremely complex to control the behavior of an animal. Luckily this is not so. We know that each actual problem contains both significant and irrelevant data upon which to base expedient behavior. For example, when we call our friend by name on the street it makes no difference to us whether we see him against the background of a grey or white house. Equally, it makes no difference whether we see him in profile or in full face. In all cases we call to him, "Hi, John." Our brain in this case transforms many situations into one action. It performs the degenerated reflection of a multiplicity of situations into a lower multiplicity of reactions.

However, not all situations require identical action from the same individual. When the author–humorist reads his new story to a group of people to determine their reaction, he is not interested in who they are but whether or not they laugh. If they laugh, it means the story is good for publication; if not, he has to rewrite it. In another situation, the Euclidian distance to some man may be of importance, but not his name or his mood. In still another case, the problem may have to do with the clothes worn by a man, etc.

Let us attempt now to separate the transformation process performed upon input signals into two stages. First is the division of situations into classes requiring identical action. The second stage is the selection (synthesis) of actions that are expedient for an entire class of situations.

The first stage is called *recognition*. To this large block—a part of the thinking process—this book is devoted.

The second stage, *synthesis*, has been studied very little. The problem is briefly touched upon in Chapter 4. It is of interest, however, that this stage apparently includes blocks of a type usually associated with the recognition stage.

3. Intuitive representation of the problem of recognition

Suppose Fig. 3 is shown to some individual who has been instructed that the shapes in the left part of Fig. 3 are called *figures of the first class*,

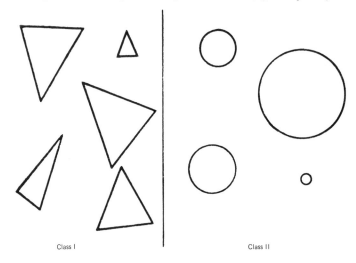

Class I   Class II

Figure 3.

and that those in the right-hand part are called *figures of the second class*. The individual is asked to determine to which class each of the figures shown in Fig. 4 belong. Practically without thinking anybody will answer that figure 4*a* belongs to the first class, 4*b* to the second, 4*c* to the second, and 4*d* to the first.

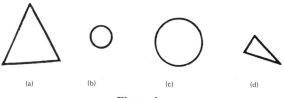

(a)   (b)   (c)   (d)

Figure 4.

Note that we did not give the tested individual any formal definition according to which the figures were divided into classes. The individual himself created a hypothesis regarding the principle for making the division into classes, by using examples from Fig. 3. The hypothesis is used for classifying the shapes in Fig. 4. The success of such a test obviously depends upon the closeness of the hypothesis to the principle used in designing the problem.

Sometimes a system is called a *recognizing device* when it performs classification by using only some constant principle. Such a system can solve only one problem, and it knows all the information about the problem ahead of time. Any coin automat is an example of such an untrained recognizing system. It checks the size, weight, and material of coins, and accepts only those for which it is designed. Such a system differentiates good coins from false ones and ones of other denominations.

[The author is here making a clear-cut distinction between inductive and deductive systems. While he might agree that a more complex coin automat for, say, classifying coins and paper money of all denominations and national currencies is no trivial recognition problem, he would probably ask what the same machine would do when asked to classify, say, pictures of men and women. If it is unable to form a reasonable hypothesis on the basis of some samples, then it is relegated to the status of a deductive "recognizing device" of little interest in this book.

—EDITOR.]

We are not interested in such systems. This book concerns only devices aimed at solving many different problems. The main difficulty for such inductive devices lies in the fact that the information regarding the principles for classifying objects is given to the device not in the form of a formal definition, but is presented by means of examples, as in Figs. 3 and 4. The process of deriving the classification principle to be used during test is called *training*. Objects used during test are called *test material*. Wherever possible, we will deal for simplicity's sake with examples in which objects are divided into two classes.

It is of interest that evolution in the animal world also progressed toward the perfection of specialized, almost untrained systems, as well as toward systems capable of solving many different problems. The animals also learn to some extent, but the acquired knowledge tends to be small compared to inherited knowledge. A newly born baby "knows" immediately how to breathe, digest food, contract the pupils, etc. However, in the life of an adult the most significant part of its overall activity is learned. Without training a man cannot talk, work, nor even walk on two limbs. Compared to more primitive animals, man is born with little knowledge, but is born with the ability to learn. Thanks to this ability, a man is able to adapt to various problems.

4. "Creative" problems and recognition

During the solution of the problems shown in Figs. 3 and 4, a man recognizes correctly not only the figures 4a and 4c, which represent exact copies of figures from the training material, but also the figures 4*b* and 4*d*, which differ to some extent from those previously encountered. The psychologist would "explain" this phenomenon as follows: "A man looking at Fig. 3 develops two abstract notions—'triangle' and 'circle'—that constitute a generalized description of all figures in the training material. These notions become applicable during test not only to specific shapes present in the training material, but also to all other triangles and circles. Therefore, a man is able to classify the shapes of the figures 4*b* and 4*d*." The word "explain" is in quotation marks because the psychologist's statement represents simply a description in other terms of the fact that a man recognizes not only objects present in the training material but much more. The psychologist's description is important because it establishes relationships between such "creative" acts as generalization, abstraction, and recognition. In reality they are different names for one and the same process. More precisely, *generalization* is another name for that part of the recognition process which is called *training*. In other words, a machine capable of solving a great number of recognition problems must also know how to create a corresponding set of abstract notions.

There is still another area of contact between the "creative process" (for example, that of the scientist) and recognition. In principle, many scientific discoveries could have been made by trial and error. In the simplest case, different wordings of a particular law could be tried. The third Kepler law (the periods of revolution of the planets around the Sun) serves as a good example. With a sufficient set of empirical data, and by patiently transforming different formulas, it is possible to find simple relationships that will adequately describe the experimental material. In more complex cases, unfortunately, the number of possibilities becomes too cumbersome to handle.

If we observe our own actions under similar conditions, we note that not all possible methods are subject to consideration. First, we separate those methods that have nothing to do with the problem from those that may provide some leads. One mathematician worded this thought in the form: "When dealing with difficult mathematical problems, nobody will find the right solution by sweeping the floor." It is quite clear that the difference between blind search and clever search is related to methods for finding common characteristics between a new problem and those solved previously, i.e., it requires recognition.

We have tried to show in Chapter 1 that the recognition process plays an unusually important role in the entire activity of the brain, starting with the most primitive forms of behavior and ending with the work of the scientist. There are also indications that the synthesis of actions contains some recognition steps.

Despite an undisputable relation between the recognition problem and neurophysiology or psychology, we will not use physiological data in considering ways to construct recognition systems. The scarcity of physiological information related to our problem of interest is the principal reason for this. Our approach is not that of the scientist studying how nature solved certain problems, but that of the engineer trying to solve the same problems independently.

It may be of interest, therefore, to compare the results of such an "engineering" approach to those obtained by physiologists. It can be hoped that such a comparison may facilitate efforts to find those elementary operations that are used for recognition in man's nervous system.

CHAPTER 2

Different Approaches

1. Initial descriptions of objects

EACH RECOGNIZING DEVICE receives information about objects in the environment in the form of readings from a transducer or data unit. In principle, these may be arbitrary measuring devices such as photoelements, microphones, thermocouples, concentration meters, etc. In analogy with the terms used in physiology, we will call these data units simply receptors. After analyzing the properties of the objects the receptor transmits a number. (For simplicity we will not consider in this chapter objects that change with respect to time.)

The numbers appearing at the outputs of the receptors constitute the information on the basis of which the recognizing device will solve the problem at hand, i.e., will decide to which class the given object belongs. In order to solve the problem, the receptor data must be processed somehow. The algorithm for this processing depends upon two circumstances. First, on the nature of the problem, and second, on the available set of receptors.

Obviously, a problem that requires complex processing in the case of one set of receptors may require quite simple processing in the case of another set. Suppose we must determine, for example, the specific weight of some crystalline substance. Assume that the receptors at our command can measure the change in intensity of x-rays scattered by the crystal at different angles, and can determine the chemical composition of the crystal. These data are often sufficient to determine specific weight. But the calculations will be very complex, because the structure of the crystal lattice must be calculated on the basis of the x-ray data, and then the locations of atoms at the lattice points must be inferred. Only after this procedure can the specific weight of a given crystal be determined.

The matter is greatly simplified, however, if we have a precision balance

10

and a device for measuring volume. In this case, the processing of the receptor signals requires only the division of one number by another.

A question comes up at this point: Is not the recognition problem, therefore, reduced to the selection of suitable receptors? Unfortunately, in a majority of cases the selection of receptors is determined not by what "should" be measured for the solution of a given problem but by what "can" be measured. For example, in order to recognize surrounding objects, it is of advantage to know the reflection coefficients of their surfaces, particularly as a function of wavelength. To determine the reflection coefficient, it is necessary to measure separately both the intensity of light incident on the object surface and the intensity of reflected light. However, for "technological reasons" (the structure of the eye), only reflected light can be measured. The brain, following a complex procedure, must compare the light reflected from different points of one object and from many objects, while simultaneously considering the shapes of objects, etc., in order to determine approximately the reflection coefficient of the object surface.

Still another factor mitigates against the creation of special receptors as a substitute for complex signal processing, particularly when we wish to design systems capable of solving a wide variety of problems. If we select receptors for individual problems, we will need a very large number of different receptors. In the above example we would need a photoelement to measure the intensity of incident light. To determine distances to objects we would need something like a radiolocator. In order to differentiate a rough surface from a smooth surface, a device would be needed to measure the reflection coefficient in different directions, etc.

A man solves these problems using one and the same receptor—the retina of the eye. Universality is achieved not by means of different types of receptors, but by the use of different algorithms for processing the signals produced by the retinal rods and cones. For example, in order to determine the distance to some object, the brain compares signals coming from both eyes (stereoscopic effect) while at the same time considering dynamics, paying attention to which object is projected onto which other objects, etc. As a result we establish the spatial locations of objects using only two-dimensional images on the retina.

With our aim being to construct a recognizing system for some group of problems, we will in this book assume that a set of receptors has been determined beforehand. For example, all systems that model the visual analyzer of man receive information in the following form: The visual field of the system is divided into a certain number of areas, and information about the amount of light incident on each area is passed to the system. We can consider that memory cells containing numbers characterizing the quantity of light at different areas of the visual field are the basic system receptors.

Thus, we assume that the initial description of objects is already given before the work of the engineer or programmer designing the system begins. It is within his power only to select the processing method. This chapter considers a number of possible principles for the processing of such input information.

2. Remembering the training material

An attempt may be made to solve the problem of recognition by remembering the initial descriptions of all objects in the training set (for example, shapes shown in Fig. 3), together with class membership. During test, the description of an unknown object is compared with descriptions accumulated in memory during training. If the description of an unknown object coincides completely with the description of an object of one of the classes, it is assigned to that class.

For a system working on this principle, a description of the class of triangles means a listing of the initial sensory descriptions of all triangles previously encountered, similarly for circles, etc. Obviously this method can be used for recognizing only those objects that were encountered in the training material. For example, the figures 4b and 4d would not be recognized.

A psychologist would say that such a system does not develop any abstract notions. In fact, in order to recognize new objects that were not encountered during training, it is necessary to find something common between all objects of one class. It is necessary to ignore the differences inside of one class, and to pay special attention to characteristics that differentiate one class from another. The machine that can only remember the initial descriptions of objects cannot accomplish this.

Our original interest in the recognition problem was to model such functions as "generalization," "reasoning by analogy," etc. Therefore, memorization systems are not considered further in this book.

3. Search for identity within the receptor space

In this section and in others to follow, systems will be discussed that are designed for the recognition of plane geometric objects. Information about objects is considered to be in the form of a distribution of dark and light areas on a limited plane region. We will consider the system to have finite spatial resolution. In this case, a finite set of numbers adequately describes any object. If we consider that each measurement is a coordinate in a multidimensional space (the number of measurements equals the number of dimensions) then the object is represented by some point within this space. Following established tradition, this space is called the *receptor space*.

It is always possible to divide the degree of brightness into a finite number of levels. In many recent works, the authors use only two levels. Such an idealization is quite permissible at the present stage because many (although not all) principal difficulties of the problem of recognition of geometric objects are preserved in this case.

It would be good, of course, to determine distances between points in the receptor space in such a manner that objects of any one class are close to one another, but the distances between objects of different classes are large. This situation should be true for all problems of interest.

It would be sufficient, then, to determine approximately the space corresponding to different classes (for example, by observing where points corresponding to the training material are located). Boundaries of these regions could be remembered for simplicity. "Centers of gravity" of these regions could be found, and distances from an unknown point to centers of gravity could be measured during test, etc.

Unfortunately, different problems present different requirements regarding "closeness of points." For some problems it is necessary that those objects be close that would almost coincide when superimposed, i.e., those that have many common and only few noncoincident points. For other problems, it is necessary that two objects be close in receptor space if they can be produced from each other by a translation or rotation process. Another class of problems might require that similar geometric figures be close in the receptor space. Among various problems, one might require that pictures of men be close to one another and at a great distance from pictures of women. Of course there could be an opposite requirement.

A resemblance requirement between all circles, regardless of diameter, and remoteness of them from triangles, leads to the contradiction that all small figures should resemble each other (regardless of shape), and be remote from large figures.

Sometimes, rather than the resemblance of points, their separation in receptor space by hyperplanes or other smooth surfaces is considered. (The hyperplane in n-dimensional space is the set of points $X [x_1, x_2, \ldots, x_3]$ the coordinates of which satisfy $A_1x_1 + A_2x_2 + \ldots + A_nx_n = B$. In particular, for $n = 2$ a straight line represents the hyperplane, and for $n = 3$ an ordinary plane.) However, the difficulty in this case does not disappear but is masked. The fact is, that points belonging to different classes are (for many problems) "mixed" within the receptor space. In other words, their relation resembles that between a sponge and water when water penetrates the sponge. It is absolutely impossible to draw a completely smooth surface in such a way that on one side of it lies only water, and on another, only the sponge.

[This is an extremely apt mental image for anyone in the field of automatic pattern recognition to carry with him. Despite the enormous amount of attention given to the fine details of optimal adjustment of hyperplanes or other simple "smooth" classification boundaries in all sorts of spaces (receptor, feature, characteristic function, etc.) the fact remains that few real pattern recognition problems are so simple. Relatively minute details can spell the crucial difference between classes (the *O* and *Q* are classical examples), while large distances in the measurement space may normally separate members of the same class (in a binary receptor space a black pattern on a white background and its complement, a white pattern on a black background, are as far apart as they can get, yet they are usually placed in the same class). John Munson[1] of Stanford Research Institute recently expressed a viewpoint similar to the author's by describing the decision space as "wormy" or composed of tightly interwoven, highly convoluted class regions. These graphic concepts probably come as close as any to depicting most real situations.

—EDITOR.]

Despite this difficulty, a division into classes directly within the receptor space is indicated in some works. Let us recall the system using the "compactness hypothesis" ("compactness" not in a mathematical sense), the algorithm of crossing planes of E. M. Braverman. In this system, the receptor space is considered as a multidimensional Euclidian space. The distance between points in it is equal to the squares of the coordinate differences (or of some monotonic function of this value). A division surface in this algorithm consists of sections of hyperplanes.

It is easy to see that such a metric is good only when it is profitable to consider those figures as similar that have a small number of noncoincident points, i.e., are almost identical. In fact, good results were obtained from a field containing 60 elements (6 by 10) with the Braverman program. This field contained numerals that satisfied the following conditions: Each number touched both the upper and lower edges of the field (standard height), and was centered along the horizontal line. It is of little wonder that in this case numerals belonging to a single class had many common points.

However, if we look at Fig. 5, we see that the numeral 2 in the upper

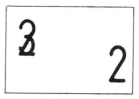

Figure 5. Digit 3 is "closer" (in receptor space) to one of the 2's than the 2's are to each other.

left corner of the field is much closer (in the sense of degree of overlap) to the numeral 3 than to the numeral 2 at the lower right corner. Therefore, this system cannot recognize, for example, numerals of any arbitrary size, arbitrarily located in the machine's field of view.

In contrast to the above situation, the "compactness hypothesis" assumes that there will be no such "bad" distribution of classes in the

such a transformation exists nevertheless. For the problems shown in Figs. 7 and 8 there are no "good" transformations. No matter how we

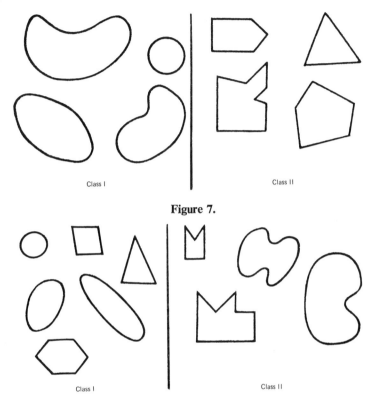

Class I   Class II

Figure 7.

Class I   Class II

Figure 8.

change the scale or turn or shift the shapes in the field, we cannot collect all the various polygons within the receptor field in such a way that they can be easily separated from curvilinear figures (Fig. 7). The same can be said about the problem shown in Fig. 8. Convex and concave figures do not form compact regions within the receptor field, and the matter cannot be improved by any turns, shifts or displacements.

A man solves such problems with ease. And this disproves directly the underlying assumptions of the theory of compactness. Thus, various problems in which classes divide "badly" within the receptor space can still be solved. The word *badly* means that points belonging to different classes cannot be separated from one another by a plane, or by some surface of simple geometric description, requiring substantially fewer parameters to specify than the number of objects in each class.

Thus, we conclude that a resemblance search within the receptor space for a wide range of problems is hopeless.

receptor space. In essence, it assumes that if such a "mixing" of points belonging to different classes occurs, then the problem cannot be solved by any means! What do we do then with the case shown in Fig. 5? Points are "mixed" in this figure but there exists a system—man!—that can easily solve the problem. Supporters of the hypothesis of compactness reason as follows. It is true that there are some transformations of figures, for example a parallel translation, for which some figures remain similar for man even though they are far apart within the receptor space. However, there are only a few such transformations, such as translation, rotation, scale change, etc. Let us perform all these transformations beforehand, namely, transfer a figure to the center of the field, make its size standard, and turn it into a standard position. In this way everything is "compact" within the receptor field.

This approach may be satisfactory for digits. But there are many problems that cannot be solved by this method. Let us give several examples.

A man examining Fig. 6 notices in no time that the first class differs

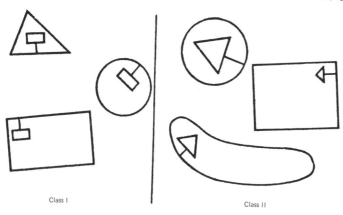

Class I   Class II

Figure 6.

from the second by the shape of the inside figure. If the inside figure is a triangle, the object belongs to the second class; if it is rectangular, to the first class. Let us try to solve this problem by reducing it to a "compact" form. In order to do this we need to place not the whole figure but only its internal part onto the same spot on the receptor field, make it of standard size, and rotate it into a standard position. Only after such a transformation will all objects of the first class be separated easily from objects of the second class (by a hyperplane, for example). A difficulty lies, however, in the fact that the system does not know which parts of the figure should be transformed into the standard position. The system must know beforehand what characteristics differentiate the given classes in order to do this. As a result we have a vicious circle.

In the problem shown in Fig. 6, it is impossible to find a good transformation for the objects without knowing the classification criterion, but

4. Standard (independent of an actual problem) transformations of the receptor field: the Perceptron

It was pointed out in the preceding section that classes can be separated within the receptor space only for very simple problems. We may now reasonably ask whether the receptor field could not be transformed into another field in which it would be easy to obtain classes for a broader range of problems.

Evidently, the first work along this line was the Perceptron. There are tendencies presently to call all adaptive recognizing systems *Perceptrons*. We think that this is not quite suitable, and so we reserve the term *Perceptron* only for the original Rosenblatt Perceptron.

The Perceptron (see Fig. 9) consists of elements of three types called S,

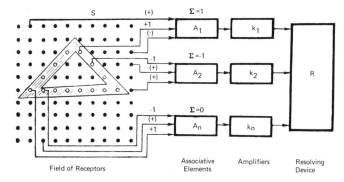

Figure 9. Scheme of the Perceptron. The images of objects during training and test are projected onto the field of S receptors. Each receptor signals either a 0 or 1 state, depending upon the picture elements centered on it. All receptors are connected with associative elements ($A_1, \ldots, A_n$) by connections which may be either "excitatory" ($+$) or "inhibitory" ($-$). For simplicity, only a few connections are shown here. The excitatory connection, depending on the receptor state, transfers either a 0 or a $+1$ signal; the inhibitory connection, either a 0 or a -1. Each A element sums up all incoming signals. If this sum exceeds some threshold, then the corresponding element becomes excited. A system of connections for A elements, and their excitation thresholds, are selected beforehand (arbitrarily, for example). They are not changed during the solution of a given problem. If an A element is not excited, it does not transmit any signal. All excited A elements send signals to the resolving device (summation) R through amplifiers that can change both the value and the polarity (sign) of signals. All amplification coefficients k of all amplifiers are equal to zero prior to adaptation. Black dots in this figure designate unexcited receptors and white dots excited receptors. Signals coming only from excited receptors (designated by $+1$ and -1) enter the associative elements.

A, and R elements. S elements are receptors, and they are joined with A elements by connections that may be either excitatory or inhibitory. Each receptor can be in one of two states designated by 0 and 1. The excitatory connection transmits the receptor state to the A element without any change, but the inhibitory connection changes the sign of the signal. A elements (associative elements) of the Perceptron are summation devices with thresholds. Each A element becomes excited if the sum of the incoming signals from its receptors exceeds some threshold. The signals from the excited A elements are transmitted into the summation device R; the signal coming from element A_i is transmitted with the coefficient k_i.

Connections for all A elements and their thresholds are selected beforehand (randomly, for example). These connections do not change during the particular problem.

Adaptation involves only the modification of the coefficients k_i. This proceeds in the following manner. At first all coefficients are assumed to be zero. Then an object of the first class is "shown" to the Perceptron. At this stage only some A elements are excited, and the coefficients k that correspond to these A elements are increased by 1. Then an object of the second class is shown, and the coefficients corresponding to the excited A elements are decreased by 1. This process is repeated until all of the training material is used. As a result, the final value of the coefficients k that will be used during test are formed. During test an unknown object is shown to the Perceptron. Each excited A element now transmits to the R summation unit a signal that is equal to the corresponding coefficient k. If the sum of signals is positive, then it is decided that the unknown object belongs to the first class; if negative, to the second class.

The states of the A elements (0 or 1) may be considered as coordinates of an n-dimensional space (A space). The system of connections and thresholds from S to A elements sets some fixed (for a given Perceptron) transformation of the receptor field into A space. This transformation is one-valued, but not necessarily mutually one-to-one. The k coefficients in turn establish an n-dimensional hyperplane in A space. Thus, the general scheme of the Perceptron is first, to transform the receptor field into A space in some standard way independent of the problem. Then, it locates a hyperplane in A space by means of adaptation; this latter decision hopefully separates objects of one class from another.

An attempt is made below to comprehend the sense of these operations and perceive the possibilities of the Perceptron.

[What the author has described here is an early version of the Perceptron with a "forced-learning" adaptation rule. Somewhat more sophisticated versions differ in at least two respects: (1) both sensory S-unit and associative A-unit signals are assigned the symmetrical values $+1$ and -1 (rather than 1 and 0), and (2) modification of the "weights" or coefficients k occurs only when the decision made by the final output resolving device R is incorrect ("error correcting" procedure). In any case, a number of investigators (see, for example, Nilsson[2]) have succeeded in proving one fundamental theorem about this system, as follows. Regardless of the transformation between S and A units, if the decision function between the outputs of the A units and the output of the R unit demanded by the particular classification problem is one for which some possible set of coefficients k exists (such a function is usually called a linear threshold logic function), then the adaptation process will, in fact, cause the coefficients to converge to a set of values that implement the function perfectly (without error). Nothing can be said about what happens if no such "solution" set of coefficients k exists for the given problem. However, experience indicates that under this condition system performance improves up to some imperfect terminal level, and tends to remain approximately there. Further, the details of the individual unit behavior and of the training algorithm do not appear to make a great deal of difference in performance (see for example Darling and Joseph[3] for a comparison of the performance of several techniques on the same pattern classification problems). The author's statement in the first paragraph below is strictly confined to the forced-learning Perceptron, and a slightly better performance would be expected with the use of the error-correcting procedure. Again, however, experience indicates that the differences are not great, and that in either case system performance is not satisfactory for most practical pattern recognition problems.

—Editor.]

Assume at the beginning that all A elements have only one excitatory connection each, and no inhibitory connections. Let the threshold of each of them be 1, that is, each A element simply repeats the output of some S element. Under these conditions, what is the meaning of the coefficients k formed at the end of adaptation? Clearly, k_i indicates how often a certain point was encountered on the field of view among pictures of one class as compared with pictures of the other class. The sign of k_i shows which class (first or second) the point occurred in most often. During test, the Perceptron essentially verifies which points comprise the unknown pictures. If a picture consists of those points that were mostly present in pictures of the first class, then it is classified as belonging to the first class. The severe limitations of this system hardly require any comment.

Assume now that A elements have two connections each, and both are positive. All thresholds are equal to 2. Now k_i accumulates information regarding the frequency of appearance of the combination of some two points in the field. Which points are accounted for is set up by the construction of the Perceptron (connections of the A elements). The "voting" during test deals with those pairs of points encountered in the unknown picture.

In general, information is accumulated in k_i regarding the number of pictures in which certain fragments

[n-tuples.

—Editor.]

of excited and unexcited S elements are encountered. In the case of low thresholds, the element A_i can respond to several different fragments.

Roughly speaking, the value of k_i will represent the number of appearances of at least one of these fragments.

Now it is clear that for a Perceptron those problems should be accessible in which objects of one class have many common fragments. A "resemblance" for the Perceptron is the resemblance resulting from superposition of one picture over another. In this case, coincidence is not with respect to points but with respect to fragments (according to those fragments responded to by A elements). It is quite natural, therefore, to expect that generalizations such as translations or similar transformations are unaccessible to the Perceptron.

[Indeed, Minsky and Papert[4] have succeeded in proving that, under somewhat specialized mathematical conditions, the Perceptron is totally incapable of learning to classify rigid objects subjected to *any* generalized transformation. The only "pattern" classification of which the Perceptron is capable when the patterns are subjected to all possible values of some transformation (e.g., translation) is that involving a decision as to whether more than or less than some number of points is active on the input field of view. Such amorphous "patterns" hardly fall within our usual definition of the term.

—Editor.]

Rosenblatt has not described problems which are "difficult" for the Perceptron. A. P. Petrov tried to find examples of such problems. All experiments were carried out with a field of 16 by 16 elements. The Perceptron had from 400 to 1,300 A elements in different versions. The number of connections to each A element (both the excitatory and inhibitory) was changed from 5 to 30.

Since the results practically did not depend upon these parameters, the results of only one version are given. They can be considered as representative of any three-layer Perceptron.

1st problem. It was required to distinguish between rectangles elongated in the horizontal direction and rectangles elongated in the vertical direction. Similar experiments were also performed by Rosenblatt. The Perceptron made 6% errors during test on 30 figures when only 15 figures were shown to it originally. This result, in general, is satisfactory.

2nd problem. It was required to distinguish between triangles and circles. Both shapes were of arbitrary size and arbitrarily located on the field. The Perceptron in this case made 33% errors, although the training material included 45 figures of each class. This problem is inaccessible to the Perceptron.

3rd problem. The problem required distinguishing between rectangles and ellipses. Both figures were arbitrarily rotated and situated. The Perceptron made 50% errors when the training material included 45 figures of each type.

How could the Perceptron satisfactorily solve the first problem? Rectangles in that problem were of different size and different location. It should be remembered, however, that the whole field had 16 vertical and

16 horizontal lines. Therefore, for any particular pattern arrangement, for example, vertically, a given rectangle inevitably had many common fragments with some figures from the training material. These were simply remembered exactly by the Perceptron. (Remember that the memory volume in the case of 1,300 A elements is practically sufficient to remember all the training material. That is, for just one picture 256 bits are needed, and for 30 pictures approximately 7,500 bits. On the other hand, 1,300 elements with 5 bits each amount to approximately 6,500 bits.) This situation helped the Perceptron, probably, to find common fragments in the second problem, and to keep the percentage of errors below 50%. In the case of a large field, for example 100 by 100, the Perceptron would not be able to solve even the first problem with the same training material. We see that a transformation from the Perceptron field to A space does not help the matter. Correlation based upon the compactness of points is equally unsatisfactory in A space for objects of the same class for sufficiently different problems. Therefore, the search for a plane dividing classes in A space for many problems is hopeless. This is not because the search method is unsatisfactory, but because there is no such plane.

We conclude that the Perceptron is a system that performs a standard transformation on the receptor field, which brings us very little closer to the solution of the recognition problem.

[T. Cover[5] has succeeded in proving, under certain special mathematical conditions, that the number of independent patterns that can be learned by a Perceptron is, on the average, approximately equal to twice the number of variable weights. While Cover's conditions are usually violated in practical problems, experience has nevertheless shown that this general limit is frequently encountered.

—Editor.]

5. Changeable (different for different problems) transformations of the receptor field

Let us go back and examine the problem shown in Fig. 6. Why is this problem difficult for a system searching for a close resemblance within the receptor field (and also for the Perceptron)? One of the reasons is that the pictures in Fig. 6 contain much unnecessary information. In fact, each picture contains information regarding the size of the picture, its convex or concave shape, the location of the external figure with respect to the internal, etc. All of this information is not needed for the solution of the given problem.

We must find a way to make the system stop paying attention to irrelevant circumstances. This means that pictorial representation methods should be found in which all unnecessary information is lost.

No matter how paradoxical it sounds, the basic task of any recognizing system is not the preservation of information, but the maximum decrease of irrelevant information about each object. From this point of view every transformation of the input data that secures success should be degenerate.

[Or "convergent"; that is, should throw away information.

—EDITOR.]

This can be contradicted by saying that what is needed in order to solve the problem of Fig. 6 is a filter that will pass only the internal figure and stop the external. However, for other problems this filter could become unnecessary and even harmful, e.g., it could eliminate significant information. For other problems other degenerate images are needed, and nobody knows in advance precisely which image is profitable for a given problem.

[It is worth emphasizing that the author here has introduced the notion of an image-to-image transformation possessing certain information-reduction properties. The idea of preserving spatial relationships by maintaining image coordinates while successively extracting more complex—and therefore more degenerate—descriptions of the original pattern is one that has found a certain appeal among workers in the field of "picture linguistics." See for example Narasimhan,[6] or Evans.[7]

—EDITOR.]

This contradiction is valid, but let us recall that we are considering systems that do not know beforehand (prior to adaptation) which transformations are useful for a given problem. It is sufficient that a system finds some degenerate representation, e.g., by trial and error, that will help to separate classes.

In daily life, we often use incomplete descriptions that characterize only some aspect of an object. A distinctive peculiarity of such descriptions is the fact that identical characteristics can correspond to different objects (the transformation of many objects into a few characteristics is the phenomenon of degeneration). For example, the characteristic *white* can be applied to a horse, cat, or cup. In these cases, we say that a certain property of an object is present. Strictly speaking, the word *white* contains two completely different meanings. The first indicates what instruments are needed to obtain the information. For example, the reflection coefficient at the surface of an object may be measured at different wavelengths. The second is the result of this measurement. In the above case *white* means that "the reflection coefficient over the entire visible spectrum is sufficiently high and is approximately identical for different wavelengths."

The same procedure holds for the characteristic *green* but the result of the measurement is different. In everyday language, these characteristics are not distinguished clearly. In order to avoid confusion the algorithm or procedure involved in making the information-reducing measurement (degenerate transformation) will be referred to as the *feature*. The result of performing the measurement or transformation will be referred to as the *characteristic* of the object with respect to the given feature. Thus, the feature in our case will be, for example, a program that measures the areas of figures, or a program that counts angles, or a program that checks the parity of a number.

The characteristic (the result of operating the program) with respect to the first feature can be represented by a nonnegative number, with respect to the second feature by a whole nonnegative number, and with respect to the third feature by the judgement *yes* or *no*. In addition, each of the programs can refuse to provide an answer, because the feature may not be applicable to the object at hand. For example, for the number 7.32 the third feature cannot say either *yes* or *no* because it is applicable only to whole numbers.

How, then, can we determine features that are useful for a given problem? Let us consider the following problem. Five stands containing test tubes are on a table. Several test tubes in each stand are filled with some substance. The test tubes in different stands contain different substances. Now we get an unknown test tube containing one of these five substances. We want to place it in an appropriate stand ("sort it" or "recognize it"). At the same time, we have many incomplete characteristics for the substances in the test tubes. Features include color, smell, the state of the substance (liquid or solid), specific weight, flammability, etc.

Assume that three stands contain liquids in their test tubes, and two contain solid substances, one white and the other blue. Two of the liquids are transparent, and the third is blue. Liquids on one stand have a strong smell, and the remaining ones have no smell at all. Now we can compile a table listing the descriptions of classes in the above terms.

TABLE 1

Number of Stand	State	Color	Smell
1	1	0	0
2	1	1	0
3	0	0	0
4	0	0	1
5	0	1	0

In this table in the column "State," a 1 designates a solid while a 0 means a liquid; in the column "Color," a 1 designates blue while a 0 means the absence of any color; in the column "Smell," a 1 means the presence of smell and a 0 means the absence of smell. There are no two identical rows in this table. Therefore, the selection of three features makes it possible to classify the new test tube.

During the classification procedure, the new substance should be tested according to all three features. The set of resulting characteristics is then compared with the rows of Table 1, and the new tube is placed in the stand whose characteristics coincide with those of the unknown substance. Clearly, the selection process for useful features is one of trial and error. First we make a hypothesis concerning the usefulness of a given feature; then we check it. The criterion for usefulness is whether or not the characteristic resulting from the given feature produces a separation among the set of objects. As a potentially useful feature, we considered the "state" because we had liquid and solid substances. The feature "color" turned out to be also useful. But if all five stands had transparent liquids, the features "color" and "state" would be eliminated as useless.

The above example is excessively simple. That is, among those features that were tested, some produced identical characteristics for all of the objects in the same class (all test tubes in one stand had identical color, smell, etc.). The problem would be more complex if substances on the same stand occurred in both solid and liquid form. Further difficulties would be encountered in the case of blue vitriol which is white in the solid state and blue in solution, etc. In this case, the description of classes in terms of features would not be simply an enumeration of characteristics according to these features, but would be some more complex logic function of the characteristics.

This potential complexity will inevitably have an impact on methods for evaluating the usefulness of features. In general, it will be necessary to consider not only the diversity of characteristics of the objects belonging to different classes with respect to a given feature, but also the degree of similarity among the characteristics of objects of the same class. Different programs use different criteria for evaluating the usefulness of features. These criteria will be pointed out at appropriate places in this book, and Chapter 11 is practically dedicated to this problem.

We see that training must lead to a description of the classes of objects. However, the description of a given class depends not only upon which objects belong to it, but also upon which objects are present in other classes (by what characteristic a given class can be distinguished from other classes). This follows from the selection of useful features. Let us attempt now to describe the operation of the Perceptron in these terms.

It can be assumed in principle that a hyperplane within the A space of the Perceptron is a feature. A characteristic with respect to this feature is the position of a point on one or another side of the plane. It might appear from this that the Perceptron "arsenal" contains a variety of different features. However, we have already seen that many needed features cannot be found there. In contrast to a widely accepted point of view, the Perceptron is not a system with an a priori set of useful features, but is a system with a very rigid, poor, and unsuccessful selection of features for many problems. The erroneous point of view originated, probably, because the Perceptron designers trusted the arbitrary S unit to A unit interconnection process to form an arsenal of useful features. After interconnections are made, however, the Perceptron becomes a system with a strictly fixed set of features. No matter how this process is realized, there still remain many needed features that are missing and not among those accessible to the Perceptron for many problems encountered. This is the price we pay for "memory economy" during Perceptron design.

Thus, as opposed to other systems searching for pattern similarity within a rigidly given feature space, we will attempt below to construct systems that will perform selection and verification of a great number of degenerate transformations of the receptor field. Only those features will be selected during adaptation that are useful for a given problem.

Since we are interested in systems capable of solving many different problems, it is necessary that many diversified features be selected during adaptation. In other words, a system should be able to produce a great variety of degenerate transformations. It is clear that it is practically impossible to keep algorithms of all these transformations readily available in memory. Therefore, it is necessary to divide the possible transformations into elementary operations, and to preserve only the methods for constructing the various features using these elementary "blocks."

Roughly speaking, features should be assembled of blocks in the same way that children build bridges, cars, lifting cranes, etc., from parts of a toy Erector set. Only in this way is it possible to make accessible to the system a great number of different features. Precisely such systems will be discussed in the chapters to follow.

[Again, the author here is advocating a pattern "parsing" or subdivision approach that is capable of constructing a variety of picture descriptions or features from a modest number of more rudimentary elements. In the case of the picture linguistics school, the rudimentary image elements have tended to be lines, vertices, corners, etc. (see references 6, 7, and 8), while those dealing with grey-level imagery have tended to use oriented grey-level transitions (edges), textures, etc. (see references 9 and 10). The combinations or structures built upon these rudimentary "blocks" have been of great variety, reflecting in each case the particular image classification problem at hand. Thus the author's concepts and approach are very powerful and general, but at the same time are difficult to analyze and implement.

—EDITOR.]

REFERENCES

1. J. Munson, "Some Views on Pattern Recognition Methodology," *Methodologies of Pattern Recognition*, S. Watanabe, Ed., (New York: Academic Press, 1969), pp. 417–436.
2. N. J. Nilsson, *Learning Machines* (New York: McGraw-Hill, 1965).
3. E. M. Darling, R. D. Joseph, "Pattern Recognition from Satellite Altitudes," (IEEE Trans. Syst. Science and Cyb., SSC-4, No. 1, March, 1968), pp. 38–47.

4. M. L. Minsky, S. Papert, "Linearly Unrecognizable Patterns," (Proc. Symp. on Appl. Math. 19, Amer. Math. Soc., 1967), pp. 176–217.
5. T. M. Cover, "Geometrical and Statistical Properties of Systems of Linear Inequalities with Applications to Pattern Recognition." (IEEE Trans., Vol. EC-14, No. 3, June, 1965), pp. 326–333.
6. R. Narasimhan, "Labeling Schemata and Syntactic Descriptions of Pictures," (Information and Control, Vol. 7, July, 1964), pp. 151–179.
7. T. G. Evans, "A Program for the Solution of a Class of Geometric Analogy Intelligence-Test Questions," (Report AFCRL-64-884, U.S. Air Force Cambridge Research Labs., L. G. Hanscom Field, Massachusetts, November, 1964).
8. A. C. Shaw, "The Formal Description and Parsing of Pictures," (Report No. 84, Stanford Linear Accelerator Center, Stanford, California, March, 1968).
9. R. S. Ledley, "High Speed Automatic Analysis of Biomedical Pictures," (*Science*, Vol. 146, No. 3641, October, 1964), pp. 216–223.
10. J. K. Hawkins, "Space-sharing Sampled-data Parallel Picture Processing," *Pattern Recognition*, (Grenoble: L.E.T.I., 1969), pp. 251–267.

CHAPTER 3

The Program, *Arithmetic*

1. *Presentation of the problem*

IN THIS CHAPTER, we consider a computer program designed to recognize (classify) tables of numbers that are constructed according to different arithmetic rules. These objects (numerical tables) were selected for recognition experiments because their use permitted us to generate a large number of features from a small number of basic building blocks. It was also easy and natural to use logic functions for constructing the features. It is of interest to note that some of the program blocks turned out to be useful, with slight modification, in other programs for recognizing geometric objects and for the solution of geophysical problems. It appears that these blocks solve some aspects of the recognition problem common to different tasks.

The basic objects to be classified by the program *Arithmetic* were numerical tables consisting of several rows, each containing three numbers, see for example Table 2. Numbers in column C in each row of this table were

<table>
<tr><th colspan="3">TABLE 2</th></tr>
<tr><th>A</th><th>B</th><th>C</th></tr>
<tr><td>4</td><td>1</td><td>12</td></tr>
<tr><td>3</td><td>5</td><td>-30</td></tr>
<tr><td>2</td><td>7</td><td>-70</td></tr>
<tr><td>5.5</td><td>3</td><td>41.25</td></tr>
<tr><td>6</td><td>6.3</td><td>-11.34</td></tr>
</table>

<table>
<tr><th colspan="3">TABLE 3</th></tr>
<tr><th>A</th><th>B</th><th>C</th></tr>
<tr><td>4</td><td>1</td><td>9</td></tr>
<tr><td>3</td><td>4</td><td>7.75</td></tr>
<tr><td>-6</td><td>2</td><td>-7</td></tr>
<tr><td>5</td><td>2.5</td><td>9.5</td></tr>
<tr><td>2.5</td><td>-2</td><td>-0.75</td></tr>
</table>

obtained from the numbers in columns A and B by using one and the same rule. For example, it is easy to see that all rows of Table 2 satisfy the rule

27

$AB(A - B) = C$. Using different numbers for A and B it is possible with this same rule to construct an unlimited number of different tables. All tables constructed according to the same rule are considered to be objects of one class.

Table 3 does not belong to the same class as Table 2 because it is constructed according to another law. In this table

$$C = \frac{A}{B} + A + B.$$

Originally the program was intended to recognize tables in which C was formed from A and B by the use of any three arithmetic operations applied in sequence. In this case, the number of possible different classes is equal to the number of different arithmetic "three-way-operations" on A and B (note that this is not the same as the number of different mathematical symbol arrangements since, for example, $(A + B)(A - B)$ is identical to $A^2 - B^2$).

Our aim is to show the program several objects of the first class (tables constructed according to a single rule), several objects of the second class, etc. At the same time the program is not informed as to the rule according to which the tables are constructed. Classes are simply numbered. During test, the program is shown a new table (not from the training material) belonging to one of the classes used during training. The program should indicate the class number of this table.

[The author has posed here an exciting problem in both pattern recognition and artificial intelligence, namely, that of induction. Can a machine find a rule (or make up a simple theory) describing a complex situation, based only on examples of data derived from the application of some fixed principle? It may be that more than one rule or theory will "fit" the data, in which case the principle of parsimony prevails—the simplest theory (algorithm) for transforming the set of data to the correct classification is desired. This is an extremely difficult problem, and touches upon what we usually think of as insight, inspiration, or stroke of genius. The fact is that present models of this function—for example incorporated in theorem-proving and problem-solving programs—are quite limited, although some notable successes have been achieved. The author further constrains himself by limiting the possible "theories" that the program can consider, and by evaluating them in a rather brute-force manner. Nevertheless, what the author is striving for is nothing less than mechanized inductive thought. While he necessarily falls short of that goal, some rudimentary elements are retained. The reader is encouraged to evaluate for himself the degree to which success is achieved, and to consider the distinctions the author draws between his own and other approaches.

—EDITOR.]

What methods should be used to solve this problem? It is clear from the start that remembering the training material will not bring us the necessary solution, because a new table is shown during test. Comparing the new table with the training material retained in memory will not produce coincidence with any previous record. The program will always give the same answer: "This was not taught to me."

Suppose we consider each number in a table to be a coordinate. Then any table can be considered to be a point in a multidimensional receptor space. For example, Tables 2 and 3 represent points in a fifteen-dimensional space. Would points corresponding to objects of one class be distributed compactly within this space? No, there is not the slightest hope of this. For example, two tables that belong to different classes could be considerably closer to each other (e.g., on account of coincidence of the numbers A and B) than different tables of the same class. The situation of the "sponge and water" no doubt has a place here.

Perhaps some standard arbitrary transformation of the receptor space (Perceptron) would be of help in this case. Assume that the receptor space is transformed into some other space by means of some such transformations. For example, one transformation may take the A number from the fourth row, the B number from the first row, and the C number from the third row and sum them; another transformation may use the B number from the second row and sum it with the A number from the first row; still a third transformation takes the sum of A numbers from the first and fifth rows and subtracts it from the B number on the second row, etc. Then each operator checks to see if the result exceeds some threshold. We see immediately that the classification problem has not been rendered easier by this kind of transformation.

Notice that the procedure described above is not a parody of the Perceptron, but is an accurate "in spirit and letter" application of the method to a given problem. In particular, one of the supposed attractions of the Perceptron lies in the fact that a simple rather than a directed transformation of the receptor space is performed in the hope that an easy divisibility of classes in A-unit space will be accomplished.

Even if we do not follow very strictly "the spirit and letter" of the Perceptron, and try to find not meaningless but standard transformations of the receptor space, then it is not known beforehand whether or not universal transformations for many different problems can be found. Who can assure us that separating the classes $\dfrac{A - B}{AB}$ and $\dfrac{A^2}{B} + B$ will require the same kind of transformation as separating the classes $(A + B + B) B$ and $\dfrac{A + B}{A - B}$?

Therefore we decided to devise a program that searches for features useful for a specific problem each time. At the same time, provision should be made so that among the features accessible to the program would be those that fit any problem from some total set of problems for which the program was created. At the beginning, the work was based primarily on the intuition of the experimenters because many features were given in implicit form, and it was impossible (because of the large number) to know beforehand what consequences the selection of this or that feature had.

2. Formal description of the program

THE PATTERNS

Numerical tables described in the preceding section are used. The program can be taught to distinguish from 2 to 24 classes of objects. Each class is represented by two tables during training. The program is informed that the first two tables belong to the first class, the following two to the second class. Each table can have from one to eight rows.

During test, the program is presented with other tables that are constructed according to the same or different rules. The number of rows in the table presented for recognition can be from one to eight, and it is not necessary that the number of rows be the same as during training. The program's task is to determine, with respect to each table presented during test, that "this table most resembles class X." From 1 to 24 tables can be presented for recognition.

GENERATION OF FEATURES

Let us recall that a feature is an algorithm that carries out a degenerate transformation of an object. The characteristic assigned to a given numerical table by this program with respect to some feature can have only two values, 0 or 1. The features are constructed in the following manner. A simple arithmetic function of A, B, and C (A, B, and C are numbers from one row of the table) is generated, for example, $A + B$ or $C \div B$, etc. The resulting number is substituted in one of three logic operators described below. A logic operator transforms this number into a binary variable.

The program uses three logic operators: L_1 determines whether or not the number is integral; L_2 checks the sign; L_3 compares the magnitude of the number to unity. Thus,

$$L_1 N = 1 , \quad \text{if } N \text{ is whole} ,$$
$$L_1 N = 0 , \quad \text{if } N \text{ is fractional} ,$$
$$L_2 N = 1 , \quad \text{if } N \geqslant 0 ,$$
$$L_2 N = 0 , \quad \text{if } N < 0 ,$$
$$L_3 N = 1 , \quad \text{if } N \geqslant 1 ,$$
$$L_3 N = 0 , \quad \text{if } N < 1 .$$

Consider an example. Let $f_i (A, B, C)$ be $B \div A$, then

$$L_1 f_i (7, 9, 3) = 0 ,$$
$$L_2 f_i (7, 9, 3) = 1 ,$$
$$L_3 f_i (7, 9, 3) = 1 .$$

Obviously, not all combinations of arithmetic functions and logic operators will be independent. For example, $L_2 AB = L_2 \dfrac{A}{B} = L_2 \dfrac{B}{A}$ (i.e., the product sign coincides with the quotient sign). Altogether 33 different combinations of arithmetic functions and logic operators are used. (Experiments were carried out on the machine M-2 INEUM AN USSR, the words of which are 33 bits long, and it was convenient to fill one machine word with logic variables related to one row of the table.)

Designate $L_j f_i$ by $L_{ji} (L_{ji} = L_{ji} [A, B, C])$. Take two logic variables L_{ji} and L_{qp} that can be constructed using different arithmetic functions and logic operators. Let $F_m (a, b)$ be some logic function of two variables a and b. $F_m (a, b)$ is regarded as a feature of one row of the table. That is, a row feature is $F_m (L_{ji}, L_{qp})$. Let us recall that there are 16 logic functions of two variables a and b. Among them two are always either 0 or 1 and are of no interest. Four are functions of only one variable $(a, \bar{a}, \bar{b}, b)$. Thus, there remain 10 functions of two variables. They are: ab, $\bar{a}b$, $a\bar{b}$, $\bar{a}\bar{b}$, $a \vee b$, $\bar{a} \vee b$, $a \vee \bar{b}$, $\bar{a} \vee \bar{b}$, $ab \vee \bar{a}\bar{b}$, $\bar{a}b \vee a\bar{b}$. The program considers all of these functions. The logic product of the features for all rows in a table is defined as a feature for the entire table. Thus, the kth feature for the table is:

$$F_k \equiv F_m [L_{ji} (A_1, B_1, C_1), L_{qp} (A_1, B_1, C_1)]$$
$$\wedge\ F_m [L_{ji} (A_2, B_2, C_2), L_{qp} (A_2, B_2, C_2)]$$
$$\wedge\ .\ .\ .$$
$$\wedge\ F_m [L_{ji} (A_n, B_n, C_n), L_{qp} (A_n, B_n, C_n)]\ ,$$

in which the subscripts on A, B, and C refer to the row, and there are n rows in the table. Features differ from one another by the values of i, j, p, q, and m, corresponding to the selection of different arithmetic functions f, logic operators L, and logic functions F. The program is able to select among 5,346 features.

[The author does not indicate how he arrives at this particular number. Clearly, there are constraints in the selection of i, j, p, q, and m, some combinations producing useless features. For example, if $i = p$, $j = q$, and $F_m (a, b) = a\bar{b}$, then the feature is always zero. The diagram in Fig. A may help to clarify the network structure the author is using to generate features.

—Editor.]

SELECTION OF FEATURES

Clearly, there is no sense in using any but the most useful features. Which are these?

The first requirement for a useful feature is that it should respond to a "cross section" of the objects (numerical tables) that occur during training. This means that the feature should not attribute the same characteristic (0 or 1) to all tables because such a response carries no information. No doubt the best information will be provided by a feature that characterizes half the tables by 0 and the other half by 1. In addition, features are of little use that produce cross sections identical to one already produced by a previously selected feature. (We do not consider at this time the reliability of the system. A feature that duplicates another's cross section can increase the reliability, and from this point of view it becomes useful.)

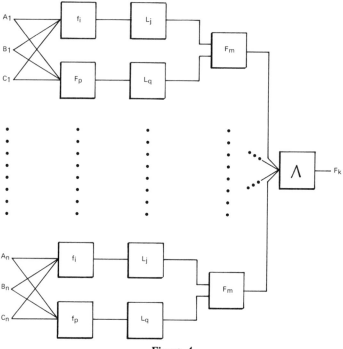

Figure A.

The second requirement for a useful feature is that it should attach identical characteristics to two tables of the same class.

In accordance with the above requirements, the program for feature selection works in the following way. All tables used in training are divided into two groups. The first group is called the performing group, the second the control group. Each group contains one table from every class. The program takes a candidate trial feature and calculates its resulting characteristic value for all tables of the performing group. Then a count is made of the number of tables having a characteristic value of 1.

Let the adaptation be carried out on S classes ($2 \leqslant S \leqslant 24$). If the number of units is not equal to $\dfrac{S}{2}$ when S is even, or $\dfrac{S}{2} \pm \dfrac{1}{2}$ when S is odd, then the feature is eliminated. If the feature survives this test, the program proceeds to calculate characteristic values of the feature for tables of the control group. Then identity between characteristics for tables of the performing and control groups is checked. If they are identical for all classes, the feature is retained, otherwise it is eliminated.

After exhausting all possible 5,346 features, the program relaxes the strictness of the first step of selection, and checks again the features previously eliminated. Features are now passed that produce $\frac{S}{2} \pm 1$ units when S is even and $\frac{S}{2} \pm 1\frac{1}{2}$ when S is odd. Later, the strictness of selection may again be reduced, etc. The whole process ends when 30 useful features are selected, or when a further reduction of the selection strictness would lead to retention of useless features.

It is easy to prove that features will be selected regardless of how the double set of tables is divided into performing and control groups. The program can also handle the case when each class is represented not by two tables but by a large number of tables.

At the conclusion of training, the memory contains lists of useful features (30 or fewer) as well as characteristic values for the numerical tables with respect to all features (within a class tables have identical characteristics).

TEST

During test, the program attaches to unknown tables characteristics according to all the features selected during training. The resulting characteristics are compared with those of tables used during training. The comparison includes counting the number of features according to which the characteristics do not coincide. As a result, the following information is obtained: the characteristics of this unfamiliar table disagree with the characteristics of tables of the first class with respect to 17 features; of the second class, with respect to 3 features; of the third class, with respect to 14 features, etc. The program selects the three smallest numbers, and prints out the corresponding classes in the order of increasing disagreement among their characteristics.

3. The meaning of features

The preceding section formally described the features accessible to the program. Emphasis was placed upon a clear presentation of the algorithm by which each feature reflects the table of numbers into a value of either 0 or 1. However, after going through "arithmetic functions," "logic operators," etc., it is very difficult to understand what these "features" are in reality. The author must confess that after such a description it would be difficult for him, too, to comprehend the whole matter. Therefore, let us look closer and analyze the given program.

For convenience, we chose features that can produce characteristic values of only 0 or 1. Thus each feature divides classes of tables into two groups (for example, up to 24 classes, each representing a different arithmetic rule, were used during training). Let us consider how different arithmetic rules may be divided in a more "natural" way.

To begin with, we may think about rules containing division and those that do not; rules containing comparatively high powers of A and B and those that do not, etc. Obviously there can be many such "natural" divisions. We do not need a great number of them to understand what form they might take. Consider first, rules that contain division and those without it. What feature is needed in this case to determine the membership of a given table in some class? We know that division is the only operation able to produce fractions from whole numbers. This means that it is not a bad idea at all to have integral-value algorithms among the basic building blocks from which the features are constructed.

It is easy to see, however, that verifying whether or not the number C has an integer value, for example, cannot serve as a feature for indicating that there are differences in the arithmetic rules for different tables. There are two types of failures in this case. First, if A and B are fractional, then C may be not a whole number even without the presence of division. On the other hand, both A and B may be whole numbers, and the division rule may be present, but C still could be integer valued. For example, if the law is expressed by $(A/B) + A + B = C$, then when $A = 6$ and $B = 2$, C is equal to 11.

Consider the first type of failure. The essence of it is that a fractional value of C occurs only when division is present and when certain constraints on A and B are satisfied. The true statement is not, "if C is fractional then the law contains division," but the statement is "if A and B are whole and C is fractional at the same time, then the law contains division." If we expect the program to produce such statements, then the simplest way is to make it possible for the program to construct logic functions based on more elementary statements. It should be able to construct features of the type "if $\left|\dfrac{A}{C}\right| < 1$ and $A + B \geqslant 0$, then produce the characteristic value 0; otherwise, 1." The program should not "hesitate" over the appropriateness of such features from the standpoint of arithmetic rules. The appropriateness criterion (or absence of it) should be whether or not tables can be divided by this feature into groups, and whether or not the characteristic with respect to this feature within a class is stable.

Consider now the second type of failure. It follows from the fact that the situation in which A and B are whole and C fractional is not a necessary but only a sufficient feature for the presence of division in the rule. Therefore, it is advantageous to state with respect not to one line but to the whole table, "if A and B are whole even in one line of the table and C is fractional, then the rule contains division." This is the reason why a logic function (product) of characteristic values for individual lines is used as a feature for the table as a whole.

It might appear that to construct an adequate feature it is necessary to use the logic sum (not product) of lines. But since all logic functions are being sought for lines, then among them a negation may be encountered, and of course the product of negations is the same as the negation of the sum. Since we do not care what characteristic value a feature attaches to a given group of tables, the use of a logic product provides for both necessary and sufficient features.

Clearly, it is not the same to show the program two tables of one class each containing three lines, or one table consisting of six lines that is a combination of two tables of three lines each. It is possible that a table consisting of six lines possesses a certain sufficient feature, but that after it is divided, only one of the two new tables possesses this same feature. The program will decide that the feature is unstable and will eliminate it.

4. Experimental results

DEPENDENCE OF SELECTED FEATURES
ON THE TRAINING MATERIAL

First experiments have shown that the selection of features depends not only on the set of classes participating in training but also on the actual numbers used during the construction of the tables. For example, if all lines of all tables contain only integer values of A and B, then a feature is likely to be selected which asks, "Is C fractional in any line?" However, if we add lines containing fractional values of A and B to the tables then this feature ceases to be useful. What will the program substitute for it? An ideal feature from the point of view of arithmetic would sound like this: "If A and B are whole and C is fractional even in one line of the table then respond with a 0." But this feature is a function of three variables, and the program under consideration can construct functions of no more than two variables. Therefore, the program finds a "substitute" for the ideal feature. In our case it has selected such features as: "Is $A \times B$ whole and C fractional in any line?" Instead of integer values for A and B individually, the program requires an integer value for the product of A and B.

From the point of view of mathematics this feature is not bad. In fact, if A and B are not selected deliberately, then it is unlikely that A and B will be fractional and their product whole. Among fractional A's and B's shown to the program, it happened that there were no such cases. If such cases had happened, then this feature would not have been selected, and something more suitable would have been selected.

Broadening the regions from which A and B can be taken sometimes prevents the program from introducing necessary "reservations" regarding the features. It is not surprising, therefore, that when A and B can have whole, fractional, positive, or negative values, the program does not classify tables as well after training, as when A and B can have only positive integer values. It is of interest that the program adapts *itself* to the region of allowable values of A and B. We emphasize *itself* because the program is not informed about which features are good in the world of whole numbers, or in the world of fractional numbers. As soon as constraints appear on the possible values of A and B, the program immediately uses the "released reserve" of logic possibilities for the construction of a greater variety of features.

RECOGNITION OF ARITHMETIC RULES

In experiments of this series, tables containing natural A and B numbers were introduced into the machine during training. All rows of tables belonging to the same class were constructed according to the same arithmetic rule. Tables of different classes were constructed according to different rules. Tables of the same classes that participated in training containing other A and B numbers were presented to the program during test.

Two sets with 24 arithmetic rules in each were used; they are presented in Table 4. Adaptation experiments were carried out with 6, 8, 9, and 24 classes. During adaptation with 6, 8, and 9 classes the first 6, 8, or 9 rules from the first set were used. When the number of classes was 9 or below, completely correct classification of the tables was achieved. This means that the number of the correct class was always printed in first place. In the case of 24 classes, not all tables were recognized correctly.

What parameter can we use to characterize the quality of recognition? Sometimes the measure of interest is the percentage of times the correct class number is in first place. However, this quantity is not very convenient, especially when it is necessary to compare the performance of two programs that select from a different number of classes. In fact, we cannot say that a program selecting from two classes and producing 60% correct recognition performs better than one selecting from 1,000 classes with 10% correct recognition. Furthermore, we consider a program excellent even if it never prints the correct number in first place, if this number is always included among the first 10 numbers, say, in the case of 1,000 classes.

It would be convenient to compare program performance after adaptation with a standard program "guessing arbitrarily." In fact, we can imagine that there exists a program that during test does not even look at the table. It performs arbitrarily and by some random process arranges numbers in order from 1 to S, where S is the number of classes from which the selection is made. The correct class number will, on the average, appear at the location $M_r = \dfrac{S+1}{2}$ in the list. Clearly, the average position of correct class numbers produced by a program for which teaching was of no benefit will also be M_r.

TABLE 4

	Set I				Set II		
1	$(A - B)AB$	II	I	1	$A - A \equiv 0$	III	IV
2	$\dfrac{A}{B} + A + B$	VI	I	2	$\dfrac{A}{B} - \dfrac{1}{A}$	III	IV
3	$\dfrac{B - A}{A} - A$	IV	II	3	$AB^2 - A$	I	VI
4	$(A + B)(A - B)$	II	I	4	$B^2 - B^4$	II	I
5	$\dfrac{A - B}{A + B}$	III	IV	5	$\dfrac{A + B}{A - B}$	III	IV
6	$\dfrac{AB}{A + B}$	III	V	6	$(B - A)^2 - B$	V	I
7	$(A + B)AB$	I	VI	7	$(B - A)^2 + B$	VI	I
8	$\dfrac{A + B}{A} + B$	III	IV	8	$\dfrac{B}{(A - B)^2}$	III	IV
9	$\dfrac{(A - B)A}{B}$	II	III	9	$\left(\dfrac{B}{A - B}\right)^2$	III	IV
10	$\dfrac{A}{B}\left(A - \dfrac{A}{B}\right)$	VI	I	10	$\left(\dfrac{A}{B}\right)^2 - \dfrac{A}{B}$	III	IV
11	$\dfrac{A + B}{AB}$	III	IV	11	$\left(\dfrac{A}{B}\right)^2 + \dfrac{A}{B}$	III	IV
12	$\dfrac{A - B}{AB}$	IV	III	12	$B^3 - B^2$	I	VI
13	$\dfrac{B - 2A}{B}$	IV	II	13	$\dfrac{A}{B^4}$	III	IV
14	$\dfrac{2A^2}{B}$	I	III	14	$\dfrac{B}{B^4}$	III	IV
15	$AB - B + A$	I	VI	15	A^3B^2	V	I
16	$(A - AB)B$	II	I	16	$4B$	I	VI
17	$(A - 2B)A$	II	I	17	$6B$	I	VI
18	$\dfrac{AB}{B^2 + A}$	III	IV	18	$4A^2B^2$	V	VI
19	$\dfrac{A + B}{B^2}$	III	IV	19	$5B$	I	VI
20	$\dfrac{B}{A}\left(\dfrac{A}{A} + \dfrac{B}{A}\right)$	III	IV	20	$\dfrac{(B - A)^2}{A}$	III	I
21	$\dfrac{B}{B + 2A}$	III	V	21	$\dfrac{B}{A} - \dfrac{A}{B}$	III	IV
22	$AB + B^2$	I	VI	22	$\dfrac{A}{B - B^2}$	IV	III
23	$4A^2B^2$	V	VI	23	$\dfrac{A}{3B}$	IV	III
24	$\dfrac{A^4}{B}$	V	I	24	$\dfrac{A}{4B}$	IV	III

In an ideal case the recognizing program always places the correct class number at the position $M_0 = 1$. Let the actual program produce the average position M_c during selection from S classes. The program's ratio of "guessing" to "knowing" during test can then be characterized by the value

$$\eta = \frac{M_c - M_0}{M_r - M_0} = \frac{M_c - 1}{M_r - 1}.$$

In the ideal case we will have $\eta = 0$, while for random guessing, $\eta = 1$.

Let us go back now to the recognition of tables. After the program on 24 classes of the first set (Table 4) testing on other tables of the same classes produced $\eta = 0.025$. In the case of the second set, $\eta = 0.036$ (Table 4). Thus, random guessing amounted to about 3% when the selection was made from 24 classes.

RECOGNITION OF ARITHMETIC LAWS NOT PARTICIPATING
IN THE SELECTION OF FEATURES

During adaptation on rules of the second set, the program selected features which were mostly different from those of the first set. The question of degree of specificity of selected features was therefore raised.

Let us define the question more accurately. Thirty features selected during adaptation, for example in the case of the second set of rules, transform every table into one apex of a thirty-dimensional cube. Note that distance in this space is measured in the Hamming sense. The distance between two apexes of an n-dimensional cube is the number of noncoinciding coordinates. For example, the distance between the four-dimensional points $(1, 1, 0, 0)$ and $(0, 1, 0, 0)$ is 1, and between the points $(1, 1, 0, 0)$ and $(1, 0, 1, 0)$ is 2. It follows that this measure can encompass only whole nonnegative values that do not exceed the space dimensionality (i.e., coordinate numbers of a point). For the particular transformation produced by the experiments, tables of one class tend to enter either the same points or points close to one another. Different classes enter, on the average, into regions that are far from one another. (Cases were encountered when the program was unable to separate some classes; for example, rules 16, 17, and 19 from the second set were projected onto one and the same space point.) In other words, the classes of objects, which are not compact within the receptor field, become compact within the feature space after transformation.

The question of specificity thus becomes as follows: Will the transformation found when adaptation was carried out on the second set of rules also produce a compact distribution of classes within the thirty-dimensional space of characteristics on the first set of rules? Or is this transformation suitable only for classes from the training set and not for others?

To answer these questions experiments were carried out with the 24 classes of the second set (Table 4). Thirty useful features were selected and retained in memory, and could not be changed for the duration of the experiment. Then tables were introduced into the machine that were constructed according to the rules of the first set. The program gave them characteristics according to the already defined features, and all characteristics were retained in memory. Other tables constructed according to the rules of the first set were then introduced for test. Their characteristics were calculated and were compared with those present in memory. The result was $\eta = 0.029$. Comparison with experimental results of the prior series ($\eta = 0.025$, and $\eta = 0.036$) shows that recognition using "foreign" features is no worse than in the case of "related" features. This means that the transformation found during adaptation turned out to be good also for classes of the first set.

In other words, one kind of arithmetic rules was presented to the program, and it proceeded to find a space in which not only these but other arithmetic rules could be successfully divided. It was of interest to see if identical results could be obtained with fewer rules. In subsequent experiments, 6 arithmetic rules were used during adaptation (the first 6 from the first set). Then recognition of 24 rules was carried out according to the selected features (as in the previous experiment). Testing produced: $\eta = 0.007$ in the case of the first set, and $\eta = 0.025$ for the second set.

Notice that in this experiment with foreign features a result even better than with features especially selected is obtained. The reason is not that features selected during adaptation on 6 rules perform more reliably than those selected during adaptation on 24 rules. On the contrary, evaluation of the results shows that the number of errors obtained during adaptation on 6 rules is 4.2%, whereas it is only 1.4% for characteristics obtained during adaptation on 24 rules. But what, then, is the reason that a more reliably performing feature sometimes produces poorer recognition? The answer is that the quality of recognition is determined not only by the reliability of individual features, but also by the quantity of features by which two classes differ (how distant their transformations are located). When adaptation is carried out on 24 classes, the characteristics of some classes with respect to all features may be nearly identical (this shortcoming can be corrected by some changes in the "novelty" criterion for features). Under these conditions errors in a small number of features can lead to a worsening of the test results. On the other hand, features selected during adaptation on 6 classes produced transformations far from one other for different classes, although they performed less reliably. In this particular case it led to some improvement in recognition.

In any case, the transformation discovered during adaptation on 6 arithmetic rules turned out to be suitable for satisfactory recognition of at least 48 rules, and probably for many more.

Does this not contradict the idea that there cannot exist a universal transformation of the receptor field suitable for a wide range of problems? A final answer to this question will be given later in this section when describing problems requiring another transformation of the receptor field. At the present stage we can say only that recognition problems of different arithmetic rules resemble each other for this program, and can be solved sometimes by one and the same transformation.

CLASSIFICATION OF ARITHMETIC RULES

In this experiment, six groups of rules were introduced into the machine during adaptation (Table 5). Each group consisted of two rules resembling each other with respect to arithmetic operations. Tables constructed according to the rules of each group were used in the same way as in the preceding series of experiments. The program generated features during adaptation, producing characteristics for the rules of any one group.

During test, 24 rules were introduced, and the program decided which group a given rule resembled most. Table 4 (Roman numerals) shows the program's choices for the two first places. The reader can compare the "opinion" of the program with his own concerning the separation of arithmetic rules into the groups of Table 5.

TABLE 5

I	II	III	IV	V	VI
$(A + B)AB$	$(B - A)AB$	$\dfrac{A + B}{AB}$	$\dfrac{A - B}{AB}$	A^2B^3	$2A + 3B$
$AB + A + B$	$A - AB - B$	$\dfrac{A}{(A + B)B}$	$\dfrac{B - 2A}{A}$	A^3B^2	$3A + 2B$

RECOGNITION OF LOGIC RULES

This program was designed for the recognition of tables constructed according to arithmetic rules. But perhaps it might have wider application. To test this possibility, experiments were conducted on tables constructed in accordance with other types of rules, in particular, *logic rules*. Tables 6 and 7 give examples of such rules. The quantity C in Table 6 is equivalent

TABLE 6

A	B	C
2	3	1
7	-2	0
-3	5	0
5	2	1
-1	-3	0

TABLE 7

A	B	C
2	3	0
7	-2	1
-3	5	0
5	2	1
-1	-3	1

to the statement, "*A* and *B* are positive." In Table 7, it is equivalent to the statement, "*A* is larger than *B*."

Adaptation was performed on tables constructed according to four different logic rules. During test, different tables constructed according to the same four logic rules were presented. All four rules were recognized correctly ($\eta = 0$). Thus, the program found a good transformation of the receptor field for the given problem. Could it be that the transformation produced during adaptation on arithmetic rules would also be suitable for this problem? To test this possibility, features were selected during adaptation on nine arithmetic rules. Then tables constructed according to logic rules were introduced into the machine for test. The result was $\eta = 1.0$! After adaptation of arithmetic rules, the program became completely incapable of classifying logic rules.

A comparison of characteristic values of the four logic rules showed that all four hit one and the same point in feature space. Under these circumstances, recognition was out of the question!

Thus, both those transformations suitable for arithmetic rules and those suitable for logic rules are accessible to the program, but they are different. It is necessary for the program to use different transformations of the receptor field when solving different groups of problems. It is of interest to notice that the point in feature space corresponding to all four logic rules turned out to be at a considerable distance from points corresponding to different arithmetic rules. Therefore, the program stated during test that logic rules "do not resemble" any of the arithmetic rules but "resemble" logic rules (without noticing a difference between them).

This situation is analogous to that in which a Caucasian finds himself when he first encounters Chinese people. He cannot recognize and distinguish them according to their facial features. All the features in the mind of a Caucasian are those useful for recognizing Caucasians, and this prevents him from differentiating among Chinese people. A Chinese person feels the same way when placed among Caucasians for the first time. However, the presence of certain images in the brain of man is not determined by genetics. The Chinese brought up in Europe, or the Caucasian brought up in China easily recognize faces of either race.

MIXED LAWS (A TRAP FOR THE PROGRAM)

Some readers may want to "trap" the program *Arithmetic*. They reason that it should be a difficult task for the program if different lines of the same table are constructed according to different arithmetic rules in accordance with some additional logic conditions.

Examples of tables constructed according to such "mixed" logic and arithmetic rules are given in Tables 8 and 9. Lines of Table 8 are constructed according to the following rules:

$C = A + B$ if $A \geqslant 0$ and $B \geqslant 0$; $C = A - B$ if $A \geqslant 0$ and $B < 0$;
$C = A \div B$ if $A < 0$ and $B \geqslant 0$; $C = AB$ if $A < 0$ and $B < 0$.

Table 9 is constructed according to different rules of the same type.

TABLE 8

A	B	C
2	3	5
7	−2	9
−3	5	−0.6
5	2	7
−2	−3	6

TABLE 9

A	B	C
2	3	−1
7	−2	−3.5
−3	5	−15
5	2	3
−2	−3	−5

Ten mixed problems were used during adaptation, and ten new problems constructed according to the same rules were used during test. All ten tables were recognized correctly. Thus, although different lines of each table were constructed according to different arithmetic rules, the program had enough logic alternatives to avoid a trap.

Experiments on arithmetic and logic rules using features selected on mixed problems during adaptation were also carried out. Results of these and similar experiments are shown in Table 10.

TABLE 10

Recognition Test Performance (η)

Material Used for Feature Selection	Arithmetic Rules (9)	Mixed Rules (10)	Logic Rules (4)
Arithmetic (9 rules)	0.00	0.20	1.00
Mixed (10 rules)	0.06	0.00	0.83
Logic (4 rules)	—	—	0.00

It is clear that mixed problems for a given program are intermediate in difficulty between the arithmetic and logic rules to some extent. At the same time, although mixed rules are closer to arithmetic than to logic rules, the transformation that best suits arithmetic rules is not the best for the mixed, and vice versa.

5. Characteristics of the algorithm

THE TEST ALGORITHM

Until now we have talked about the selection of different transformations of the receptor field into feature space after different kinds of adaptation (arithmetic and logic rules). The program selects 30-dimensional subfields within the 5,346-dimensional feature space accessible to it.

However, there is another way of describing the adaptation process. We might say that the separation of classes is always carried out in the same 5,346-dimensional field, but the method of class separation is selected during adaptation. If no limitations are imposed on the possible complexity of the classification method, then we can consider the rigid transformation (independent of the problem) of the receptor field into a 5,346-dimensional feature space to reduce the whole matter to finding a classification method within the receptor field.

[In other words, if every possible "pattern" is mapped onto a unique point in feature space, then we are back to the original problem. This is of course the essence of the feature-selection or feature-design (synthesis) problem, namely, how to break up or operate upon the pattern dimensionality to simplify classification without inadvertently throwing out some essential information. In the absence of any applicable theory to cover this situation, workers in the field have been generally guided, as the author notes below, by two principles: (1) break up the problem (and usually the receptor field) so that it is more comprehensible to the designer, and (2) break up the problem so that erroneous behavior of isolated parts of the decision networks is not catastrophic, and so that individual errors can be identified.

—EDITOR.]

If we want to describe the program in terms that facilitate understanding, then considering the classification algorithm as a single "black box" is not likely to be productive. Therefore, we try to divide the classification algorithm into several stages that can be easily comprehended. This kind of division is, of course, conditional, but makes it possible to compare corresponding parts of different algorithms.

Consider that the separation of classes always occurs in some Euclidean space. Classification methods either divide the space into parts (one per class) by planes, or by indicating some points ("class centers") and adjacent regions around these centers. Only points inside of these adjacent regions can be classified; all others do not belong to any class. The space within which the separation of classes takes place is called the feature space.

A projection of the receptor field into feature space can be also subdivided into parts. That part of the transformation always encountered during test regardless of the problem or the actual adaptation process is called the *rigid part*. The algorithm for the rigid transformation is entirely determined by the programmer.

That part of the transformation that can be absent during test (when adaptation is carried out on some other classes) is called the *adaptive part*. The adaptive part of a transformation is always some subset of the possible transformations determined by the programmer. The adaptation program selects this subset and the selection result depends on the training material.

The method for separating classes within the feature space is also usually *adaptive* because either the parameters of hyperplanes performing the separation or class centers and radii of possible regions are found during training.

Experiments described above illustrate the advantages of considering the formation of the receptor field transformation and the formation of the classification method, as independent processes. In these experiments, the transformation of the receptor field was formed during adaptation on rules of one type (arithmetic, for example). But formation of the classification method took place during training on rules of another type (mixed, for example). Let us see now how the test algorithm in the program *Arithmetic* is divided. Distance from the image of an unknown table in feature space is the dividing rule in this program. Selecting the minimum among these distances is one method of class separation. Another assigns an object to a class when the distance to the center of the class is less than some constant.

The feature space within which any of these resolving rules performs is a 30-dimensional field. Because different problems use different sets of features, the transformation of the receptor field is not completely rigid but contains an adaptive part. In the program *Arithmetic*, the rigid transformations are those using the arithmetic functions f_i and logic operators L_j. If a table has t lines ($1 \leqslant t \leqslant 8$), then it can be rigidly projected onto a $33t$-dimensional field. Finding 30 logic functions using table coordinates in this $33t$-dimensional field is the adaptive operation.

By comparison, consider the structures of the algorithms in the Braverman program and in the Perceptron, using the same scheme.

In the Braverman program, a rule of the first type (a set of planes) is used. It is formed during adaptation. The field of useful features coincides with the receptor field. Thus, in the Braverman program there is neither a rigid nor an adaptive transformation of the receptor field.

Separation of classes in the Perceptron is carried out using one plane in A-space. Therefore, feature space coincides with A-space. The transformation of the receptor field into feature space is rigid. Only the classification rule adapts in the Perceptron during training (i.e., parameters of the dividing plane).

Let us deliberate for a while on the possibility of describing the work of the program *Arithmetic* without using the statement: "an adaptive transformation of the receptor field." In the actual program, as was demonstrated, this was impossible to do. Therefore, let us "supplement" the program with some operations so that it contains a rigid transformation. Let the supplemented program project the receptor fields not onto the 30-dimensional but onto the 5,346-dimensional field of all possible features (this projection will be a rigid one).

It is easy to see that there is no simple and reliable classification rule in this supplemented space. The reason is that the addition of new coordinates is an operation that influences the distance between points. Points present in a 30-dimensional space in the vicinity of the class center may be at a great distance from one another in the supplemented field. The average characteristic distance value in an increased field will be on the order 2,500 in the Hamming sense. However, only part of this value, on the order of 100, will depend on important factors (belong to some class), and all the rest will depend only on the random circumstances associated with a given problem.

Notice that broadening the space from 30 to 5,346 measurements is possible only if any of the 5,346 features can be applied to any table. There are, however, features that are not applicable to all objects. For example, the property, "A is larger than the least common multiple of B and C," is not applicable to tables containing even one fractional value of B or C. (Recall that nonapplicability does not mean that the feature produces a characteristic value of zero, but that it cannot produce any characteristic value.)

THE AMOUNT OF MEMORY OCCUPIED AFTER ADAPTATION

It is often said that the creation of "thinking machines" is hindered by the small memory of modern computers. Let us examine the amount of information stored in the machine memory in the course of adaptation.

This information is divided into two separate groups. The first group contains information about useful features. It determines the transformation of the receptor field into the feature space during test.

The second group contains information about the locations of class centers within feature space. This information is used during test for determining the resemblance of an unknown object to some class.

Up to 30 features are selected during adaptation. All the information about the structure of any one feature can be stacked easily into 16 bits. Thus, all the information regarding transformation of the receptor field can be contained in 15 machine cells. (In actual practice, for convenience, this information occupies 30 cells.) This volume depends only modestly on the number of classes (it increases logarithmically with the number of classes).

Coordinates of the class centers within feature space occupy 30 bits each. Thus, the amount of memory occupied by information of the second group should be approximately equivalent to the number of classes (in reality it increases somewhat faster because of the increase in the number of features).

Now compare the memory volume per class after adaptation with the volume required for recording tables. After adaptation 50 bits are required for each of the 24 classes of tables (30 are center coordinates and 20 are the share of one class in the 480 digits occupied for recording features).

Adaptation in this case was carried out with two tables of each class. This amounts to 48 ($3 \times 8 \times 2$) bits per class. Actually each number was recorded in a separate cell (33 bits); however, in principle, each number could be recorded in 17 bits with an accuracy sufficient for this problem. (Further reduction of accuracy may lead to acceptance of fractional numbers as whole numbers.) Thus, some $17 \times 48 \approx 800$ bits are required for recording tables belonging to one class.

It has been stated that the principal aim of any recognizing system is to stop paying attention to irrelevant circumstances in any given problem. By any standard, this should lead to a reduction in memory requirements in going from the original problem statement to its classification essentials, and indeed, such appears to be the case in the experimental program.

DESCRIPTION OF CLASSES

A set of class characteristics with respect to all features can be considered as a description of this class in some language. Descriptions in this case are short. This is because of the special language selected by the program (from the set of languages accessible to it), which suits the given set of classes. In some cases, the language selected for a few arithmetic rules is quite suitable for many arithmetic rules. On the other hand, this language is not acceptable for logic rules, because their descriptions in this language are identical.

[The author alludes here again to the notion of pattern "languages" and pattern "descriptions." These concepts are close to those currently being pursued in this country under the general titles of *picture linguistics, picture syntax, picture parsing,* etc. Works in this area by Narasimhan, Ledley, Evans, and Shaw are listed at the end of Chapter 2. The general notion is to develop languages especially suited for describing pictures and their elements in a hierarchy of successively more abstract terms. It is useful to read the remaining paragraphs of this section with the word "picture" substituted for the words "pattern" or "object." The author returns to this theme in later chapters, and indeed this viewpoint appears to open one of the most promising present avenues for future development in the field of image recognition.

—EDITOR.]

Let us see this in an everyday example. Let the difference between elephants, giraffes, cats, hares, and geese be based on statements: weight more than 30 kg, length of neck 50% longer than trunk, length of tail 20% longer than trunk, etc. All the above animals when described by this language will have different descriptions. However, try to use the same language to distinguish tigers, lions, and panthers. These animals can also be described by the language but their descriptions are identical.

We might say then that languages selected by the program for arithmetic and logic rules are applicable in principle for all objects (tables above), but they are inconvenient for other types of rules. This is a serious shortcoming of this program. In fact, the problem of adaptation can be defined as that of creating a short description of the material, on the one hand, while preserving the possibility of class differentiation, on the other hand. Brevity requires the elimination of information regarding individual differences between objects of one class in the overall description. This is precisely what makes it possible to extrapolate to the description of new objects during test. It is easy to obtain a lengthy description of the material, for example, a logic sum (disjunction) of detailed descriptions of all objects (from the training material) of a given class. But in this case the possibility of extrapolation is lost, and with it the ability to recognize objects absent in the training material.

The shorter the description of classes, the higher the degree of abstraction, and the less information is retained regarding random properties of the training material.

Consider now what languages make short descriptions possible. We often use specialized languages that are useful in comparatively narrow subject areas but that make it possible to produce short descriptions of objects within that subject. The language used in court is completely unacceptable for describing the operation of a steam engine, and vice versa. Such terms as *attorney, crime, verdict, strong argument,* etc. cannot be applied to the steam engine. Is there a universal language suitable for both these subjects? Evidently yes, but it is beyond our comprehension, and we cannot even imagine it from a rational point of view. Perhaps a description in terms of such a universal language would contain information about the coordinates of all the elementary parts present in the system (a court or a steam engine) for a given time interval. But descriptions would be long. In addition, it would be extremely difficult to distinguish between a trial in which the defendant was acquitted and one in which he was found guilty using this type of description. The same thing would happen if we tried to distinguish a diesel from a steam engine.

It can be said then that short descriptions depend upon the use of specialized languages that are mainly unacceptable for a large range of questions. It is no accident that all specialized regions of knowledge create their own jargons, and terrify philologists by the fact that they "spread" into other regions of our life.

In Chapter 9, an algorithm will be considered that creates for one kind of problem a language that is acceptable for objects present in other problems. The result is that still shorter descriptions can be obtained. The program *Arithmetic* does not have this property, and this constitutes its shortcoming.

THE STRUCTURE OF FEATURES

All the various features in the program *Arithmetic* are obtained in the form of combinations of a small number of algorithms. They work in sequence and are divided into three groups: (1) arithmetic functions f_i, 12 to 16 of them in different variants; (2) logic operators L_j, 3 of them; (3) logic functions F_m, 10 of them. This makes it possible to retain in memory a small number of very simple algorithms (approximately 30).

Although the "bricks" from which features are constructed are simple, they are not selected at random. Here lies the difference between the program *Arithmetic* and the Perceptron. The program starts at a high level of organization. (We do not agree with the point of view that the Perceptron does not have any initial organization. It is simply on a very low level, and masked by the arbitrary selection of relationships.)

THE FLEXIBILITY OF THE PROGRAM

One might question the degree to which the selection of arithmetic functions and logic operators is critical in the program *Arithmetic*. Could the reason for success be that the authors were lucky enough to find precisely those 33 combinations that secured good performance for the system? In order to check this, 20 of these combinations were replaced by others, and selected experiments were repeated. After adaptation on arithmetic rules, the recognition rate of the program was no worse then before (with the old set of combinations).

An experiment was also carried out with fewer logic operators accessible to the program. Only two were used instead of three. Even in this case no significant change in test results occurred.

It was also of interest to see how the program would behave in the presence of slight machine defects. If these defects did not lead to a complete machine stoppage, and produced only computational errors, then after repeated adaptation different features were selected. Recognition was as good as before with these new features. An outsider could not tell that the machine had any defects. It appeared rather that the machine possessed a "free will" or "phantasy" that did not interfere with the attainment of the goal, but only made the road to it more heterogeneous.

CHAPTER 4

Recognition and Imitation

1. Description of recognizing systems in terms of the theory of automata

AT THIS POINT the reader may wonder why the author needs one additional method for describing recognizing systems. Why are automata needed?

The fact is, different aspects of the recognizing system performance are described more easily (more briefly) by using different languages. Translation from one language into another is simple. Therefore, in many places in this book we will use different methods of description.

In this section, we consider a recognizing system in the process of adaptation as an automaton consisting of two parts (Fig. 10). The part K is an automaton with many states. Selection of states is accomplished by a "push button." Different push buttons are designated by arrows at the top of block K. The automaton K classifies objects according to some rigid algorithm associated with each state. Each pattern or object at the input to K will be classified as belonging to either the first or the second class, or to neither of them ("trash").

Adaptation consists of selecting the state of K, i.e., selecting which push button should be pressed. This selection is carried out by the block L on the basis of knowledge of the teaching or training material. Only the block K operates during test or "examination."

Dividing the recognizing system into blocks K and L is arbitrary to a large extent. For example, in the majority of actual systems, the block L contains almost a complete copy of the block K as an integral part, in order to be able to check the result on the training material of "pressing" any given button. However, we are not interested at the moment in how blocks are designed.

At the input to block L there is a set of patterns, together with an indication of the class to which each of them belongs. At the output of block L there is a selection of one of the states of block K.

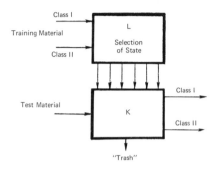

Figure 10. Scheme of an adaptive recognizing system. Block K performs classification. Block L selects the state of block K.

At the input of block K there is a sequence of patterns or objects about which no class membership information is given. At the output of block K there is a statement assigning patterns to classes, or to "trash."

2. Possible causes of poor performance of the recognition system

Assume that we have a large number of objects from two classes. Some of them are presented to the input of block L. One of the block K buttons will be pressed. All the remaining objects are then presented to the input of block K. Each of them will be assigned to some class. Assume that the system makes many errors. This could occur for two reasons.

First, the block K may not have a state necessary for the solution of the given problem. No matter what button we press, classification of the objects by the block K will differ from the classification given initially. Second, the block L may not be able to find the needed state, although it exists.

It is beside the point that the system may have a very poor set of states for a given problem. For example, if a system has only three states, (1) separation of large figures from small, (2) those in the left part of the frame from those in the right, and (3) convex from concave, then it will never learn how to differentiate circles from triangles. No amount of optimization by the block L will help in this matter.

It would be a surprise to some readers that man is an example of a system possessing shortcomings of the second type. Let us show by an experiment the limitation of block L in man.

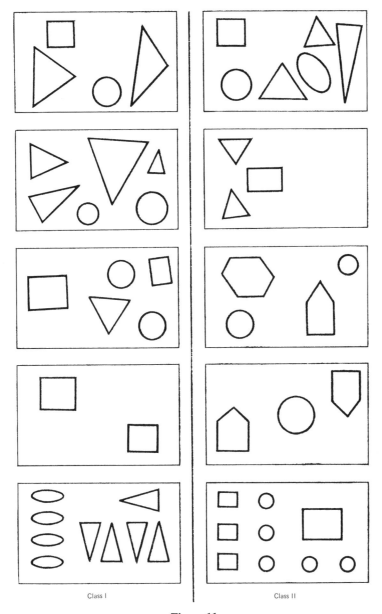

Class I   Class II

Figure 11.

Examine Fig. 11. The five pictures on the left are assigned to the first class; those on the right belong to the second class. See if you can find a principle on the basis of which you could recognize new objects by studying these examples. Do not read the explanation below until you find the principle by yourself.

The majority of people cannot solve this problem in ten minutes. The reason is not the small number of examples given for adaptation. If this were so, you would be able to find several features that would make it possible to separate pictures of the first class in Fig. 11 from those of the second class. ("Block L" would be able to find several different states.) I assume that you probably did not find even a single suitable state for "block K." Even increasing the number of training samples would not, probably, simplify the task.

It never occurs to you to check the feature *the difference in the number of all angles and the number of all figures in the picture*. The characteristic of all pictures of Class I with respect to this feature is equal to 6, and of pictures in Class II, to 7.

[This is not only a good illustration of the author's point about the difficulty of finding suitable features, it also illustrates beautifully two other factors important in pattern recognition. One is that the same objects can be seen from quite different viewpoints by different people (and pattern recognition machines). The other is the high value we place on a parsimonious description of the classification criteria, in other words, the importance of a simple theory. These factors can be demonstrated by taking a look at the editor's response to the author's challenge. The editor chose to try out a classification scheme based upon the presence or absence of different types of figures in each picture. The result is given in Table *A* (patterns are numbered from top to bottom, left

TABLE *A*

Are there one or more of the following figures in the picture?

Pattern Number	Triangle (X_1)	Circle (X_2)	Oval (X_3)	Rectangle (X_4)	Polygon with more than 4 sides (X_5)	Class I = 0 II = 1
1	1	1	0	1	0	0
2	1	1	0	0	0	0
3	1	1	0	1	0	0
4	0	0	0	1	0	0
5	1	0	1	1	0	0
6	1	1	1	1	0	1
7	1	0	0	1	0	1
8	0	1	0	0	1	1
9	0	1	0	0	1	1
10	0	1	0	1	0	1

column first). From this table the class can be written as a Boolean function, namely,

$$
\begin{aligned}
C = \; & X_1 X_2 X_3 X_4 \overline{X}_5 \\
+ \; & X_1 \overline{X}_2 \overline{X}_3 X_4 \overline{X}_5 \\
+ \; & \overline{X}_1 X_2 \overline{X}_3 \overline{X}_4 X_5 \\
+ \; & \overline{X}_1 X_2 \overline{X}_3 X_4 \overline{X}_5 \; .
\end{aligned}
$$

This can be simplified somewhat, one form being,

$$
\begin{aligned}
C = \; & \overline{X}_1 X_2 \\
+ \; & X_1 \left(X_2 X_3 + \overline{X}_2 \overline{X}_3 \right) \; .
\end{aligned}
$$

In words, this is equivalent to the statement: "The picture is Class II either when there is a circle but no triangle, or when there is a triangle accompanied either by both a circle and an oval, or by neither of them; all other pictures are Class I." Now, both the author's and the editor's "features" make it possible to correctly classify the patterns; but which is right? It is impossible to say on the basis of the existing evidence. If pictures in "nature" or "the world" are generated by the author's process, then sooner or later one will be generated that violates the editor's "hypothesis," and it will be proved wrong. It might be, however, that nature is generating pictures (and classes) according to the Boolean expression above, in which case the author is "wrong." Neither viewpoint can be proved without additional evidence, and from this standpoint both are equally correct. But they are not equally satisfactory. The author's elegant criterion can be stated in few words. It is simple, and easy to apply. The editor's clumsy expression, on the other hand, requires many words to specify, and is confusing to apply. Therefore, we prefer the former; it is the "simplest explanation" of the known facts. If further experiments do not disprove this explanation, it will greatly reduce the amount of effort that others must expend in classifying "the world" (at least, this particular world). Society rightly recognizes the importance of, and rewards, such labor-saving insights. Who would have thought that $E = mc^2$?

—Editor.]

It can be stated without reservation that the brain of any man (who has read this far) has a state necessary for the solution of this problem. But to have a required state, and to be able to find it are two different things.

Let us suggest another problem (Fig. 12) for those inventive and resourceful people who solved the previous problem. As before, see if you can find a classification principle or "theory" by studying these examples.

It is unlikely that you will discover from Fig. 12 the following classification rule: If the three principal diagonals of the hexagon in the picture intersect at a single point, AND there is an even number of circles in the picture, then it is Class I; otherwise, it is Class II. With this description you can classify the pictures without any difficulty and prove that there exists a state in your brain. However, not only Fig. 12, but also a description were needed to bring your brain into the required state.

Of course it is highly abstract to consider a human brain as consisting

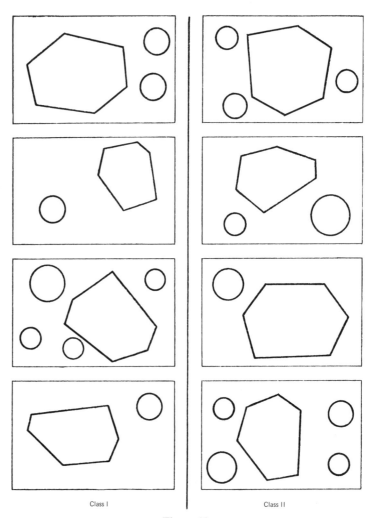

Figure 12.

of K and L blocks. Nevertheless, the mental processes equivalent to these blocks in man are different after the problem has been solved, compared to their prior state. The aim of these examples was to show that all of the possible states of block K cannot necessarily be realized at any instant simply by showing examples of the training material.

Thus, man is a good example of a system in which not all possible states can be achieved by adaptation. Are there systems in which any possible state of block L can be achieved by adaptation, but the system still is not able to learn to recognize correctly, despite the existence of the required internal state for the given problem?

Let us analyze the following system. Binary pictures on a 10 × 10 field are the patterns for this system (Fig. 13*a* and *b*). All field points are numbered. The block K has 100 states. In the state i, it assigns to Class I all pictures having no less than 51 black dots AND black on dot number i; it assigns to Class II all pictures having no less than 51 black dots AND white on dot number i; it classifies as "trash" all pictures having fewer than 51 black dots. Let us call the ith problem a set of pictures divided into classes in such a manner that they will be correctly recognized by the block K when in the ith state.

a   b

Figure 13.

Let the block L have the following algorithm: A picture of the first class is taken from the training material and superimposed on a picture from the second class. Only those black dots are left on the field that were black in both pictures (logic product of pictures). Then other pictures from the training material are placed on the same field, and the logic product is taken again, etc. The number of black dots can only decrease with each step. The number of the last remaining black dot is sought. If, however, several black dots disappear at the same time from the field and no dots are left, then the lowest number of the remaining dots is taken. The block K now is transferred into a state whose number is that of the last dot.

First, let us show that the block L never finds the required classification state. Remember that after processing the first pair of pictures (one of each class) there must be at least one black dot on the field. However, if training is carried out with patterns from the ith problem, then the ith dot without fail will be white after the first step, because any picture of Class II has a white i^{th} dot. Therefore, the remaining dots will not include the number i, and the system cannot acquire the ith state after being trained on material of the ith problem.

However, it is possible to achieve any state j of the system by an appropriate selection from the training material of the ith problem, provided

$j \neq i$. Namely, only pictures in which dot j is black are included in the training material. (At least half the pictures in each class are of such a nature.) For example, take a set with no less than one white dot on every field, except in the jth position. This is always possible, regardless of the number of the problem. After pictures of this training material intersect, only one black dot will remain. It is necessarily in the jth place, and the system attains the jth state. It can be said, therefore, that the attainment of any state during training does not guarantee good performance of the system.

The above "stupid" system can easily be transformed into a perfect one (at least for the 100 problems having a corresponding state in block K) simply by changing slightly the algorithm used by block L.

Let block L take the picture of the first class, and the "negative" of the picture of the second class at each training step for generating the logic product. In other respects, the algorithm remains unchanged. It is easy to see that the system now always learns correctly, and uses only an absolute minimum amount of training material.

3. Searching for causes of poor performance in the recognition system

Assume that we have a system that is unsatisfactory in solving some group of problems. Engineers who want to improve its performance will be looking for the causes of the errors. But it is not clear what the cause is. It may be the absence of a necessary state in block K; or block L may not be able to find this state (although it may be present).

This problem is simple if the system is primitive in the sense that there is some possibility of predicting the performance of block K in all possible states, and of block L under sufficiently varied training. Unfortunately, such an approach is not applicable to most systems. For example, suppose it was revealed that the program *Arithmetic* could not learn to recognize tables constructed according to rules that are logic functions of arithmetic rules. Assume that no other experiments were carried out prior to this one. It is very doubtful if anybody, although knowing both the training and test algorithms, could find the cause of poor recognition. This is because the number of possible states of block K is $C_{5346}^{30} \cdot (2^{30})^{24} > 10^{290}$ in the case of 24 classes. Therefore, in order to determine the quality of block K, it is necessary either to prove some theorem about the absence of the required state for the given problem, or to find by hand a suitable state. The program *Arithmetic* is by no means the most complex one; there exist others of much higher complexity at this stage in the development of recognition systems.

Is it possible to experiment with blocks K and L in such a way as to be able to use experimental results for explaining poor performance, without knowing the structure of the blocks? Consider the following experiment.

Assume that we have a second "smart" variant of the system. We know nothing about the structure of blocks K (its states) or L (its ability to find a required state). Our attempt to teach this system to differentiate vertical lines (white on black field) from horizontal lines is unsuccessful. How can we find out which of the blocks is at fault without looking inside them?

Take block $\bar{K}$, an exact copy of block K, and transfer it into some state (by pressing a button). After this the block $\bar{K}$ becomes an automaton with rigid classification. At its input there is a sequence of random pictures (Fig. 14). Some pictures will be classified as "trash." All others will be

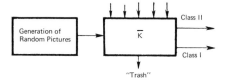

Figure 14. A system that generates problems for which block K has the necessary states beforehand.

divided into two classes. Some of the classified pictures can be used for input to block L during training, and the other part used for test (Fig. 15).

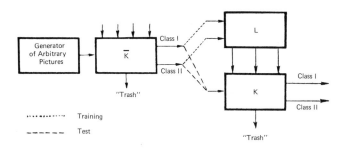

Figure 15. Scheme for verifying the performance of block L.

After training, block L will transfer its subordinate block K into some state. It will be noticed during test that the classification carried out by block K coincides with that performed by block $\bar{K}$.

In other words, there are no errors during test. Repeat the same experiment by pressing another button of the automaton $\bar{K}$. Again the system K recognizes well during test. It is clear that in both cases the block L has succeeded in finding a state of block K that is both necessary and known to exist.

Only the performance of block L is checked during these experiments. The method by which we initially divide pictures into classes guarantees that K has the required state. Therefore block L will always be responsible for failure after training. On the other hand, a sufficiently large number of successful experiments with different states of the block $\bar{K}$ will signify that the block L is not designed badly at all. (Of course, only trying all states of K will guarantee good performance of the block L during the solution of a new problem. However, we usually will trust it if it performs well 50 times out of 50 experiments with arbitrarily selected states of the block $\bar{K}$, and may do so even when the system is trained only once.)

In our example, suppose all experiments produce good results. On the basis of this, we conclude that the block L is capable of finding a required state, provided it exists. However, the system still cannot learn to distinguish horizontal lines from vertical. This means that block K does not have the necessary state.

If the first ("stupid") variant of the system were subjected to the same test, then experiments on dividing pictures into classes would show that block L is unable to find required states (even when they are available). In this case, the question about the availability of states for differentiating horizontal lines from vertical would have remained open.

Thus, experiments according to the scheme shown in Fig. 15 make it sometimes possible to "localize the defect" in one of the blocks. If both blocks are "defective," poor performance is ascribed to block L.

4. General structure of the recognition problem: Imitation

It has been said many times that such and such a system learns to solve one type of problem, and cannot solve another type. (For example, the Perceptron learned to differentiate rectangles elongated in the horizontal and vertical directions, but never learned to distinguish rectangles from ellipses.) This statement means that in one case there were many errors during test, and in another case none.

However, it is meaningless to speak about the number of errors of a system until the patterns for test are selected, and the classification algorithm is defined. Who is the supreme judge that decides whether or not the system made an error or defined a class correctly?

Some readers would undoubtedly protest by saying that in all previous problems there was no need to solve questionable problems. They would say that if the program *Arithmetic* assigned first place to the number of that rule according to which the table is constructed, then there is no need for argument.

But the reference to a supreme judge is not vain. This question was not raised until now only because we made the verification algorithm self-evident in the preceding examples.

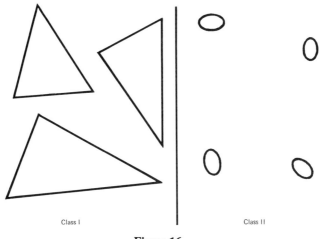

Class I   Class II

Figure 16.

Consider now an example in which there is no such self-evidence. Take a system trained on the figures shown in Fig. 16. Then another figure shown in Fig. 17 is presented to it for test. Which answer is the correct

Figure 17.

one? Three possible points of view are possible. Some people will say the figure is classified as belonging to Class I (it is big). The second point of view will classify it as belonging to the second class (ellipses). Still other people will classify it (and not without reason) as "trash." It is impossible to prove the correctness of any of these points of view.

Thus, we need a "supreme judge" no matter how the recognizing system performs. In this respect the most difficult question is: What does it mean to recognize an object that was absent in the training material? The answer to this question will be found in the formal scheme of the recognition process, and this is discussed below.

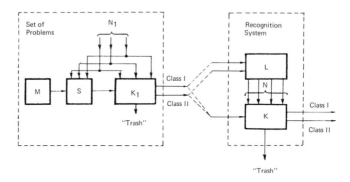

Figure 18. Diagram of the general structure of the recognition problem.

Let there be a set of patterns $M = \{m_k\}$. The block K_1 (Fig. 18) has N_1 states. The block S has the same number of states, and they are in $1:1$ correspondence with those of block K_1. When the block S is in state j it selects patterns from M with the probability distribution $p_j(m_1), p_j(m_2) \ldots$ $p_j(m_k) \ldots p_j(m_r)$, subject to the constraint,

$$\sum_{k=1}^{r} p_j(m_k) = 1 \, .$$

The selected pattern is presented to the input of block K_1, which assigns it to either one of two classes, or to "trash."

The system consisting of M and blocks S and K_1, in a fixed state, we call *the problem*. The same system, but without a fixed state specified, we call *the set of problems*.

The output of the "problem" box in Fig. 18 is some subset of the set M, separated into classes. (We will number problems to coincide with the states j of blocks S and K_1.) The recognition system, as before, consists of block K (not necessarily a copy of block K_1), an automaton with N states, and of block L, which selects states on the basis of the training material.

We will say that block K in state i *weakly imitates* block K_1 in state j when these blocks classify identically those patterns from M not rejected as "trash" by block K_1. (For simplicity, it can be assumed that block S selects such patterns with zero probability.) When the blocks classify identically *all* patterns from M, we will say that block K "strongly imitates" block K_1.

These definitions require agreement 100% of the time. However, we can also speak about strong and weak imitation with an accuracy of $1 - \epsilon$ when the corresponding classifications differ with a probability ϵ. (The number ϵ indicates the probability of disagreement between K and K_1 with respect to the total set of patterns.)

Let us introduce the notion of distance between states i_1 and i_2 of block K. Let $\epsilon_1(j)$ and $\epsilon_2(j)$ be, respectively, the probabilities of disagreement between K and K_1 when K assumes the states i_1 and i_2, and K_1 is in state j (j^{th} problem). Then we define the distance between states i_1 and i_2 with respect to problem j as $||\epsilon_1(j) - \epsilon_2(j)||$. (Note that if the distance between states with respect to problem j is zero, it does not mean that the states are identical. The material of problem j may not contain all subsets of M, and the distance between states for another problem could be nonzero.) It is easy to see that if the distance between states i_1 and i_2 is α, and block K in state i_1 weakly imitates blocks S and K_1 in state j with an accuracy β, then block K in state i_2 will also weakly imitate blocks S and K_1 in the same state with an accuracy within the range $\beta \pm \alpha$. In other words, close states differ little in their accuracy of imitation.

The above system definition (Fig. 18) precludes any conflict about correct or erroneous classification of a pattern. The correct classification is that performed by block K_1. Thus, the "supreme judge" is an inseparable part of the problem itself. Until this part is given, we cannot even speak about a given problem, and it is meaningless to try to design a system capable of solving it.

5. Interesting and noninteresting sets of problems for pattern recognition

Many experimental recognition systems have been designed recently. Each of them is adapted to solve certain sets of problems. These sets differ in sets M and in blocks K_1. Some systems handle their sets of problems well. What is the reason for their success? Is it that a sufficiently broad approach has been taken to the design of recognition systems, or are the sets of problems too easy?

We know that it is possible to describe many problems in pattern recognition terms. But some of these should be considered from other, more natural viewpoints. For example, we can say that "a lock recognizes a key" (divides it into classes). But it is hardly worth considering the design of good locks as a pattern recognition problem.

This situation is complicated by the fact that each author describes his system design in his own language. Sometimes it is difficult to understand what is new in a given design. Sometimes only the description is new. Therefore, it is of some advantage to agree beforehand about criteria for recognition problems.

Assume that block K_1 has only one state (the set of problems consists only of one problem). In this case, the recognition system can eliminate the training step, and block L is not needed. The only problem in this case is the design of a "rigid" automaton K that will imitate automata S and K_1. Interesting problems related to the design of an automaton with many different states and of block L (which selects states) are absent in this case. Therefore, the presence of many states in block K_1 is one of the first requirements for an "interesting" problem from the point of view of recognition.

There are some sets of problems that satisfy this first requirement but are still absolutely noninteresting. Let us give an example. There are automatic baggage storage compartments at big railroad stations and airports. These compartments are simply boxes with the front wall serving as a door. On the reverse side (inside) of this door, there is a numbering device consisting of four discs. Each disc has 10 fixed positions, and the device therefore has 10^4 states. The user puts his baggage into the chamber, sets the dials to any desired position (training), and memorizes the selected set of digits. An identical set of dials is located on the outside of the compartment door. After closing the door, the baggage can be removed from the compartment only by selecting the same combination of digits on the outside dials. The door opens easily after a correct combination is selected ("recognition of a pattern of the first class"). Any other combination will not open the door ("patterns of the second class").

This system can learn to solve sets of problems consisting of 10^4 problems. A selection of one state from 10,000 takes place during training. All other states are unacceptable. Nevertheless, nobody calls this a recognizing system. What property does this system lack?

One of the classes into which the system divides numbers after training consists of only one pattern. Therefore all "training" can be reduced to remembering this one number. Test is reduced to comparing an unknown pattern with the contents of memory. But recognition systems differ from "remembering" systems in their ability to recognize new patterns that did not participate in training. We tend to associate recognition with generalization and with the extrapolation of regularity noted during training to a new area. There is no generalization performed by the baggage compartment mechanism, and for this reason we do not count it as a recognizing system.

Therefore, the second requirement for significant pattern recognition problems is that one class contains many different objects. Only a small portion of them are shown during training; test is carried out with new objects.

There are sets of problems that satisfy both the first and the second requirements but still remain noninteresting for recognition. Assume that the mechanism of the baggage compartment is redesigned somehow. The door will now open only when the two first digits coincide on both sides of the door. Now the set of problems consists of 100 problems, and the first class of each problem contains not one but 100 patterns. It is sufficient to show only one of 100 during training. If the number 4,726 is set at the inside dials, the door will open when the combination is 4,711 or 4,794. We have here a "generalization," but we are not very excited about it. This is simply nondifferentiation among patterns within a class, and amounts to the same situation as when the class contains only one object.

Therefore, to the second requirement we may add that only those pairs of patterns are considered to be different that are encountered in different classes in at least one problem from the set.

Let us evaluate some systems that are considered to be recognizing on the basis of these criteria.

What set of problems is accessible to a letter-reading system? For example, consider a system that inputs printed text into a computer.

Such a machine always divides objects into classes (there are more than two classes). In other words, the set of problems consists of only one problem. (The first requirement is not obeyed.) The system can be made "rigid" without any training. The design of a reliable reading system requires, probably, overcoming many technological difficulties, but they are not necessarily related to the design of recognition systems.

Another case would be a system that could solve a set of problems requiring both recognition of letters and other problems. The design of such a system would be a real achievement in the field of pattern recognition.

Evidently the Perceptron was intended for this type of problem. But we know now that it cannot solve many specific problems taken from given sets of problems. What is the reason for this? Which of the Perceptron blocks (K or L) is at fault? If the Perceptron has many A elements, then block L can cope somehow with training. This means that if there is a suitable state of block K, then the Perceptron will take this state or another near it after a short training period. But the Perceptron with only a small number of A elements does not have states suitable for many problems.

On the other hand, with a very large number of A elements ($\sim 2^m$ where m is the number of receptor cells) and some changes in the design of A elements, the Perceptron may have all the necessary states for the solution of any problem. But in this case a complete set of objects must be shown during training. The second requirement will be broken, and the system again becomes noninteresting.

6. "Self-teaching"

We do not tell the recognition system the principle according to which block K_1 classifies objects. A well-performing system will discover this principle by itself, after seeing several objects and what block K_1 does with them. Can we go further in this direction and design a self-teaching system for which simply seeing objects—without knowing what the block K_1 does with them—will suffice?

For simplicity, we start with the case in which block S selects patterns from set M with equal probabilities.

In order to prevent block L from getting information about the treatment of patterns by block K_1, all patterns are input to block L, including those classified as "trash" by block K_1. "Self-teaching" is impossible in this case because the teaching material does not depend in general on the problem (a state of block K_1).

[Training an adaptive system without benefit of outside information about class membership of patterns is generally referred to as "unsupervised learning" in this country. The author's categorical denial of this possibility must be tempered somewhat in light of the present status of this field. The reader can be indebted to Dr. Paul W. Cooper,[1,2] one of the authorities in the field, for the following statement summarizing current status.

Nonsupervised learning cannot be done in arbitrary situations. It *can* be done in many cases of interest, and in some measure of generality. The model is as follows. A set of unlabeled samples is drawn from an aggregate probability distribution consisting of the sum of the individual class distributions. From these samples we wish to estimate the parameters required for defining the class decision rule, or, loosely speaking, we wish to estimate the individual category distributions (in which case the decision rule is determined). The question of whether this is possible at all boils down to the following: given an estimate of the overall distribution of the aggregate, can it be uniquely decomposed into its component category distributions? The answer is that it can in a number of interesting situations, but not in general. Among the interesting cases are large classes of parameterized distributions. For example, it can be done for multivariate normal distributions that differ in means and covariance matrices. It can be done for other parameterized classes, but not all (e.g., trouble arises with uniform distributions). It can be done when there is adequate structure relating the distributions (e.g., when two distributions of any unknown form differ only in location). The fact that it is theoretically possible doesn't mean that an actual procedure is easy. In general it is difficult and requires the use of a computer.

Readers interested in more details on unsupervised learning systems are directed to the references[3-5] listed at the end of this chapter.

—EDITOR.]

Now let only those patterns enter the input of block L (those selected by S) that are not classified as "trash" by block K_1 (Fig. 19). By doing this we provide the recognition system with some information about the relation of block K_1 to objects. In this case there are the following possible situations:

a) Block K_1 classifies as "trash" one and the same subset of set M in all its states. This situation coincides with the already considered case of "self-teaching." The only difference in the training material for different problems lies in the classification of patterns that escape the "wastebasket." But block L does not receive this information. As an example, Fig. 20 shows training material for three different problems. It is easy to see that the training material for all three problems contains one and the same eight objects. These problems differ only in the classification method. The system shown in Fig. 19 cannot solve this problem.

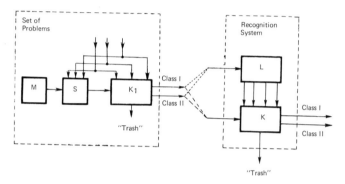

Figure 19. Scheme in which block L obtains information about "nontrash" classification of the training material, but does not receive information about the class of objects.

b) There is only one unique state of block K_1 in which it divides objects into "trash" and "nontrash." The scheme shown in Fig. 19 can in principle solve this problem. But then there is no sense in speaking about self-teaching. The information that a given set of objects is not "trash" tells the whole story about the state of block K_1 including its rule for separating classes. Block L receives this information by the same method as in Fig. 18.

[This is unclear, and does not appear to make sense unless the author is equating the class assignment rule of block K_1 with its separation of "trash" from "nontrash," as he also seems to do in point (*c*) below.

—EDITOR.]

c) There is an intermediate case in which several states of block K_1 are available (more than one but less than N_1) in which one and the same subset of set M is classified as "trash." Under this situation the scheme in Fig. 19 makes it possible to select a group of states in block K that can separate "trash" from "nontrash," but excludes the possibility of selecting one state among this group.

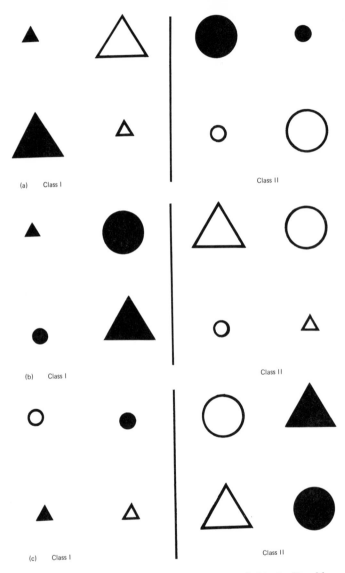

Figure 20. Different classifications using the same set of objects. Teaching according to the scheme shown in Fig. 19 is impossible here.

If we lift the restriction that block S select patterns with equal probability, then nothing changes in principle. Now we can get information not only about the classification of objects, but also about the frequency of appearance of different objects. However, this does not influence our basic conclusion that the situation where teaching is possible is not self-teaching, and where "self-teaching" exists there cannot be teaching.

[Obscure, even in Russian.

—TRANSLATOR.]

The question of the possibility or impossibility of self-teaching has nothing to do with participation of man in the teaching process. A man, another automaton, or nature can be teachers for an automaton. Of importance is the fact that a teacher is necessary. From the correlations considered under (b) and (c), above, it is evident that attention should also be paid to the separation of objects into "nontrash," in addition to the separation of objects into classes. In other words, a strong imitation of block K_1 should be attempted.

In fact, if the set of problems is such that there are few problems with an identical division of objects into "trash" and "nontrash," then preliminary work with the scheme of Fig. 19 may noticeably decrease the amount of computation involved in the final selection of the state of block K. Part of the next chapter is devoted to this problem.

This problem is closely related to the creation of specialized languages by the recognition system for the description of patterns in a given problem that would be unacceptable for patterns in some other problems. Such systems are discussed in detail in Chapter 9. It should only be emphasized here that the term "self-teaching" is very unsuitable. It contradicts the teaching process during which the recognition system gets information for block K by observing patterns together with what block K does with them. Sometimes the information is about class membership; in other cases it is about "trash." However, in all cases observation of the object about which something is said is of advantage. (We think that the recognition system does not need information about set M. In fact, this set can be regarded as one and the same for all problems, and therefore there is no need to obtain information about it by teaching. This information can be rigidly incorporated into the system. If, for example, the system is designated to recognize geometric figures on a 100×100 field, then it is incorporated into the design. Therefore, simply showing a picture without indicating its class does not carry new information for the recognition system.)

Thus, no question about self-teaching exists. Discussions about teaching without a teacher are vain.

[Again, the author seems to take too strong a stand on this issue. In fact, he himself creates an excellent counterexample in Chapter 5.

—EDITOR.]

7. *Ambiguous problems and imitation*

In order to check the intelligence of children, psychologists often use a test in which a group of words is shown to them, and children are asked to cross out one "unwanted word" (or a group of pictures). For example, the following group of words may be selected:

1) bed
2) cupboard
3) suitcase
4) table
5) divan

and the child should guess that *suitcase* be crossed out.

What kind of a problem does the child solve in this case? It is certainly wrong to think that a suitcase differs more from the other items than they differ among themselves. It all depends on what feature we consider to be the most important. It is very hard to convince a child that he made an error by crossing out the word *cupboard* because the latter is taller than the other items. The problem is not clear in this case, and we cannot prove which answer is right and which is wrong.

Therefore, the only sensible solution for the child is to guess which feature is of importance to the author of the problem. In other words, imitation of the examiner's thinking is required.

It is clear that the information needed for imitation is missing from the list of items. The examiner could be thinking that the "unwanted" item is *bed* (as the only metal object), or *divan* (as the only upholstered item), etc. Despite this, the majority of people are able to give the correct answer. This means that the different states of the block K_1 (examiner) are not equally probable, and the most probable state of the block K, which solves the problem, coincides with the most probable state of the block K_1 after observation of the training material.

The solution of this problem is possible because of the fact that all people are "designed" to some extent identically. Individual deviation of reasoning is easily discovered during such tests. In fact, psychiatrists have discovered that a different distribution in the probabilities of the states of block K exists in schizophrenia. For example, if a schizophrenic person is shown the following four pictures: a cake of soap, a tube of toothpaste, a whisk broom, and a pear, he finds that the whisk broom is "unwanted" in this group. He will base his answer on the grounds that all other items have a strong odor, with the exception of the whisk broom. Nobody can prove that he is wrong. For the majority of people such an answer is unexpected. A schizophrenic person does a poor job of imitating the reasoning of other people, although it is difficult to prove whose reasoning is "more correct."

Scientists are often faced with similar, nonclearly defined problems. Strictly speaking, these problems are impossible to "solve" because of information insufficiency in the training material. Almost every time the solution is reduced to one of imitating the problem generator, or creating a mental model of the process under consideration. Suppose we want to design a machine that would substitute for a man in this task. If the machine selected the first state of block K that did not contradict the teaching material it would seem to us that the machine suffered from schizophrenia. In order to avoid this, the block L should possess some information about the entire set of problems from the very beginning.

Therefore, the machine designer should try to create a machine with as much information as possible stored in blocks L and K—not about an individual problem, but about entire sets of problems. Information about limitations imposed on certain problems by the design of block K_1 should be stored in a form readily available for use. This means that selecting the state of block K will be accomplished with as few operations and as little teaching material as possible. The designed system should be judged not on the basis of how much information it stores, but on how large are the sets of problems it can solve, what teaching material it uses, and how many trials are needed for it to find the state of the block K.

REFERENCES

1. D. B. Cooper, P. W. Cooper, "Adaptive Pattern Recognition and Signal Detection without Supervision," (IEEE Intl. Conv. Record, Part I, March, 1964), pp. 246–256.
2. D. B. Cooper, P. W. Cooper, "Nonsupervised Adaptive Signal Detection and Pattern Recognition," (*Information and Control*, Vol. 7, September, 1964), pp. 416–444.
3. S. C. Fralick, "Learning to Recognize Patterns without a Teacher," (IEEE Trans. on Info. Theory, Vol. IT- , No. 1, March, 1967), pp. 57–64.
4. P. W. Cooper, "Some Topics on Nonsupervised Adaptive Detection for Multivariate Normal Distributions," *Computers and Information Sciences— II*, J. Tou, Ed., (New York: Academic Press, 1967), pp. 123–146.
5. P. W. Cooper, "Nonsupervised Learning in Adaptive Statistical Pattern Recognition," (Proceedings IFIP Congress 68, Edinburgh, Scotland, August, 1968, to be published).

CHAPTER 5

Sifting

SIFTING DURING TEST

1. Remembering the training set

IN CHAPTER 2, SECTION 2, a system that remembered the positions of patterns in the training set with respect to the receptor field was considered. The memory retained as references (standards) all patterns shown during training. The description of all patterns in the training set is the description of a given class; it is a function of the training set.

The unknown pattern in this case is compared during test with all references stored in memory. Consequently, the number of machine operations during test depends on the number of objects shown during training, and not on the number of classes. (We assume here that comparisons with stored references occur sequentially. In principle, searches can be accomplished by some type of decoder in less time. But in most cases, the search is conducted for close similarity rather than complete identity. Decreasing operations in this manner during test is not considered further in this book.)

The large amount of "sifting" required in programs of this type is a direct result of the low degree of abstraction involved in the class descriptions generated during training.

2. Remembering the classification rule

The Perceptron is free from this shortcoming. The classification rule is already stored in its memory, although in a very cumbersome form. The length of the description of classes depends on the number of A elements,

70

and not on the size of the training set. Therefore, the time needed to recognize a pattern does not depend on the number of patterns used during training.

This is even more obvious in the case of the program *Arithmetic*, which remembers the positions of patterns (numerical tables) in feature space. Points corresponding to individual lines or tables in the training material are not remembered; rather, only one point per class is stored. This is possible because the program searches for features until it finds some space in which all patterns of a given class transform to one and the same point. Comparisons with respect to distances to class centers are performed during test. Therefore, the test time depends only on the number of classes, and not on the number of tables given during training.

3. Synthesis of the class name

During training, we always inform block L as to which class a given pattern belongs. The coding of this information was until now of no particular importance. For example, the number assigned to different rules has no significance for the program *Arithmetic*. Because the program is required to relay its "opinion" regarding the class of the test pattern in the same code, it simply recodes the set of feature characteristics into the class number ("name").

The situation changes if the class name is no longer arbitrarily coded. If some set of properties of the class is chosen to serve as the communication language between man and machine, then the machine need only remember class properties, not class name. There will usually be fewer class properties than classes, and in this way the sifting time is reduced. Let us give some examples.

Let the machine consider six classes of objects (Fig. 21, *a–f*). The first class (*a*) is called, *objects located at the right-hand side of the picture, solid rectangles;* the second class (*b*), *contour rectangles at the left side;* the third class (*c*), *contour ellipses at the right-hand side,* etc.

There is no need to tell the machine the names of the classes in the Russian language. It is sufficient to code the phrases *at the right-hand side* by 1, and *at the left-hand side* by 0; the words *solid* by 1, *contour* by 0, *rectangle* by 1, and *ellipse* by 0. The name of the class will then be replaced by a three-bit binary number. These are listed in Fig. 21.

Now the program searches not for characteristics indicating that the pattern belongs to a given class, but for characteristics indicating that the picture contains a figure either on the right-hand or left-hand side, is solid or contour, or is rectangular or elliptical.

In other words, characteristics correspond to whether digits 1 or 0 occupy the first place in the class name. The same holds for the second place, etc. When all features are found, the program is able to synthesize the name of the class. In this case, there is no need for class references. Only class properties need be "sifted." In a successful case, the number of properties may be on the order of the base two logarithm of the number of classes, and this can lead to a noticeable decrease in the required number of decisions during test. The program that synthesizes class names

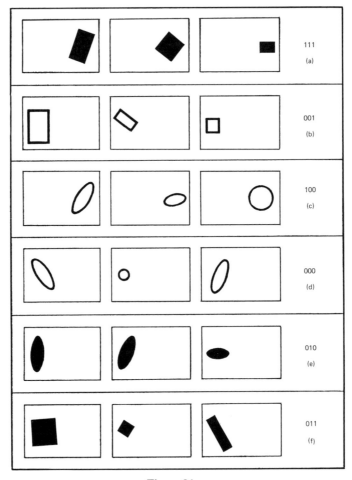

Figure 21.

part-wise in an acceptable language possesses one additional important feature. It can "recognize" (name correctly) patterns belonging to classes not shown to it during training. If a program trained on the six classes of Fig. 21 is asked to recognize the pattern in Fig. 22, it will not assign it to any of the six classes. Rather, it will establish that a 1 occupies the first place, a 0 the second place, and a 1 the third place in the machine name of the class. In man's language, this means that the figure resembles a contour rectangle on the right-hand side. And the answer is *right*.

Thus, the following hierarchy is obtained:

a) systems that remember the training material and recognize only those patterns participating in training

b) the "usual" recognition systems that also recognize patterns which did not participate in training, provided they belong to classes present in the training material

c) systems that "synthesize the name of the class," and "recognize" patterns belonging to classes not present in the training material.

We put the word *recognize*, above, in quotation marks because recognition in this case does not correspond exactly to the formal definition of this word given in Section 4 of the preceding chapter. It is of interest to note that the program *Arithmetic* seems to resemble programs that synthesize class names. Let us recall an example considered in "Recognition of Arithmetic Rules," in Chapter 3, Section 4. The program was trained on six arithmetic rules, after which it was able to recognize 24 arithmetic rules. What does "was able to recognize" mean in this case? Tables constructed according to new rules were shown to the program. The program attached sets of characteristics (class names in machine language) to them. However, these names were incomprehensible to man. And the program was forced to remember these sets together with terms expressed in man's language (their numbers). After that the program knew how to translate the names from its own language (a set of characteristics) into man's language (the rule number).

Figure 22.

Thus, the program *Arithmetic* lacks a language common with man's language, which would enable it to synthesize the names of classes. Chapter 6 is devoted to the design of a program able to synthesize classes using the language of ordinary algebra.

SIFTING DURING TRAINING

The number of operations performed by a machine during training increases with the number of patterns in the training material. This is common to all kinds of programs, and we are not going to discuss it now.

For simplicity we consider, in the following sections, that training is carried out with minimum but sufficient material. This means that there exists only one state in block K_1 for the set of problems, and the training material is divided into classes by that method.

4. Searching for classification rules in a fixed space

Most of the systems to date have tried to separate pattern classes by means of a hyperplane or several hyperplanes. The Perceptron generates a plane within a fixed feature space (A-space). The Braverman program performs separation directly on the receptor field. Training for these algorithms is reduced to a search for the parameters of the dividing plane or system of planes.

The author of the Perceptron chose the simplest approach to the search for a plane. Coefficients k_i (see Fig. 9) are the normal coordinates of the hyperplane used during test. During training, each coefficient is adapted independently from others. Therefore, the number of operations performed by the program during training is on the order of the product of the number of A elements and the number of patterns in the training set. This product is smaller than the total number of different states of the Perceptron. But a high price is paid for this decreased "sifting" during training, namely, the Perceptron sometimes cannot find a plane separating the training material, even if such a plane exists.

[This is not quite true. A basic Perceptron theorem that has been proved in a number of ways[1] states essentially that if such a plane exists then a Perceptron adapted according to the error-correcting training algorithm[2] is guaranteed to find it. However, the author appears to think of the Perceptron training rule as equivalent to that for the Adaline,[3] similar to what was originally called the "forced-learning" adaptation rule, in which coefficients are adapted after each pattern presentation regardless of whether the classification decision is right or wrong. It is true that problems can be constructed for which a solution (hyperplane) exists, and in which the latter rules will not find it (but the error-correcting will). In practical pattern recognition problems, the difference in performance between the two approaches has generally proved to be negligible. In particular, both fall far short of desired performance for the reasons the author gives below.
—EDITOR.]

However, we already know that for many problems the patterns belonging to different classes cannot be separated by a hyperplane or any other dividing plane within the receptor field. Furthermore, for many sets of problems there does not even exist a fixed transformation of the receptor field onto some space in which the classes of many problems can be simply divided (by a plane, for example). The aim of training in this case is not that of finding a separating rule (for example, the hyperplane), but rather that of finding a feature space in which separation is possible. Notice that during the search for useful features, separability of the training set patterns within feature space is the criterion for value. Therefore, after finding a satisfactory transformation of the receptor field into feature space there is practically no need for finding a classification rule; it is already found.

5. Sifting during transformation of the receptor field

Only a limited number of transformations of the receptor field are accessible to any given system. In principle, therefore, it is possible to find the needed transformation simply by checking all possible transformations (complete sifting). However, if the number of possible transformations is very large, then it is impossible to do this within a reasonable time. How, then, can we decrease sifting (search, checking) time?

Would it perhaps be simpler to use a random selection of transformations instead of systematic sifting? Sometimes this might reduce the expected maximum number of trials. Assume that a system is capable of performing 10^8 different transformations of the receptor field. Let 10^5 be satisfactory for our problem. Then on the average we will need 10^3 trials if we select and test them randomly. "Poor luck" could increase that number to 10^4. But in the case of systematic sifting, it could happen that all 10^5 "good" transformations are located at the end of the lists, and this would increase the number of trials to almost 10^8. Thus, the random approach could be useful, provided there are many available useful transformations. However, this condition contradicts our second pattern-recognition-system requirement, which states that a good recognition system's block K should contain a state identical (if possible) with that of the problems set's block K_1. Therefore, it does not make sense to count on the advantages of random search of the receptor field transformations when the system solving a given set of problems is logically designed.

If a recognition system ought to have many different features in its repertoire, then the best way to do this is to construct features from a relatively small number of basic building blocks or operators.

For example, the 5,000 different features of the program *Arithmetic* are obtained from combinations of less than 30 operators (12 arithmetic functions, 3 logic operators, 10 logic functions). And the transformation of a pattern (table) into a 0 or 1 is realized in several steps. First, the top row of a table is represented by 1 of 12 numbers, then each number is represented by 0 or 1, etc.

In principle, such a method for constructing features makes it possible to perform selection at each step, and to consider only a portion of the transformations for further processing. If such a procedure is possible, then sifting would be sharply reduced. However, a question arises about the selection criterion at intermediate steps for the construction of features. How can we guess, for example, whether the processed results of the C/B operator (in the program *Arithmetic*) should be subjected to further processing? Or will this only increase the amount of sifting that must be done in later stages?

There is one condition sufficient for eliminating intermediate results, namely, when the transformation results in the same representation for all objects. If, for example, number C in all rows of all tables is fractional, then there is no need to construct logic functions that use this situation as an argument.

A second sufficient condition for rejecting trial transformations is the inapplicability of the corresponding feature to patterns in the training set. For example, let the program be able to produce an operator that can compare all angles of a figure with respect to their value. This operator, in combination with others, will clearly be useful, provided there is a need to differentiate regular polygons from irregular, or rectangles from rhombuses. However, if all patterns in the training set are curvilinear figures without precisely defined angles, then it is pointless to use this operator. The inapplicability of an operator to only a portion of the patterns does not mean that it should be rejected. As an example, consider regular polygons and circles as belonging to one class, and irregular polygons as belonging to another.

It is difficult to name additional absolute criteria whereby intermediate results can so easily be rejected, and further processing avoided. Therefore, we must search for criteria involving a certain risk. In this case it may happen that the "half-finished structure" of some useful feature will be

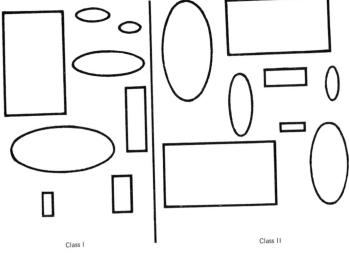

Class I   Class II

Figure 23.

rejected. A good criterion for intermediate selection should reflect in some sense the structure of block K_1 of the problem set. We discuss below some situations that make it possible to decrease the amount of sifting (feature evaluation) in cases where a man or some physical process is the "problem generator."

In order to decrease sifting during training, the features can be constructed by a gradual accumulation of chains of comparatively simple operators. Because each chain can be built up in many ways, the process is analogous to climbing a tree. Some branches will be chopped off in the process without checking all the features "growing" on them. It can be said that the search for a suitable "pruning" criterion during the construction of features is one of the most important tasks in the field of pattern recognition.

6. Correspondence between complexity of classes and training material: Postulate of training set sufficiency

Suppose a friend suggests a problem in which classes can be described in words: *large, small, figure, rectangle, ellipse, horizontal, vertical, outline, solid,* and logical connectors *and* and *or*.

He shows you a figure and says that "large solid figures" belong to one class, and "large outline figures or small figures" belong to another. See the problem in Fig. 23.

TABLE B

Solid?	Large?	Vertical?	Rectangle	Friend's Class	Training Material
0	0	0	0	II	I
0	0	0	1	II	II
0	0	1	0	II	II
0	0	1	1	II	I
0	1	0	0	II	I
0	1	0	1	II	II
0	1	1	0	II	II
0	1	1	1	II	I
1	0	0	0	II	(I)
1	0	0	1	II	(II)
1	0	1	0	II	(II)
1	0	1	1	II	(I)
1	1	0	0	I	(I)
1	1	0	1	I	(II)
1	1	1	0	I	(II)
1	1	1	1	I	(I)

[I'd say that's no friend. The author apparently inadvertently confused the issue here. His statements and Fig. 23 are depicted in truth-table form in Table *B*, in which *no* = 0 and *yes* = 1. Clearly, the friend's advice contradicts the training material. Furthermore, the author's simplified classification criterion, below, only makes matters worse since it assigns patterns not appearing in the training material (in parentheses in Table *B*) to classes that are in further conflict with the so-called friend.

—EDITOR.]

The fact that all objects in the training set are outline figures makes it unnecessary to check for the features outline or solid. This decreases the search area and we find that the first class can be described by the phrase "horizontal ellipses or vertical rectangles," and the second class by the phrase "horizontal rectangles or vertical ellipses."

If you produced a correct answer to the first problem, consider another one shown in Fig. 24.

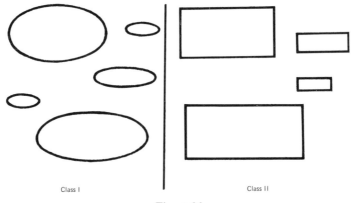

Class I   Class II

Figure 24.

All people possess a certain "inertia of thinking." By trying to apply the same approach to the problem as in Fig. 23 we get nowhere. Without this "inertia of thinking" we would never apply the same approach to the problem in Fig. 24. Instead, we would say that ellipses belong to the first class, and rectangles to the second class. Still another careful observer might say that outline horizontal ellipses belong to the first class, and outline horizontal rectangles to the second class.

As opposed to the problem shown in Fig. 23, the material of Fig. 24 is insufficient to determine a single description from all possible descriptions. For the problem shown in Fig. 24, the following descriptions could be used:

1) Horizontal ellipses or vertical figures belong to the first class.
2) Horizontal rectangles belong to the second class.

3) Horizontal ellipses belong to the first class; horizontal rectangles or vertical figures belong to the second class.
4) Outline ellipses or solid rectangles belong to the first class.
5) Outline rectangles or solid ellipses belong to the second class.

Many similar descriptions can be devised, and the material shown in Fig. 24 will not contradict them. This means that it is impossible to choose just one description on the basis of the training set.

[The author's heart is in the right place here, but his examples are terrible. For example, it is *not* strictly true that Fig. 23 determines a single class description. An equally valid (but more complicated and thus less desirable) description that does not violate the training material is (ignoring that "friend"): "vertical rectangles, or horizontal ellipses, or solid figures belong to the first class, others belong to the second." This would convert all entries in parentheses in Table *B* to Class I. What the author appears to be getting at is his previous theme that the "best" description is the simplest one not in violation of the facts. Below, he contends that the training material should *uniquely* determine the description. This is very unlikely in practice, and violates the author's own notion that many "viewpoints" are generally possible with regard to the same training material. The uniqueness of a description should therefore reside in its being some minimum-energy (information) state within the energetic boundary conditions (constraints) imposed by the training material.

—Editor.]

While solving the problem, we assume, naturally, that the training set is sufficient for the selection of just one description. In this way, the initial set of descriptions is restricted additionally. In other words, we limit the complexity of the description to such an extent that the training set starts to limit uniquely the description of classes. The region of different descriptions of classes (in which the search is going on) changes, depending on the actual training set. It can be said that we use the *postulate of sufficiency of the training set for the solution of a given problem.*

Curiously enough, this process is unnoticeable to a person, if no special attention is paid to it. Probably very few people have noticed that the description of classes in Fig. 23 was derived using the sufficiency postulate.

In fact, the training set in Fig. 23 does not contradict the following description of class: "To the first class belong horizontal outline ellipses or vertical outline rectangles, or vertical solid ellipses, or horizontal solid rectangles. To the second class belong horizontal outline rectangles, or vertical outline ellipses, or vertical solid rectangles, or horizontal solid ellipses."

Intuitively, we reject such a description as being too complex. (The complexity of the description does not correspond to that of the training set. In the case of another training set, we could supply an identical description.) Formally this description was disproved because the figures in

Fig. 23 are all outline. Therefore, we have not considered descriptions containing the words *outline* and *solid*.

Let use generalize this formal rule. We assume that the description of a class is in the form of a disjunction of several statements (these statements are connected by "or"). Then each statement (each disjunction term) should be true for at least one object of the training set from a given class. In fact, if the description of a class contains a disjunction term that does not satisfy this requirement, then we can eliminate it from the description of the given class, and include it as a new disjunction term in the description of the opposite class. If the initial description of classes correctly classified objects from the training set, then the new description will also classify them correctly. The training set does not provide enough data to choose between these two descriptions, and this means that the initial description was too complex, and did not satisfy the sufficiency postulate.

[The author's "sufficiency postulate" appears to be the equivalent of certain formal procedures for simplifying Boolean expressions. An example based on Fig. 23 may clarify this. Suppose no rectangles appeared in the Class II patterns. Then the truth table would appear as in Table C. There are four possible ways

TABLE C

Large?	Vertical	Rectangle?	Training Material	A	B	C	D
0	0	0	I				
0	0	1		I	II	I	II
0	1	0	II				
0	1	1	I				
1	0	0	I				
1	0	1		I	II	II	I
1	1	0	II				
1	1	1	I				

of assigning the blanks in the training material, as indicated in the columns A through D. They are equivalent to the Class II descriptions:

1) A: vertical ellipses
2) B: horizontal rectangles or vertical ellipses
3) C: vertical ellipses or large horizontal rectangles
4) D: vertical ellipses or small horizontal rectangles.

The author's sufficiency test is as follows: (1) Do any vertical ellipses appear in Class II training material? and (2) Do any rectangles (large or small) appear? The answer to the first is *yes*, so this disjunction is retained. The answer to the second is *no*, so it is eliminated, converting all descriptions to that of A, the simplest. —EDITOR.]

Notice that if the training set is limited by external conditions (with respect to the system undergoing training), then actions designed on the basis of the sufficiency postulate have no hidden danger of worsening system performance. The reason is simply that if the postulate is false, then no other actions will help. It is another matter if the system can ask for additional training material. In this case, the system should be able to evaluate the degree of sufficiency of the processed training material, and ask for new material when the evaluation is unsatisfactory.

7. Retrieving information from the test material

We have discussed so far the case in which the recognition system first studies the training set, finds the description of classes (sets the block K into some state), and only after this are patterns from the test material presented to it.

Now consider a case in which the system can also observe the test material while being trained. It might appear that no advantage can be derived from this situation. Remember, however, that observation of the test material makes it possible to tell which objects are present and which absent in the "world of a given problem." This knowledge can sometimes decrease the description of classes.

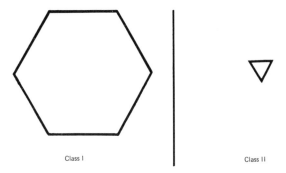

Class I   Class II

Figure 25.

Let us try to solve the problem shown in Fig. 25. Only one object from each class is shown during training. By looking at them it is impossible to determine the concept of the problem's author. Do these classes differ by figure size or by number of angles, or by some other feature? The training set is insufficient for the selection of a description of the classes, even from a very small initial set. It can only be expected that these descriptions will be very simple.

Assume, however, that Fig. 26 is shown together with Fig. 25 with the instructions that all patterns are from the test material.

Now the hypothesis of training-set sufficiency can help us select a description of classes. For example, it is impossible to assume that patterns of different classes differ by the number of angles. It is also impossible to assume that classification should be done according to some other feature (e.g., a side or an angle at the bottom) because it would be unclear how circles and ellipses should be classified, etc. On the other hand, if we assume that classes differ in the size of figures, then the training set will be sufficient. Therefore, if a man looks simultaneously at Figs. 25 and 26, he starts to classify figures in Fig. 26 according to their sizes.

Figure 26.

A quite different description of classes is developed by a man if other test material is shown to him together with the training material (Figs. 25 and 27). It is impossible to assume in this case that the patterns shown will be classified according to their size. Instead, a man starts with the classification of figures into triangles and hexagons.

Thus, some descriptions of classes may be rejected on the basis that the training material is insufficient to select one description from among many that are similar. Therefore, it can be an advantage to observe objects from the test material during training, even without any information as to their class membership.

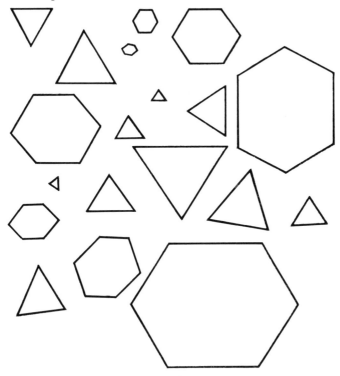

Figure 27.

[The foregoing seems to be an example of "self-teaching" or unsupervised learning, against which the author railed in Chapter 4. In fact, we hardly need Fig. 25 to generate a "natural" separation of Fig. 26 into large and small figures, and of Fig. 27 into triangles and hexagons. Of course this assumes, as the author points out in the next section, that in the "society" of pattern recognition machines, certain transformations will occur with higher probability than others; in other words, a priori bias. But it contradicts the author's statement in Chapter 4 that recognition systems do not need information about the set M; he has just demonstrated that this very information is extremely useful, even without a teacher.

—EDITOR.]

8. Breaking down into groups

Let there be among the operators available to a program for constructing features, those which transform a pattern into a number capable of assuming many values. This is sometimes called having "a continuous value." Programs that measure areas of figures, ratios of their sides, different angles, diameters, lengths, etc., are good examples of such operators.

The resulting presence of continuous-valued parameters in the program's arsenal makes training extremely difficult. There are two reasons for this. First, selection must be made from the enormous set of class descriptions that may be composed from combinations of continuous parameter values. Many more combinations of characteristics must be checked during training because it is not easy to tell which parameters are of importance and which not.

Second, the training material must be extensive enough to make a selection of class descriptions possible. Furthermore, the amount of training material increases not only because of an increase in significant parameters (increase in description complexity), but also because of an increase in irrelevant parameters. Many examples are needed in order to show that a given parameter or a given combination of parameters are not significant.

This difficulty exists in the general case when no limitations are imposed on the values of the continuous parameters. However, there are cases when a parameter that assumes arbitrary values within a set of problems is not arbitrary at all in a given problem.

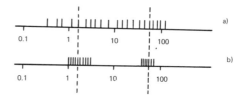

Figure 28. Cases when some parameters either break down into groups or not.

For example, Fig. 28a shows the distribution of figure areas for the patterns in Figs. 25 and 27. Figure 28b shows the same distribution for the patterns in Figs. 25 and 26. The vertical dotted lines correspond to the areas of the patterns in the training material (Fig. 25). It is evident that in case a the area can be of any value (within some limits, of course). On the other hand, the area value in b is broken down into groups. But this is exactly the same problem (Figs. 25 and 26) in which we assumed the sufficiency hypothesis for the training material, and classified patterns according to area! Only a small number of examples is adequate in this case to determine a classification principle according to area. In Figs. 25 and 27 the areas of patterns are such (Fig. 28a) that it is impossible to state a classification principle according to area. On the other hand, graphs similar to those in Fig. 28 would make the parameter (the number of angles) in Figs. 25 and 27 break down into groups, but this would not happen in Figs. 25 and 26.

Thus, a small amount of material can suffice in cases where some parameter assumes few values for a given problem (but not necessarily for the entire set). In the case of the continuous parameter, breaking into groups is inevitable. This is facilitated by the fact that the block K_1 passes only patterns with certain parameter values. The reason for success in selecting correct states for block K with only a small amount of training material is that the selection is carried out among states that also classify as "trash" objects with "forbidden" parameter values. In other words, states of block K are considered that strongly imitate block K_1.

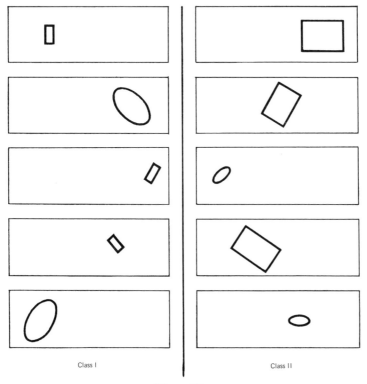

Class I   Class II

Figure 29.

It should not be thought that parameter grouping necessarily indicates pattern classification. Consider the problem in Fig. 29. Patterns differ here in their location with respect to the frame, figure shape (rectangles or ellipses), inclination angle of the large diameter to vertical, and by area. It is evident from this material that the vertical coordinate of the center of gravity of all figures is the same. This means that it can be omitted from consideration. The inclination angle of figures varies, i.e., this parameter does not break down into groups. The same can be said about the horizontal coordinate of the center of gravity. On the other hand, the areas of figures break down into groups very easily. The number of angles is 4 for a rectangle and 0 for an ellipse. (Nothing is changed if we assume that ellipses have an indefinite number of angles.) However, it is impossible

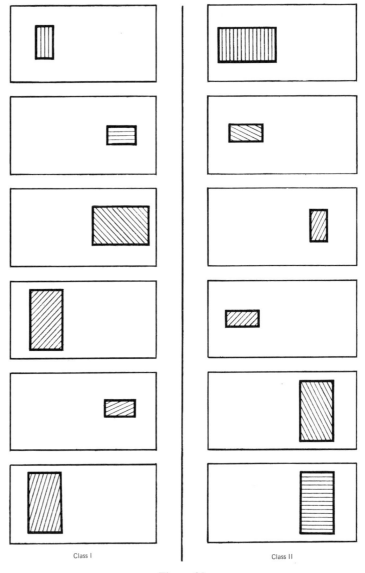

Class I   Class II

Figure 30.

to determine class membership, either according to size, or according to number of angles. Patterns of both classes are present in each group.

A description of classes can be achieved by simultaneously considering both parameters that break down into groups. The first class can be designated as "large ellipses or small rectangles," and the second as "large rectangles or small ellipses." In order to find this description, different functions of the elementary statements are evaluated. But the amount of "sifting" in this case is comparatively small because only those parameters that break down into groups are considered as arguments.

Rigid adherence to this approach may cause us to lose the ability to find a description of classes in which parameters do not break down into groups. However, in the case of large numbers of parameters with many values, the selection of a unique description of classes is possible only with a very large amount of training material. Therefore, if the amount of training material is small, and we have postulated its sufficiency for finding a description of classes, then it is worthwhile to consider only parameters that break down into groups.

It is quite possible that future studies will show the numbers of patterns and parameter properties at which it is profitable to consider only parameters breaking down into groups.

Not all parameters capable of breaking down into groups are necessarily present in the description of classes, as was the case in Fig. 29. Figure 30 shows a problem in which three parameters (horizontal coordinate, area, and the inclination of a figure) break down into groups, but only two of them (horizontal coordinate and inclination) are present in the description of classes. The inclination of hatched lines does not break down into groups. The problem in Fig. 30 is an example of the rapid growth of indeterminacy in the description of classes when parameters that do not break down into groups are considered. If the inclination of hatched lines is not eliminated from consideration, then a great many descriptions are valid that do not contradict the training material of Fig. 30.

Breaking down into groups has been considered here from the point of view of decreasing the amount of "sifting," in particular, as related to the training-material sufficiency postulate. However, this question has still another side, namely, the derivation of short descriptions of classes. This problem will be considered again in Chapter 9.

REFERENCES

1. N. J. Nilsson, *Learning Machines*, (New York: McGraw-Hill, 1965).
2. F. Rosenblatt, "Principles of Neurodynamics," (Cornell Aeronautical Lab., Report No. VG-1196-G-8, March, 1961).
3. B. Widrow, "Generalization and Information Storage in Networks of Adaline Neurons," *Self-Organizing Systems—1962*, Yovits, Jacobi, and Goldstein, Eds., (New York: Spartan Books, 1962).

CHAPTER 6

Synthesis of Formulas

1. Discovering a law

LET US CONSIDER now a trivial playing-card game for kindergarten children. An adult places playing cards in front of a child, dividing them into two stacks according to some principle. This could be according to color, one group being black, and the other red; or one group could contain face cards and the other nonface cards; or all even nonface cards could be placed in one group, and odd nonface cards in the other, etc. After letting the child observe for a while, we ask him where the next card goes. By answering this question the child, in fact, solves a typical recognition problem. We may ask him, instead, to formulate the law according to which the cards are divided. He may not give you a short definition of a principle, but may say, "jacks, queens, kings, and aces," instead of defining them as "face cards." (It should not be thought that a child does not make use of generalization in this case. This can be verified by dividing cards into two stacks, placing in one of them only jacks, queens, and aces, but eliminating kings. If we ask the child where to put kings, he will point to the stack containing face cards.)

Applied to numerical tables constructed according to arithmetic rules, the game would sound like this: All rows in Table 11 are constructed according to the same not very complex arithmetic formula; find the formula.

Looking at the first two rows, we think immediately that $C = A \times B$ is the answer. But the next row disproves our hypothesis. After some deliberation, we can produce the right answer, $C = \dfrac{A^2}{B}$.

It is easy to see that this game is related to serious problems. In fact, if the numbers of A, B, and C in the first row represent measurements of some physical quantity (for example, the average distance of some planet from the sun, and its rotation period), and the remaining three rows represent the same meaurements but for other objects (distances and rotation periods of other planets), then finding a generalized law for all rows is equivalent to the discovery of a natural law (in this case, the third Kepler law). In the case of other tables constructed according to different principles, this would lead to discovery of other natural phenomena.

TABLE 11

A	B	C
4	2	8
9	3	27
6	4	9
15	9	25

When a man makes such discoveries it is said that he performs "creative analysis of the experimental data." Usually it is difficult to point to any uniform approach to finding such generalized laws. It all depends to a great extent on intuition, and some peculiar approach to the problem. There are few people capable of discovering the Balmer formula, $\lambda = 3646 \, N^2 / (N^2 - 4)$, $N > 2$, for the wavelengths λ of the spectral lines in hydrogen. Therefore, it is of special interest to try to design a machine that would be able to discover this law.

2. Random search for a law

The first program constructed to search for arithmetic rules for tables of numbers uses a certain arbitrary chain of arithmetic commands. First, it selects at random one of the numbers, A or B, to occupy first place in the first arithmetic operation. Second place is decided in the same way. Then the arithmetic operation itself is randomly selected. The machine command for the second arithmetic operation is decided in an analogous way, except that not only A and B, but also the results of the first operation are considered as possible arguments for the second operation. Arguments for the third operation include A and B, the results of the first operation, the results of the second operation, etc. After the construction of each command, it is decided at random whether or not to discontinue the chain (a three-address machine was used; therefore, one command corresponds to each arithmetic operation).

It is obvious that with this algorithm, a chain can be constructed corresponding to any law that can be expressed in a finite number of arithmetic operations. The occurrence of every possible formula has nonzero probability. The more complex the formula, the less its probability of occurrence.

After the chain is constructed, the program checks to see if the formula fits a given table. Numbers from the first row of the table are substituted for A and B, and the chain of commands is carried out. The number obtained is compared with the value of C from the same row. If they are not identical, the formula does not fit. If they are identical, the program goes onto the second row, etc. If all rows of the table satisfy the formula, the program prints it out and stops. If even one line is unsuitable, the formula is rejected, and the program starts to construct a new formula (again at random), and this goes on and on.

In short, the program consists of a generator of arbitrary noise that is interpreted as a hypothesis for a given rule, and the hypothesis is tested by substituting numbers from the table.

This program was tried on a machine performing 2,000 three-address operations per second. To discover a rule containing only one arithmetic operation, the machine spent about 2 seconds. In the case of two arithmetic operations, 20 seconds were spent on the average; in the case of three arithmetic operations, 10–20 minutes. Repeated solution of one and the same problem required different times. Because of the random approach involved, the answer was sometimes produced in 5 seconds, but sometimes the machine was "thinking" for a whole minute.

The above time is average. In addition, the rule $AB(A + B)$, which can be written as $(B + A)AB$, and as $B(A + B)A$, etc., is found much sooner than the rule $\dfrac{A - B}{A} - B$, which in the case of three arithmetic operations can be represented in only one form.

The machine was not tested on more complex problems because of a shortage of machine time.

Notice that the third Kepler law is a three-operation problem; the law of gravitation is a two-operation problem.

3. Behavior of man and of a random search program in the "discover a law" game

A program of the above type finds a formula suitable for a given table in the process of many trials. A man also checks several formulas before he finds a suitable one. However, a man reaches the goal in a considerably fewer number of trials. This can be seen from the amount of time needed for a man and for the machine to solve one and the same problem. In many cases the time will be identical, because the speed of machine computation is much faster. This means that a man cannot test anywhere near the same number of formulas as the machine can. How does the man manage to decrease the number of trials?

Let us consider several tables constructed according to the same principle, but using different numbers A and B. Tables 12 and 13 are con-

| TABLE 12 | | | TABLE 13 | | |

TABLE 12

A	B	C
3	4	2.25
4	3	5.33
9	5	16.2
4	8	2

TABLE 13

A	B	C
3. 1	4. 2	2.29
4. 3	3. 8	4.86
8. 9	5. 6	14.16
4. 7	8. 4	2.63

structed according to the same rule as Table 11. Experience shows that if Table 12 is presented to a man instead of Table 11, he finds the rule $\frac{A^2}{B}$ noticeably faster. (The program for random generation of arithmetic rules was first designed by the author and his colleagues in 1958. It was not designed very skillfully, and performs many unnecessary operations. Eliminating these could decrease machine time by a factor of ten. This, however, would not change the validity of our conclusions.) The reason is quite simple. Both numbers A and B in Table 11 are selected in such a way that the presence of division is masked. Despite the presence of division, all numbers C are whole. Loss of time in this case is due to the fact that a man starts with formulas not containing division.

On the other hand, the presence of division is immediately evident in Table 12. Furthermore, a careful observer always notices that the product of C and B is a whole number. It is then concluded that the formula contains division by B. Evidently these and analogous deliberations help man to select the needed formula more quickly.

Table 13 is more difficult than Table 11. In the presence of fractional values of A and B, simple characteristics that signify the presence of division disappear. As a result the number of trials increases.

We see that man makes hypotheses about the formula, but not at random. He first applies "features" of whole classes of formulas, and accordingly selects an order in which to test formulas (i.e., an order depending upon table characteristics). The program behaves differently. Regardless of the contents of Tables 11, 12, 13, or any other constructed according to other laws, the program checks various formulas in the same random manner. The program uses the table only for checking the hypotheses. Numbers present in the table do not at all influence the construction of the hypotheses.

The program loses because it does not use the information contained in the table. Clearly, in order to decrease the number of operations performed by the machine during the search for a needed law, we have to eliminate this shortcoming. We need to design a program that can decide just by "glancing" at the table whether or not it is profitable to check, for example, those laws containing division by *B*. This is discussed in the next section.

4. *Ways to decrease the number of selection steps*

We have already observed that a considerable decrease in the number of trials can be achieved if information of the following type is used: "the formula contains division by *B*," or "the formula does not contain subtraction, but it contains several multiplication steps," etc. Can we use the program *Arithmetic* to obtain this information? We have seen that it was successful in searching for characteristics of a similar nature (Chapter 3, Section 3).

Unfortunately, the matter is not so simple. The program *Arithmetic* finds features after training on material in which, for example, one group contains rules with division, and another group contains rules without division. However, the program will never know the principle upon which these rules are separated into groups. Naturally, the program cannot know because it is not informed of the formula according to which the tables are constructed.

If we want the program to find formulas in a small number of trials after training, we need evidently, not only to show it the tables, but also to inform it of the principles according to which the tables are constructed. What language should we use in this case?

Let us present information about the formula in coded form. Let the value of the first code digit signify, for example, whether or not addition is the first operation in the formula. Let the second digit signify whether or not subtraction is the first operation, etc. In this manner, it is possible step-by-step to describe what should be done with *A* and *B* in order to obtain *C*, i.e., to code the formula. Several methods of coding can be devised with various advantages and shortcomings. Three-step arithmetic formulas can be described by 14–30 binary digits.

Now add another idea. Let us make the program first search for features to represent the digit occupying first place in the code, then for features to represent the digit occupying second place in the code, etc. If we succeed in finding such features, the problem is solved. In fact, during test the program would determine the value of the first digit in the code using the first group of features; the second digit, using the second group of features, and the entire coded formula in this manner. The results of "voting" by the features could be used to control the probability distribution with which the program selects rules for testing. Now the probability of occurrence of any formula would depend on the table shown. If the majority of code digits were determined correctly, the number of trials would be smaller.

Approximately such a program was indeed designed. However, it performed very "unevenly." In some cases, it considerably decreased the number of trials, but in other cases the number of trials did not differ at all from random guessing. Why did we get this result?

The absence of $1 : 1$ correspondence between rules and formulas for them is to blame. That is, different formulas can express one and the same rule; $(A + B) \cdot A \cdot B$ and $A \cdot B \cdot (B + A)$ are the same from the point of view of the features, but they are different things from the point of view of formula codes. One code may indicate that the first operation is addition, while another will claim that the first operation is multiplication, etc. Furthermore, $A - (B - A)$ does not contain addition, but $A + A - B$ does contain that operation. And there are no features, for example, that would indicate that the second operation is the division of some number by A, etc.

At the present time, a new program is being prepared that will search for features that can detect the presence of combinations of digits occurring in different positions in the code. All equivalent formulas will be shown to this program during training. The program will effectively describe a given rule by constructing other formulas from one equivalent formula.

We hope that in considering such formulas as $(A + B) \cdot A$ and $A \cdot (A + B)$ the program will find that the first operation may be either multiplication or addition, but the second operation will be multiplication if the first was addition, and vice versa.

Our hopes can be justified only by experiments. But even if this fails, it makes sense to continue the search. We need programs that are able to recognize classes not shown during adaptation, and that can substantially decrease the number of steps involved in search.

CHAPTER 7

Useful Information

1. *Amount of information and usefulness of communication*

IN THE PRECEDING CHAPTER, we considered a program that was able to find arithmetic rules by trial and error. A table of numbers was used only for verifying hypotheses. This approach required many trials. At the same time, the possibility of finding some logical order in the derivation of hypotheses (logical in the sense that it would lead to a decrease in the number of trials) was also discussed. It is proper to state here that the program can decrease the number of trials only on the basis of information contained in the table.

Let us analyze the word *information* in the preceding sentence. If we consider this word as not having any exact meaning, like the word *knowledge*, then there is no doubt about the meaning of the sentence. However, in this case it becomes of little value. It would be beneficial if the word *information* had a quantitative measure in order to relate it to a changing number of trials. Can we use the measure of information suggested by Shannon? No, entropy as the measure of indeterminacy will not always suit us if we wish to connect this measure with program performance during problem solution.

The fact is that information theory came into being as a theory for information transfer along communication channels. A communication engineer does not worry about how the information will be used at the reception end of the channel. Therefore, the telegraph office charges a set amount per word both for very important events and for trifling messages.

Additional difficulties arise if we try to relate the amount of information received to the behavior of a recipient trying to solve some problem. In this case, two completely different reports carry different information from the point of view of the recipient. For example, a report about the victory of a weak football team over a much stronger one has no value for a broker concerned about oil stocks. He is much more interested in reports about a new oil line.

News about a new oil line can make him rich or lead to bankruptcy, depending on how he interprets the report. He can either buy more stock if he believes the report, or sell all his shares if he suspects that the information is false. The report contains for him both information and disinformation.

Thus, we want to have a measure of information that reflects the usefulness of a message to the recipient. This measure should depend on the problems the recipient is involved in, his knowledge about the subject prior to the message, and his interpretation of the message. This chapter is devoted primarily to the problem of "useful information" satisfying the above requirements.

We are going to consider a model system that carries out experimental work (by trial and error) during the solution of a problem, and derives some information in this way. A function of the number of trials necessary to solve the problem is used as the "measure of difficulty" of a problem for this system. Furthermore, the system can get information about the problem through a communication channel. As a result, the sequence of trials changes. The number of required trials will also change, and with it the measure of problem difficulty.

The logarithm of the average number of trials is used in this chapter as the measure of difficulty. In this case, we obtain simple relationships between the capacity of the communication channel and the maximum decrease in difficulty that can result from using the channel. The measures of indeterminacy and of channel capacity suggested by Shannon are limiting cases of more general expressions.

Basic ideas are introduced, in general, independent of the form of the actual value function for difficulty (e.g., logarithmic), and can be applied to a large class of value functions. Some aspects of this problem are considered in Appendix 2.

The traditional meaning of the word *information* is closer to the measure discussed below than to Shannon's meaning. However, in this chapter we use *useful information* instead of simply *information*.

2. Solution algorithms and uncertainty

Assume we have a finite set of patterns $M = \{m_k\}$, that occur with a given probability distribution, $p(m_1), \ldots, p(m_k), \ldots, p(m_r)$. This set of patterns is divided into n subsets A_i such that $A_1 \cup A_2 \cup, \ldots,$ $\cup A_i \cup, \ldots, \cup A_n = M$, and $A_i \cap A_j = \phi$ when $i \neq j$. Such a system is called the *problem* **A**. This definition is identical to that given in Chapter 4, Section 4, except for the subsets into which M is divided.

The solution of the problem with respect to some pattern m_k is to find an i such that $m_k \in A_i$ (the pattern m_k is a member of subset A_i).

Assume that there exists a *testing algorithm* that can determine the truth or falsity of the statement $m_k \in A_i$. We will refer to this as the W algorithm.

Assume further that there exists a class of algorithms called *solution algorithms*, which operate in the following way. First, one pattern m_k and one subset A_i are chosen at random. They are both substituted into the W algorithm. If the answer is *true*, then the problem is solved with respect to pattern m_k. If the answer is *false*, the selection of other subsets proceeds at random, etc.

The solution algorithm determines the probability distribution for the selection of the A_i. This distribution may remain constant, or may change from one step to another. Different solution algorithms differ from one another both in their initial probability distributions, and in their rules for change.

Solution algorithms are used here as a model by means of which concepts regarding *useful information* can be discussed.

If the pattern m_k, subsets A_i, and the solution algorithm are given, then the number of times (trials) that the W algorithm must be applied before a *true* answer is obtained is some number $K(m_k)$. We define the *problem uncertainty with respect to pattern* $\mathrm{m_k}$ *for a given solution algorithm* to be the logarithm of the mathematical expectation of this number of trials, $\bar{K}(m_k)$. That is, by definition,

$$N(m_k) \equiv \log \bar{K}(m_k). \tag{1}$$

The total problem **A** *indefiniteness (uncertainty) for a given solution algorithm* is defined as the mathematical expectation of the uncertainty with respect to all patterns, namely,

$$N(A) \equiv \sum_k p(m_k) N(m_k) = \sum_k p(m_k) \log \bar{K}(m_k). \tag{2}$$

3. Relationship between uncertainty and entropy

In Sections 3 through 5, we will consider only those solution algorithms having constant probability distributions for the selection of the A_i (no change from step to step).

Designate the probability of selection of A_i for a given solution algorithm by the quantity q_i. Note the constraint

$$\sum_{i=1}^{n} q_i = 1.$$

With respect to any pattern present in A_i, the average number of trials before reaching the problem solution will be $1/q_i$. That is, the problem uncertainty with respect to each pattern in A_i is the same. Designate this uncertainty by $N(A_i)$. Then

$$N(A_i) = -\log q_i .$$

Now let p_i be the sum of the probabilities of occurrence $p(m_k)$ for all $m_k \epsilon A_i$. In other words, p_i is the probability that a pattern comes from class i. Then the total problem uncertainty can be written as

$$N(A) = \sum_{i=1}^{n} p_i N(A_i) = -\sum_{i=1}^{n} p_i \log q_i . \tag{3}$$

Since we will be constantly using expressions of this type, let us define the following quantities:

$$N(\boldsymbol{p}/\boldsymbol{q}) = -\sum_{i=1}^{n} p_i \log q_i$$

$$H(\boldsymbol{p}) = -\sum_{i=1}^{n} p_i \log p_i .$$

The latter is of course the common designation for the entropy of a probability distribution $p_1, p_2, \ldots, p_n$. Thus $H(\boldsymbol{p}) = N(\boldsymbol{p}/\boldsymbol{p})$.

We wish to construct the best solution algorithm possible. Which probability distribution will lead to the lowest uncertainty?

It is easy to see (A. M. Yaglom and I. M. Yaglom, *Probability and Information*, Fizmatgiz, Moscow, 1960) that if the p_i are fixed, problem uncertainty is minimal when $q_i = p_i$. In this case $N(\boldsymbol{p}/\boldsymbol{q}) = N(\boldsymbol{p}/\boldsymbol{p}) = H(\boldsymbol{p})$, i.e., the problem uncertainty is equal to the entropy of the answer probabilities. Thus, if we know the probabilities p_i during construction of the solution algorithm, we can simply select $q_i = p_i$.

In the general case, however,

$$N(\boldsymbol{p}/\boldsymbol{q}) \geqslant N(\boldsymbol{p}/\boldsymbol{p}) = H(\boldsymbol{p}) . \tag{4}$$

Assume now that we deal with a problem with the probability distribution $p_1, p_2, \ldots, p_n$, but we think that the distribution is $p'_1, p'_2, \ldots, p'_n$ (generally speaking $p'_i \neq p_i$). In attempting to construct the best solution algorithm, we decide that $q_i = p'_i$ $(i = 1, 2, \ldots, n)$. The uncertainty in this case is $N(A) = N(\boldsymbol{p}/\boldsymbol{p}')$.

The expression $N(\boldsymbol{p}/\boldsymbol{q})$ can be considered as the problem uncertainty when the answer probability distribution is $\boldsymbol{p}$, but an observer uses the hypothesis that the distribution is $\boldsymbol{q}$. Therefore, the probability distribution $\boldsymbol{q}$ is called the *observer hypothesis*.

From this point of view the entropy $H(p)$ is a particular case of uncertainty. Entropy is the uncertainty for an algorithm that knows and uses to best advantage the probability distribution of the problem answers. If this is not known, uncertainty increases.

Generally speaking, lack of knowledge can be of two types. We can know the truth, only the truth, but not the whole truth; or we can know what actually does not exist (fallacy).

An attempt to separate these two cases is given in Appendix 1.

4. Decoding the signal—Useful information

Figure 31 shows a block diagram of the solution algorithm. Class choices are decided here by a roulette wheel divided into n sectors. Sector areas are proportional to the corresponding values of q_i. A rotatable arrow is fixed in the center of the roulette wheel. If pushed, it will make several turns, and stop with probability q_i in the ith sector. After the arrow stops, A_i is transmitted to the input of the W algorithm. Pattern m_k is simultaneously presented to the other input of the W algorithm. Depending upon whether or not $m_k \in A_i$, either the number i is printed and the solution is complete, or the arrow is pushed again, etc.

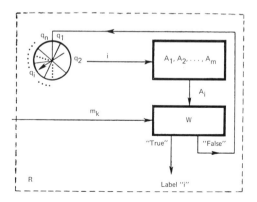

Figure 31. Scheme of the solution algorithm.

Consider now a system consisting of the solution algorithm R (Fig. 31), a communication channel C, and an algorithm D connecting the communication channel to the solution algorithm (see Fig. 32).

The additional algorithm D we call the *decoding algorithm*. It performs as follows. For every value of the incoming signal C_k, it substitutes a new value q_i' for each value of q_i, thus supplying a new probability distribution q' to the solution algorithm. In terms of Fig. 31, the decoding algorithm removes the old roulette wheel, and substitutes another one with new sector areas. Therefore, the incoming information changes the problem uncertainty.

Suppose that a problem had an uncertainty N_0 for a given solution algorithm prior to receiving information from the communication channel, and uncertainty N_1 after receipt of the information. Then we say that the amount of useful information transmitted by the channel is,

$$I_n = N_0 - N_1 .\qquad(5)$$

It follows from this that it is pointless to talk about useful information unless we know the problem, the initial state of the solution algorithm, and the properties of the decoding algorithm.

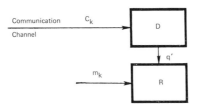

Figure 32.

A change in problem uncertainty due to the incoming signal can be interpreted as a process of accumulating useful information in the form of the probability distribution q. It is of advantage to assume that useful information is zero when $q_i = \dfrac{1}{n}$ $(i = 1, 2, \ldots, n)$ as a reference point from which useful information can be measured. (It is shown in Appendix 1 that the hypothesis $q_i = \dfrac{1}{n}$ $[i = 1, 2, \ldots, n]$ is optimal if we know nothing about the probability distribution p). The increment in useful information contained in the hypothesis q, with respect to a problem with an answer probability distribution p, is given by the expression:

$$I_n = \log n - N(p/q) .$$

Let us give an example. Suppose person X wishes to see person Y in the latter's office. The office is open from 10 A.M. to 6 P.M., but it is known that Y is in his office only two hours a day. In order to verify his information, X talks to an acquaintance who works in the same office as Y. The acquaintance tells him that Y is in the office after 2 P.M. twice as often as he is before 2 P.M. Then X calls Y's secretary and receives the following reply: "We do not have any schedule for the next month, but Y sees visitors five days a week from 12 to 2 P.M., and once a week from 2 to 4 P.M. Wait a minute. I made an error. He sees visitors once a week from 12 to 2 P.M., and five times a week from 2 to 4 P.M." The last answer was closer to reality.

What useful information has X obtained: (1) From his acquaintance? (2) From Y's secretary? (3) From the secretary's answer had she not corrected her error?

All probabilities are summarized in Table 14 for convenience.

TABLE 14

	A.M. 10–12	P.M. 12–2	P.M. 2–4	P.M. 4–6
True probability distribution	0	1/6	5/6	0
Initial hypothesis	1/4	1/4	1/4	1/4
Hypothesis after talk with acquaintance	1/6	1/6	1/3	1/3
Hypothesis after secretary's answer	0	1/6	5/6	0
Hypothesis after secretary's erroneous answer	0	5/6	1/6	0

Uncertainty and useful information will be expressed in bits. The initial uncertainty is:

$$N_0 = -1/6 \log_2 (1/4) - 5/6 \log_2 (1/4) = \log_2 4 = 2 \text{ bits.}$$

The uncertainty after the information obtained from the acquaintance is:

$$N_1 = -1/6 \log_2 1/6 - 5/6 \log_2 1/3 \approx 1.75 \text{ bits.}$$

The uncertainty after the secretary's complete answer is:

$$N_2 = -1/6 \log_2 1/6 - 5/6 \log_2 5/6 \approx 0.65 \text{ bits.}$$

If the secretary had not corrected her answer:

$$N_3 = -1/6 \log_2 5/6 - 5/6 \log_2 1/6 \approx 2.20 \text{ bits.}$$

The useful information obtained from the acquaintance is:

$$I_{n_1} = N_0 - N_1 \approx 0.25 \text{ bits.}$$

The secretary's answer contained this useful information:

$$I_{n_2} = N_1 - N_2 \approx 1.1 \text{ bits.}$$

If the same conversation with the secretary had taken place before the information supplied by the acquaintance, it would have contained $N_0 - N_2 \approx 1.35$ bits of useful information.

The erroneous answer carried this useful information: $I_{n_3} = N_1 - N_3 \approx -0.45$. In other words, it contained 0.45 bits of disinformation.

In this example, the decoding algorithm is reduced to the transfer of the received probabilities directly to the solution algorithm ("complete trust"). In the case of another decoding algorithm, the useful information contained in the communication would be different, of course. For example, it would be quite natural for X not to trust the secretary's erroneous information because of its sharp difference with the story told by his acquaintance. And even the right information cannot be trusted completely because of its discrepancy with the story of his acquaintance, and the initial error made by the secretary.

The amount of useful information also depends on the code in which information is transmitted. The same information would have been coded differently if transmitted in a language not known to X. In this case, the coding device would not have distributed q_i at all to the solution algorithm. The amount of useful information would thus be zero.

In books on the theory of information, it is emphasized that if zeros are substituted for ones and vice versa in information coded in a binary alphabet, the amount of information does not change. But this has nothing to do with useful information. The useful information will change drastically with such a transformation, and even the sign can be reversed.

One additional property distinguishes useful information from "classical information." How much information can be stored in a code composed of the numbers $q_1, q_2, \ldots, q_n$? In the case of classical theory, the answer depends on the accuracy of $q_1, q_2, \ldots, q_n$. The higher this accuracy, the more information we get. On the other hand, useful information distributed in $q_1, q_2, \ldots, q_n$ with respect to a problem with an answer probability distribution $p_1, p_2, \ldots, p_n$ is equal to $\log n - N(p/q)$, and it does not depend on the accuracy with which the q_i is known. Useful information depends on the correspondence of q to p. If q_i is known less accurately, then I_n will be of lower accuracy, but its value will not necessarily be small.

5. Transmission capacity of a communication channel for useful information

Consider now the relationship between the uncertainty of a problem after receipt of information, and the transmission capacity of a communication channel.

Two signals C_1 and C_2 are indistinguishable to a system if it enters one and the same state after receiving either C_1 or C_2. (The solution algorithm uses the same hypotheses $q_1', q_2', \ldots, q_n'$.) Using some definite measurement accuracy for q_i, we can state whether any two signals differ or not. A real system can have only a finite number of states. Let the number of distinguishable sets of $q_1, q_2, \ldots, q_n$ be t. Divide the set of all possible signals $C_1, C_2, \ldots, C_m$ into classes of indistinguishable signals. Evidently $m \leqslant t$. (Signals indistinguishable for the system in one state could become distinguishable for it in another state. However, we consider below only classes of signals indistinguishable for a system in a given state.) Properties of the decoding device for a fixed initial distribution of q can be exhaustively listed for a division of signals into classes, as shown in Table 15, which gives the distribution of q' after arrival of signals from the class C_k.

TABLE 15

	C_1	C_2	$\ldots$	C_k	$\ldots$	C_m
q'_1	d_{11}	d_{12}	$\ldots$	d_{1k}	$\ldots$	d_{1m}
q'_2	d_{21}	d_{22}	$\ldots$	d_{2k}	$\ldots$	d_{2m}
$\ldots$	$\ldots$	$\ldots$	$\ldots$	$\ldots$	$\ldots$	$\ldots$
q'_i	d_{i1}	d_{i2}	$\ldots$	d_{ik}	$\ldots$	d_{im}
$\ldots$	$\ldots$	$\ldots$	$\ldots$	$\ldots$	$\ldots$	$\ldots$
q'_n	d_{n1}	d_{n2}	$\ldots$	d_{nk}	$\ldots$	d_{nm}

Consider the situation in which, before problem solving begins, the system is somehow informed as to the class membership of pattern m_1. If $m_1 \in A_1$, then message ϕ_1 is sent; if $m_1 \in A_2$, message ϕ_2 is sent, etc. Now the probability of arrival of signals C_k is different, depending upon which message ϕ is sent. The situation can be depicted by means of the matrix, P_{ik}, Table 16.

TABLE 16

	C_1	$\ldots$	C_k	$\ldots$	C_m
ϕ_1	P_{11}	$\ldots$	P_{1k}	$\ldots$	P_{1m}
$\ldots$	$\ldots$	$\ldots$	$\ldots$	$\ldots$	$\ldots$
ϕ_i	P_{i1}	$\ldots$	P_{ik}	$\ldots$	P_{im}
$\ldots$	$\ldots$	$\ldots$	$\ldots$	$\ldots$	$\ldots$
ϕ_n	P_{n1}	$\ldots$	P_{nk}	$\ldots$	P_{nm}

The reader may ask why such a complex case is considered. Why do different signals C_k arrive after sending the message ϕ_i regarding the class membership of m_k, and only one and the same signal arrives after sending different ϕ_i? Assume that the solution algorithm searches for the formula according to which some numerical table is constructed. The table itself represents the message by means of which the decoding algorithm may try to decrease the uncertainty of the problem. Clearly, different signals can arrive regarding the membership of a pattern in one and the same class in this example. Consider another case, in which the solution algorithm must decide whether a given photograph is of a man or a woman. The message received (the photograph itself) will usually contain enough information to answer this question. However, there could be photographs from which it would be difficult to decide between a man and a woman. This could happen because of poor picture quality, or because of facial similarities of some men and women. Thus, more than one nonzero number can be encountered in the rows and columns of Table 16. Since some kind of signal must arrive after the communication ϕ_i is sent, then it is required that:

$$\sum_{k=1}^{m} P_{ik} = 1 .$$

[It is not entirely clear why the author chose to drag a "prior message" ϕ, followed by a "subsequent" signal C, into the exposition. What he appears to be saying is simply that the P_{ik}'s are the probabilities of the kth signal being sent to the decoder if in fact the pattern under consideration belongs to the ith class. Thus the column of ϕ's in Table 16 could be replaced by the title "class membership," and the column: 1, 2, . . . , i, . . . n. The sequence of events would then be more rationally described as follows. First, a pattern from Class i is picked with probability p_i. This triggers two events: (1) the pattern is presented to algorithm W, and (2) signal C_k is selected with probability P_{ik} from the ith row of Table 16, and transmitted to decoder D. Upon receipt of signal C_k, decoder D immediately replaces the roulette wheel in Fig. 31 with one proportional to the column k in Table 15. The solution algorithm then spins the arrow, which has a probability d_{ik} of pointing to the correct answer (Class i). The testing algorithm checks the actual pointer reading for veracity, and the system R proceeds as before. Clearly, the "perfect" message source and decoder would correspond to matrices in Tables 15 and 16 in which $P_{ik} = d_{ik} = 1$ if $i = k$, and zero otherwise. As the author points out, however, there is seldom this much certainty in practice. The secretary may be giving out false information to shield Mr. Y from visitors, and Mr. X may choose not to believe her anyway.
—EDITOR.]

What is the problem uncertainty if the signal transmitted along the communication channel, characterized by the matrix $||P_{ik}||$, is decoded by an algorithm characterized by the matrix $||d_{ik}||$?

Assume a pattern belongs to Class A_i. The signal C_1 arrives with the probability P_{i1}. If signal C_1 is indeed selected, then the average number of trials is $1/d_{i1}$. If signal C_2 is selected (with probability P_{i2}) then the average number of trials will be $\dfrac{1}{d_{i2}}$, etc. Thus, for the ith class the uncertainty is,

$$N_1 (A_i) = - \sum_{k=1}^{m} P_{ik} \log d_{ik} .$$

The probability of this situation occurring is p_i. Therefore, for the entire problem (all classes) the uncertainty is,

$$N_1(A) = -\sum_{i=1}^{n} p_i \sum_{k=1}^{m} P_{ik} \log d_{ik} . \tag{6}$$

We will use the notation

$$\bar{P}_k = \sum_{i=1}^{n} p_i P_{ik} , \tag{7}$$

$$\bar{d}_i = \sum_{k=1}^{m} \bar{P}_k d_{ik} . \tag{8}$$

It is evident that

$$\sum_{k=1}^{m} \bar{P}_k = 1 , \tag{9}$$

$$\sum_{i=1}^{n} \bar{d}_i = 1 . \tag{10}$$

In order to evaluate the uncertainty, (6) can be transformed to:

$$\begin{aligned}
N_1(A) &= -\sum_{i=1}^{n} p_i \sum_{k=1}^{m} P_{ik} \left(\log \bar{d}_i - \log \bar{P}_k + \log \frac{\bar{P}_k d_{ik}}{d_i} \right) \\
&= -\sum_{i=1}^{n} p_i \log \bar{d}_i \sum_{k=1}^{m} P_{ik} + \sum_{k=1}^{m} \sum_{i=1}^{n} p_i P_{ik} \log \bar{P}_k \\
&\quad - \sum_{i=1}^{n} p_i \sum_{k=1}^{m} P_{ik} \log \frac{\bar{P}_k d_{ik}}{\bar{d}_i} \\
&= N(p/\bar{d}) - H(\bar{P}) - \sum_{i=1}^{n} p_i \sum_{k=1}^{m} P_{ik} \log \frac{\bar{P}_k d_{ik}}{\bar{d}_i} .
\end{aligned}$$

Using (4) and (8) we can obtain:

$$N_1(A) \geqslant H(p) - [H(\bar{P}) - \bar{H}(P)] , \tag{11}$$

in which

$$\bar{H}(P) = -\sum_{i=1}^{n} p_i \sum_{k=1}^{m} P_{ik} \log P_{ik}$$

is the average entropy of the signals C_k.

The expression within square brackets in (11), the entropy of the average signal minus the average entropy of signals, is identical to the transmitting capacity of the channel (characterized by the matrix $||P_{ik}||$), when the probability of different communications is $p_1, p_2, \ldots, p_n$. Therefore, (11) means that no matter how we decode the signals, the problem uncertainty after decoding will not be less than the entropy of the distribution of answers minus the channel transmitting capacity.

How close can we approach this theoretical limit?

Let the matrix of the decoding algorithm be constructed according to the formula

$$d_{ik} = \frac{p_i P_{ik}}{\overline{P}_k} . \tag{12}$$

This matrix can serve as the decoding algorithm because $d_{ik} \geqslant 0$, and from (7) it follows that

$$\sum_{i=1}^{n} d_{ik} = 1 .$$

Now the problem uncertainty after decoding the signal by means of the above algorithm becomes:

$$
\left.
\begin{aligned}
N_1(A) &= - \sum_{i=1}^{n} p_i \sum_{k=1}^{m} P_{ik} \log \frac{p_i P_{ik}}{\overline{P}_k} \\
&= - \sum_{i=1}^{n} p_i \sum_{k=1}^{m} P_{ik} (\log p_i - \log \overline{P}_k + \log P_{ik}) \\
&= - \sum_{k=1}^{m} P_{ik} \sum_{i=1}^{n} p_i \log p_i + \sum_{k=1}^{m} \sum_{i=1}^{n} p_i P_{ik} \log \overline{P}_k \\
&\quad - \sum_{i=1}^{n} p_i \sum_{k=1}^{m} P_{ik} \log P_{ik} \\
&= H(P) - [H(\overline{P}) - \overline{H}(P)] .
\end{aligned}
\right\} \tag{13}
$$

Thus, if the decoding algorithm is constructed according to (12), the uncertainty reaches a minimum. The uniqueness of the optimal decoding algorithm can be also proved. It is omitted here for brevity.

In order to use formula (12), we must know beforehand all p_i and P_{ik}. In reality, this requirement is not often fulfilled. Assume that an observer has a hypothesis $q_1, q_2, \ldots, q_n$ regarding the probability of answers to the problem, and also another hypothesis indicating that the communication channel is characterized by the matrix $\|Q_{ik}\|$. In order to decrease the problem uncertainty maximally, the decoding algorithm is constructed according to the formula:

$$d_{ik} = \frac{q_i Q_{ik}}{\overline{Q}_k} , \tag{14}$$

in which

$$\bar{Q}_k = \sum_{i=1}^{k} q_i Q_{ik} .$$

As a result, the problem uncertainty for such an observer will be, omitting intermediate steps.

$$N_1(A) = - \sum_{i=1}^{n} p_i \sum_{k=1}^{m} P_{ik} \log \frac{q_i Q_{ik}}{\bar{Q}_k}$$

$$= N(p/q) - [N(\bar{P}/\bar{Q}) - \bar{N}(P/Q)], \qquad (15)$$

in which,

$$\bar{N}(P/Q) = - \sum_{i=1}^{n} p_i \sum_{k=1}^{m} P_{ik} \log Q_{ik} .$$

The formula (15) can be rewritten as

$$N(q/p) - N_1(A) = N(\bar{P}/\bar{Q}) - \bar{N}(P/Q) . \qquad (16)$$

The left part of this equality is the change in problem uncertainty after arrival of the decoding signal. That is, $N(p/q) = N_0(A)$ is the initial problem uncertainty for an observer using the hypothesis q, and $N_1(A)$ is the terminalun certainty. Thus, $N(p/q) - N_1(A) = N_0(A) - N_1(A)$ is the amount of useful information transmitted along the communication channel. Therefore, the difference

$$N(\bar{P}/\bar{Q}) - \bar{N}(P/Q) \qquad (17)$$

can be called the *transmission capacity of the channel for useful information* under situation p and P with respect to an observer using hypotheses q and Q. For an observer who knows everything about the problem and the communication channel ($q_i = p_i$; $Q_{ik} = P_{ik}$), the classical transmitting capacity is obtained:

$$H(\bar{P}) - \bar{H}(P) . \qquad (18)$$

It is of interest to note that (17) can be either smaller or larger than (18). For example, if an observer knows correctly everything about the channel ($Q_{ik} = P_{ik}$), but uses a nonoptimal hypothesis with respect to the problem ($q_i \neq p_i$), then (17) is

$$N(\bar{P}/\bar{Q}) - \bar{N}(P/Q) > H(\bar{P}) - \bar{H}(P) .$$

Such an observer will measure experimentally (by comparing the number of trials before and after the arrival of signals) a greater capacity for the communication channel than will an observer using optimal hypotheses. Despite this fact, the final problem uncertainty for such an observer will be higher than that of an "all knowledgeable observer."

The formula (16) in fact establishes the relationships among the problem properties, the signal properties, what the observer thinks about the problem beforehand, his attitude to the signal, and the benefit that he derives from the signal under these circumstances.

6. Systems with feedback

We have considered up to now those solution algorithms that do not change q_i during the solution of the problem. These algorithms "have not remembered anything." If the algorithm determines by applying the W algorithm that A_1, for example, does not contain m_k, it will still continue to use the same random approach with the old probability distribution q, despite the fact that it is now known that q_1 could become zero. The problem uncertainty remains the same both before and after a trial.

Such "stupid" algorithms were needed as models to facilitate the introduction of ideas about problem uncertainty for an observer using some quite definite hypothesis, q. In fact, if q changes in the course of the problem solution, then there is no way to compare the number of trials with any hypothesis.

However, if our aim is to construct an optimal solution algorithm, we should not disregard the information obtained from applications of the W algorithm. Systems in which the results of the W algorithm influence the probability distributions employed in successive steps are called *systems with feedback*.

An example of such a system is one in which a signal saying "not A_i," is sent along the feedback channel after an unsuccessful trial. The system receiving such a message makes $q_i' = 0$, and increases all other probabilities proportionally in such a manner that their sum remains unity. The problem uncertainty now decreases after each unsuccessful trial. The system with feedback uses a new hypothesis (perfected during experiment) during each new step. In particular, for such a system the number of trials to classify a new pattern never will be higher than n.

It was stated in Section 3 that the uncertainty is lowest for an algorithm without feedback if it uses a statistical approach with the probability distribution p. Does this mean that if this process is supplemented by eliminating rejected classes and renormalizing all other probabilities, then an optimal algorithm with feedback is obtained? Not at all. It is shown in Appendix 2 that the following algorithm with feedback is optimal: First, order the classes in such a way that $p_{t_1} \geqslant p_{t_2} \geqslant p_{t_3} \geqslant , \ldots, \geqslant p_{t_n}$. Now try class A_{t_1}. If the answer is *false*, try A_{t_2}, etc. Thus, the optimal solution algorithm with feedback actually does not need any statistical approach (all selections are carried out with unity probability). Each test result is characterized for this algorithm not by the selection of probability q_i, but by the positive integer z_i, the ordinal number for checking.

During repeated solutions of a problem with respect to an object $m_k \in A_i$, the solution algorithm with a rigid sifting order will always find the answer at one and the same step z_i. Therefore, the uncertainty $N(m_k)$ for such an algorithm is simply $\log z_i$. Therefore,

$$N(A) = \sum_{i=1}^{n} p_i \log z_i = \sum_{s=1}^{n} p_s \log s, \qquad (19)$$

where s is the position of the number p_s in the column of p_i arranged in decreasing order.

Naturally, if we use hypothesis q regarding the answer probability distribution during the construction of a solution algorithm, the q_i will also be arranged in decreasing order. According to formula (19), s should be counted as the position of the number q_s in the column of decreasing q_i.

Let us prove that in this case

$$N(A) = \sum_{s=1}^{n} p_s \log s \leqslant N(p/q). \qquad (20)$$

Ordering requires that

$$1 \geqslant q_1,$$
$$\frac{1}{2} \geqslant q_2,$$
$$\frac{1}{3} \geqslant q_3,$$
$$\ldots\ldots$$
$$\frac{1}{n} \geqslant q_n.$$

Consequently,

$$\log 1 \leqslant -\log q_1,$$
$$\log 2 \leqslant -\log q_2,$$
$$\ldots\ldots\ldots\ldots$$
$$\log n \leqslant -\log q_n.$$

Formula (20) follows automatically. Assume we have two solution algorithms with rigid sifting order, one constructed on the hypothesis q, and the other on hypothesis q'. Furthermore, assume that $q_i \neq q'_i$, but $z_i = z'_i$. It is impossible to distinguish one algorithm from another from

their behavior. Therefore, we can reasonably say that the order for checking answers constitutes the hypothesis for algorithms with feedback, not
the distribution of probabilities.

The decoding device connected to the solution algorithm should be
characterized by a table to determine the testing schedule for the answer
A_i, after the arrival of signal C_k (Table 17). In a given column $z_{1k}, z_{2k}, \ldots,$

TABLE 17

	C_1	C_2	$\ldots$	C_k	$\ldots$	C_m
A_1	z_{11}	z_{12}	$\ldots$	z_{1k}	$\ldots$	z_{1m}
A_2	z_{21}	z_{22}	$\ldots$	z_{2k}	$\ldots$	z_{2m}
$\ldots$						
A_i	z_{i1}	z_{i2}	$\ldots$	z_{ik}	$\ldots$	z_{im}
$\ldots$						
A_n	z_{n1}	z_{n2}	$\ldots$	z_{nk}	$\ldots$	z_{nm}

z_{nk}, all whole numbers from 1 to n are encountered only once. A decoding
device $||z_{ik}||$ constructed in the following manner will be optimal. Take
the matrix $||d_{ik}||$ with elements determined from (12). Arrange the elements
of the kth column in decreasing order: $d_{1k} \geqslant d_{2k} \geqslant \ldots \geqslant d_{nk}$. Number
them in the same order such that $z_{ik} = s$. Considering the expression (20),
we see that the formula (13) for the uncertainty of such an algorithm will be

$$N_1(A) \leqslant H(p) - [H(\overline{P}) - \overline{H}(P)]. \tag{21}$$

7. Two functions of the "problem conditions"

Ideas about the W algorithm, the solution algorithm, and the decoding
algorithm were introduced in Sections 2 and 4. How can we translate into
this common language, everyday statements containing "problem conditions"?

Take an elementary school problem: Two boys have 12 books. Mike
has 2 books more than Peter. How many books has Mike, and how many
has Peter?

First, *the problem condition contains the W algorithm.* In principle, the
answer could be found by generating random pairs of numbers, and
checking to see if they satisfy the condition.

Secondly, *the condition represents a signal* that can reduce the problem
uncertainty after appropriate decoding.

The presence of two completely different functions in "the condition"
is very difficult for adults to notice. But it is evident in experiments with
children and in some programs.

If this problem is given to a child 8 or 9 years old, capable of counting to 100 and knowing addition, subtraction, and division by two, but who never solved a similar problem, he, as a rule, will not use the condition as a W algorithm. He will state unchecked assumptions, and will use the adult (who gave him the problem) as the W algorithm. He will also use the conditions to decrease the search field (not always to the best advantage). In this example, the child will never use a number higher than 12. Many children will try only pairs of numbers that produce 12 when added. And sometimes pairs of numbers that differ by two will be tried. Even if a child knows fractional numbers, he will still use only whole numbers. However, if we state the condition differently, like "12 kg. of candy," then fractional numbers come into use.

This indicates that the condition may contain information not used in the W algorithm.

A correctly formulated condition in the case of the above elementary school problem can decrease the uncertainty to zero after optimal decoding. This leads to situations in which children of grades 3 or 4 can produce a correct answer, but do not know how to check it. This may be the reason why it is difficult to solve "nonstandard" problems, i.e., those problems in which optimal decoding of the condition decreases the uncertainty to such a level that it becomes impossible to try alternatives.

The program that tries to find arithmetic rules by random trials behaves differently. It uses the input table of numbers to check hypotheses, without trying to decode them, or to decrease the problem uncertainty.

Thus, different systems use different properties of the problem conditions. What kind of procedure with respect to conditions is characteristic of recognition systems?

8. Decoding and recognition

The program *Arithmetic*, after calculating the characteristic values of a table in accordance with its selected features, compares these with sets stored in memory. It then prints out the numbers of the three most similar rules. Could this program produce the number of precisely that rule according to which the table was constructed after some additional checking? The answer is *no*. The reason is that it does not know the formulas (given during training) according to which tables are constructed. Furthermore, it does not know which rules (arithmetic or logical) are used to construct tables. In other words, the program does not have a W algorithm.

Evidently, this situation is common to all recognition problems. Consider Fig. 18 which shows a scheme of the recognition process. The "supreme judge" (W algorithm) is the block K_1 located outside the recognition system. The task of the system during test is to decode the object shape in order to decrease uncertainty. But the system is incapable of telling whether or not finite uncertainty exists.

In other words, a test begins and ends with the selection of $q_1, q_2, \ldots, q_n$ because there is no W algorithm. Only the examiner (who already knows the W algorithm) can evaluate the uncertainty (or the number of necessary trials). (Of course it is possible to automate the test process by supplying an additional program equipped with a W algorithm, and entrust it to conduct the checking of hypotheses. But this addition would not really be a recognizing program. Precisely this was done when the quality of the program *Arithmetic* was evaluated.)

It can be said that testing consists of decoding some signal regarding the class to which a pattern belongs. Training, on the other hand, consists of the construction of the decoding device. The training system should synthesize by itself the decoding device suitable for a given problem.

In other words, the system should select one decoding device suitable for a given case among some set of decoding devices accessible to it. Checking the results of decoding patterns from the training set could serve as the W algorithm. Thus, the synthesis of the decoding device itself represents a problem, the uncertainty of which is higher with the greater the variety of decoding devices the system can construct.

Is it possible to decrease the uncertainty in this problem by decoding the training material? One way would be to provide an additional decoding algorithm that could select the order for checking different decoding devices just by "looking" at the training material. This additional algorithm would thus be a system for recognizing not objects, but problems.

It might appear that it is worth trying to construct such a universal decoding algorithm. Remember, however, that the set of problems contains many problems. We often do not know how many there are, and are unable to describe the whole set in any formal language. Under these conditions, the construction of a universal algorithm is hopeless. It is very doubtful that training could be reduced to a single decoding for complex sets of problems.

The most likely approach is to construct a multistage process: The first step concerns the selection of some subset of problems (to which our problem belongs). Selection takes place partially on the basis of decoding the training material, and partially on the basis of some sifting.

During the solution of the problem, the program reduces the area of search within the first stage, and is able to construct a somewhat specialized decoding device. This decoding device, however, is not suitable for all problems from a given set. It is suitable only for the selected subset. The whole process is repeated again. The selected subset is divided again in parts, etc.

The decoding device produced at each stage consists of two parts: a block that transforms individual patterns, and a block that compares the results of transformations of different patterns. The input of the block transforming the patterns at the ith stage takes the results produced by the corresponding block at the $(i - 1)$st stage, and the comparison of different patterns is repeated. The comparison of objects at the $(i - 1)$st stage has only helped to select the transformation for the ith stage.

The whole process will stop at the stage in which patterns of one class become indistinguishable among themselves after transformation. Patterns of the second class will also be indistinguishable, but the first class will differ from the second class. The transformation found in this way can, clearly, be used during test.

In the above process there is one vague point. Namely, what should be used for the W algorithm at intermediate stages? The W algorithm for the last stage is given in the preceding paragraph. But what about the other stages? What criteria should be used to select pattern transformations? Generally speaking, these criteria should differ for different sets of problems. Some of these criteria are considered in Chapters 5, 8, and 9. The same chapters discuss the sets of problems for which these criteria are useful.

CHAPTER 8

The Program, *Geometry*

1. *Perceptron lectures*

THE PERFORMANCE of the simple Rosenblatt Perceptron was considered in Chapter 2. In the same chapter, it was also shown that rectangles and ellipses are too difficult for the Perceptron. Let us analyze the poor performance of the Perceptron, and see if it cannot be improved by some change in the algorithm.

First, we notice that interconnections between A elements in Perceptrons (Fig. 9) do not depend upon the problem to be solved. In fact, these interconnections are established arbitrarily before the teaching material is shown. Therefore, the Perceptron is forced to differentiate triangles from circles, and convex figures from concave ones, using the same structural relationships among the A elements. There are too few degrees of freedom in the learning process in the Perceptron scheme, since learning influences only the amplification coefficients, k.

A supposedly better idea is therefore suggested, namely, to select the interconnections among A elements by means of the learning process itself. To accomplish this, the interconnections could be, for example, generated randomly as before. However, only those which proved useful for a given problem would be fixed in memory. It will be shown, unfortunately, that the possibility of making a good selection of A elements even in this case remains very low.

113

[The author reflects here the general conclusions reached by many investigators in this country and elsewhere. He discusses this conclusion at greater length, in forceful terms, in Sections 4 and 5.

—EDITOR.]

Assume that it is of importance in a given problem to differentiate angles from smooth lines. After several random approaches, an A element is formed with the required properties. It will recognize an angle at one particular location in the field. But the Perceptron should be able to recognize angles regardless of their location. If we persist in pursuing this same procedure, clearly much more time is needed to assemble a set of elements capable of detecting angles at any spot within the field.

Therefore, the next step is to "reproduce" suitable A elements. This can be accomplished for example by the rule: As soon as one suitable A element is found, analogous elements are created in other parts of the visual field, without further testing.

This suggests the question: Should the machine receive all its information by learning? Clearly, there are detection operations upon the picture that are seldom required (i.e., for a limited number of problems out of the total number). We feel that they should be found during learning. But there are operations that are very useful, and used frequently. Why should they be relearned every time? Would it not be better to incorporate into the program a set of such operators, and not spend machine time for repetitive learning. Identifying the figure contour, finding angles, detecting crossing points of lines, etc., are examples of such operators.

Finally, it is extremely important to note the limitations on the logical functions that can be realized by the Perceptron. All A elements vote with weights selected during learning. The weight of a given element does not depend upon whether another A element becomes excited at the same time. The Perceptron, therefore, cannot solve problems in which the weight of some situation should change in the presence or absence of another situation. An example of this type of problem is shown in Fig. 30.

[This is not completely true, since the nonlinearity introduced by the threshold operation makes the output decision a complex function of the input variables, and weights that are conditional to a limited extent upon the activity of other elements can therefore be achieved. However, the author's general intent to point out the lack of completeness of the linear threshold type of logic is, indeed, well taken. Previous investigators such as Minnick[1] and Stafford[2] have catalogued the realizable functions, which represent a small fraction of all possible functions, for up to six input variables.

—EDITOR.]

The present chapter is devoted primarily to a description of the program containing the above improvements, and experiments with it. The program was designed to divide pictures into four classes, and was prepared by M. Bongard, M. Smirnov, V. Maksimov, and G. Zenkin.

Figure 33. Examples of input patterns.

2. *Structure of the program* Geometry

Binary pictures on a 32 × 36 field make up the input patterns for the program *Geometry*. Figure 33 presents examples of such pictures for two classes.

The program consists of four blocks that treat the pictorial information in succession. The first block accepts the original picture, the second block accepts the results of the picture treated by the first block, etc.

Each block adapts after the preceding blocks have adapted, and prior to adaptation by the following blocks. As a result, during adaptation of the third block, for example, the conditions of the first and second blocks do not change. This makes it possible to consider each block individually, forgetting about others temporarily.

In naming the blocks, an analogy with the eye was used. In the retina of vertebrates, the signal from the receptors reaches first a layer of bipolar cells, then a layer of ganglion cells. Appendages of the ganglion cells extend to the subcortex in the brain, and subsequently into the cortex. The four program blocks are named accordingly. However, the reader should keep in mind that this analogy is superficial, and the terms *bipolar cells*, *ganglion cells*, *subcortex*, and *cortex* represent only arbitrary designations for the program blocks.

Bipolar cells. Bipolar cells constitute a fixed, nonadaptive block. They perform picture transformations expected heuristically to be frequently useful.

The bipolar cells are divided into three layers. Each layer transforms the original 32 × 36 picture into a field of the same dimensions. The first layer extracts the contours of the figures; the second detects the angles; the third performs smoothing to eliminate simple noise. If the picture contains an isolated black spot on a white background, or the reverse, the third layer removes it.

Consider the first layer. Assume all points in the image processed by the first layer are arranged just above the corresponding points of the original input picture. Each element (square) in the rectangular array has eight nearest neighbors in the array below it (the boundary squares have fewer).

The square in the upper field is turned on (black) whenever two conditions are fulfilled: (1) there is a black square exactly under it, and (2) at least one neighboring square is white. Other squares of the upper field remain off (white). The contour of the figure is thereby obtained, as illustrated in Fig. 34. The algorithms of the two other layers are similar, and are not considered further here.

Thus, the bipolar cells transform the 32 × 36 field into four fields of the same size (the initial field of receptors and the results of three processing layers). These four fields serve as initial data for the ganglion cells.

Ganglion cells. The ganglion cells represent the first adaptive block of the program. They are adapted only once (for the total set of problems, and not for each problem individually).

The block of ganglion cells consists of 45 layers. All layers are constructed identically, and differ only in the data used for their adaptation.

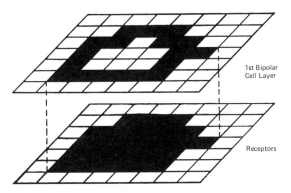

Figure 34. Illustration of contour extraction in first bipolar cell layer.

Each layer contains a field of 32 × 36 cells. Each of these 1,152 cells represents an *A* element. All *A* elements in a given layer are identical. Each ganglion cell has a certain number of exciting and inhibiting connections from receptors and bipolar cells as shown in Fig. 35. When the

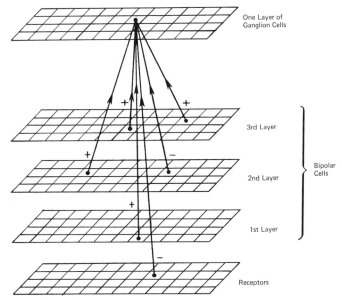

Figure 35. Connection pattern of one ganglion cell to preceding bipolar cells and receptors.

net signal to the cell exceeds a certain threshold, the ganglion cell fires (on). If all bipolar cell and receptor layers are projected onto one plane, then the cells to which a given ganglion cell connects are located within a local 8 × 8 square, as shown in Fig. 36, illustrating the connections of three

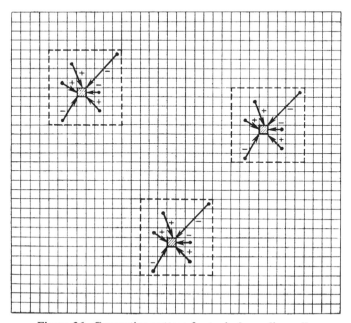

Figure 36. Connection pattern for typical ganglion cells.

typical ganglion cells (crosshatched). All ganglion cells in a given layer are connected in an identical pattern. Each ganglion cell has 12 input connections. (Figure 36 shows only six connections for simplicity. Cells near the boundary have fewer connections because signals do not come from beyond the field.) During network assembly, the number of inhibitory connections (0, 2, 4, or 6) for the cells in a given layer is chosen at random. In the same manner (randomly), a connection pattern for the twelve inputs to the (identical) cells in each layer is selected from among the 256 possibilities (8 × 8 ganglion cell input field, three bipolar layers, and one receptor layer). Due to the fact that all cells of a given layer are arranged according to one plan, the random selection is done only once for all 1,152 cells.

Adaptation consists of selecting those layers of the ganglion cells that prove useful for differentiating certain pairs of pictures. Examples are given in Fig. 37.

Adaptation is conducted in the following manner: A pair of pictures is introduced into the machine, e.g., Fig. 37 (a, b, or c). The bipolar and receptor cells transform the picture into four 32 × 36 fields. At this stage, the above random interconnections are made, and a layer of ganglion cells is formed. This layer processes both pictures. Then the program checks to see if a threshold for the ganglion cells can be found such that a number of cells excited by one picture differs substantially from the number of cells excited by the other picture. If such a threshold is found, then the memory records the interconnection pattern of the layer, together with the selected

Figure 37. Pairs of pictures used for selecting ganglion cells.

threshold. If the layer cannot readily differentiate the pair of pictures, then it is not recorded in memory, and the process of randomly generating inter-connections is repeated. Two or three layers of ganglion cells are selected on each pair of pictures; altogether 45 layers are selected.

[This procedure resembles others previously tried by Rosenblatt[3] and others to improve Perceptron performance by "evolving" good *A* units. It differs in that only one pair of samples is used in selecting acceptable units, as opposed to using the results from all or a larger portion of the training set. It also differs from a similar approach tested by Uhr,[4] who chose interconnection patterns and interconnection weights to resemble portions of the patterns themselves used in the training process.

—Editor.]

The pairs of pictures are heuristically selected in such a way as to "attract the attention" of the program to situations that often play the role of key elements in problems. Care is exercised not to distract the program by incidental circumstances. For example, in the pair of pictures shown in Fig. 37a, the number of individual lines and their total length are identical on both pictures. The aim is to differentiate between straight and curved lines.

The output of each of the 45 selected layers of ganglion cells is an integer, from 0 to 1,152 (the number of excited cells).

Subcortex. The program *Geometry* is capable of differentiating four classes. Adaptation of the block *subcortex* is carried out on the total set of training samples from all classes.

The purpose of the *subcortex* is to transform the 45 numbers (from 0 to 1,152) produced by the 45 layers of the ganglion cells, into 45 zeros and ones (0 and 1).

The *subcortex* is adapted in the following way. The interval between the highest and lowest numbers produced by a given layer of ganglion cells over the set of training patterns is divided into ten parts, making it possible to try nine thresholds. Each threshold transforms the set of numbers into a set of zeros and ones. The problem is to select an optimum threshold. It is desired that the characterization of the pictures by the binary variable carry the highest possible information regarding class membership. Using this criterion, the program selects the best threshold (discussed in detail later).

The adaptation of *subcortex* is carried out in the same manner individually for each layer of ganglion cells.

Returning now to the "informativeness"

[This novel but descriptive nomenclature is retained in the following text.

—Editor.]

criterion for threshold selection, the best situation is, evidently, when all pictures of half the classes produce zeros, and all pictures of remaining classes produce ones. In this case, indeterminateness is reduced by one bit. However, such an ideal case is seldom encountered. Consider the general case. Let the frequency of appearance of a one in the ith class be p_i^1, and of zero, p_i^0 $(p_i^1 + p_i^0 = 1)$. Designate by $H(p_i)$ the value $-p_i^1 \log p_i^1 - p_i^0 \log p_i^0$. The informativeness in this case is

$$H(\bar{p}) - \bar{H}(p) \tag{22}$$

where $\overline{p}^1$ is the average from p_i^1; $\overline{p}^0$ is the average from p_i^0; and $\overline{H}(p)$ is the average from $H(p_i)$.

If we consider that pictures from different classes will be shown with equal frequency, then

$$\overline{p}^0 = \frac{1}{n} \sum_{i=1}^{n} p_i^0, \quad \overline{p}^1 = \frac{1}{n} \sum_{i=1}^{n} p_i^1, \quad \overline{H}(p) = \frac{1}{n} \sum_{i=1}^{n} H(p_i) \qquad (23)$$

where n is the number of classes.

In principle, the informativeness can be determined directly from formula (22). However, the evaluation in the subcortex is accomplished by use of the approximate formula (24), below.

The value of $H(p)$ is closely approximated by the parabola, $4p^1(1 - p^1)$. Using this fact and expressions (23), the formula (22) can be replaced by the following expression:

$$4\left[\overline{p}^1(1 - \overline{p}^1) - \frac{1}{n}\sum p_i^1(1 - p_i^1)\right]$$

$$= 4\left[\frac{1}{n}\sum_{i=1}^{n} p_i^1\left(1 - \frac{1}{n}\sum p_i^1\right) - \frac{1}{n}\sum p_i^1(1 - p_i^1)\right]$$

$$= \frac{4}{n^2}\left[n\sum(p_i^1)^2 - (\sum p_i^1)^2\right].$$

Since the scale for measuring informativeness is of no importance, we can use the following formula

$$n\sum_{i=1}^{n}(p_i^1)^2 - (\sum_{i=1}^{n} p_i^1)^2. \qquad (24)$$

Here we can take the number of samples in the ith class instead of p_i^1. Using this method of calculation, the second term in (22) is the square of the total number of samples. The first variant of the subcortex block used formula (24).

It was discovered during the experiments that the lack of distinction between "types of information" is a serious shortcoming of this method. For example, a given characterization may either separate the 1st and 2nd classes from the 3rd and 4th, or, equally, separate the 1st and 4th from the 2nd and 3rd classes. From the point of view of informativeness, these cases are indistinguishable. However, they may possess different values, depending upon prior adaptation. For example, during the selection of the 20th characteristic, the difference would be significant if the 19 preceding characteristics already thoroughly accomplish the class division of the first type, but only poorly accomplish the separation of the second type.

In order to remove this deficiency, a second version of the subcortex considered six types of information individually (differentiation of the 1st class from 2nd, 1st from 3rd, etc.). Depending on properties of the preceding ganglion cells, the "price" for different types of information was changed. The selection of the threshold in the subcortex was accomplished on the basis of the price established at this particular "stock exchange."

Cortex. The subcortex characterizes each picture by a set of 45 zeros and ones (Table 18). The problem of the cortex is to find combinations

TABLE 18

Subcortex Responses to Training Patterns

		1st Subcortex Layer											44th Subcortex Layer	Errors (Example)
I Class	1st Pattern	1	1	0	0	1	0	1	1	0	1	0 ...	0	1
	2 »	1	0	1	1	1	1	0	0	1	1	1 ...	1	0
	3 »	1	1	0	1	1	1	1	0	0	1	0 ...	0	0
	4 »	1	0	1	0	1	0	0	1	1	1	1 ...	1	1
	5 »	1	0	0	1	1	1	0	0	1	1	0 ...	1	1
	6 »	1	1	1	0	1	0	1	1	0	1	1 ...	1	1
II Class	1 »	0	0	1	0	0	1	1	0	0	1	1 ...	0	0
	2 »	0	1	1	1	0	0	1	1	0	1	1 ...	0	0
	3 »	0	0	0	0	0	0	0	1	1	1	0 ...	0	0
	4 »	0	1	1	1	0	0	1	1	0	1	0 ...	0	1
	5 »	0	1	0	0	0	1	1	0	0	1	1 ...	1	0
	6 »	1	0	0	1	0	0	1	1	0	1	1 ...	1	1 V
III Class	1 »	0	1	0	1	0	0	1	1	1	0	0 ...	1	1
	2 »	0	1	1	0	0	1	1	1	0	0	1 ...	0	0
	3 »	0	0	0	1	0	0	1	1	1	0	1 ...	1	1
	4 »	0	0	1	0	0	0	0	0	1	0	0 ...	0	1
	5 »	1	1	1	1	0	1	0	0	0	0	0 ...	1	1 V
	6 »	1	0	0	0	0	0	0	0	1	0	1 ...	1	0 V
IV Class	1 »	1	1	1	1	1	1	0	0	1	0	0 ...	1	0
	2 »	1	0	0	0	1	1	1	0	0	0	0 ...	0	1
	3 »	1	0	0	1	1	0	1	1	0	0	0 ...	1	0
	4 »	0	0	1	0	1	0	0	1	1	0	1 ...	0	1 V
	5 »	1	1	0	0	1	1	0	0	1	0	1 ...	1	0
	6 »	1	0	1	1	1	0	0	0	0	0	1 ...	0	1

of columns in Table 18 that make it possible to decide with sufficiently high accuracy the class membership of a picture. For example, if we consider a combination of the 5th and 10th columns in Table 18, we note that by using the digits in these columns, it is possible to determine precisely the class of a particular picture. The combination 1, 1 is encountered only in Class I; the combination 0, 1, only in Class II, etc. The combination of 1st and 10th columns is not as good. Using this combination, we would make four errors. A combination of the 1st and 2nd columns would produce a still worse result.

The block *cortex* checks all combinations consisting of two and three columns.

[This means checking some 15,180 pairs and triplets for their "value" in separating the classes.

—EDITOR.]

Only those pairs and triplets are selected that produce sufficiently good information about class membership of the pictures. In the cortex, as in the subcortex, the "stock exchange" observes which classes are already satisfactorily recognized, and decreases the price for particular information. The minimum price at which a given characteristic is to be retained is inserted as a program parameter.

Assuming that the cortex selects a pair consisting of the 1st and 10th columns, how are these used during test? Let the unknown picture have the characteristic 1 in the first column, and characteristic 0 in the tenth column. Now we can deliberate in two ways. We may notice that the combination 1, 0 was encountered in Class IV more frequently than in Class III, and it was not encountered at all in the other classes. Accordingly, we may classify the picture as belonging to Class IV. On the other hand, we can refuse to answer, when we note that the combination 1, 0 is encountered in more than one class.

Each of these approaches has its advantages and shortcomings. In the case of the second approach, each characteristic will never commit an error, but it will also seldom answer. Therefore, the final judgment will be made on the basis of a small number of votes.

In the case of the first approach, a different weight may be attached to different combinations of variables. That is, the combination 0, 1 indicates with high probability that the picture belongs to Class II, while the combination 0, 0 indicates that it belongs to Class III.

The block cortex in the program *Geometry* was prepared in two variations. In the first version, the characteristics were selected according to the first method described above, and they voted during the tests with different weight. In the second version, only the "rules without exceptions" were selected, and during the test they voted in a "democratic" way (each had one vote only). The results in both cases were approximately identical.

It should be noted that the selection and weighting of characteristics was based upon the training material. Therefore, when we say "the character-istics work frequently," or "a rule without exception," we are really mak-ing an unwarranted induction about the entire problem based upon the training material. Of course, the broader and more diverse the training material, the higher the hope that this approach will not lead to errors.

3. Experiments with the program

The program *Geometry* was prepared for the machine *M*-20. Since the program contained basically logical actions, the speed of the machine was approximately 40,000 operations per second. In the machine memory (4,096 words, 40 bits per word), there was room for the entire program: 24 pictures, work fields, and learning results. However, it was necessary to place on a drum (during the subcortex instruction) the result of imaging of 24 pictures by layers of bipolar cells.

The processing time of each picture by the layers of the bipolar cells was one to two seconds. This kind of processing occurred only once, occupying about one minute. During the selection of ganglion cells, checking each type of layer on two pictures took 0.6 seconds. However, since the structure of each layer was randomly generated, only one "good" layer was found per many "bad" layers. About two hours of machine time was spent for the selection of all 45 layers.

The instruction time for the subcortex on 24 pictures was 12 minutes, and that of the cortex on 48 pictures (12 in each class) was 10 minutes.

Altogether, two hours were spent for processing related to the totality of problems (ganglion cells), and about 20 minutes for processing related to particular problems (subcortex and cortex).

Each picture for *Geometry* (Fig. 33) occupied 36 bits in each of 32 words. The preparation of material for training and test proved to be a very diffi-cult task. Therefore, all experiments were conducted with comparatively little material (6 to 12 pictures of each class). The majority of pictures represented letters. Different forms of the letter *A*, for example, are shown in Fig. 38.

In experiments with letters, the subcortex was always trained on four classes. In one set of experiments, the cortex was trained on the same pictures as the subcortex. The result was correct classification of 75% of the letters. This result differs from random guessing, but nevertheless is poor. In a second set of experiments, the cortex was trained on samples different from those used to train the subcortex. During the test of this case, 77% of the letters were correctly recognized.

[These results are indeed remarkably poor considering the richness and com-plexity of the network structure postulated. The author discusses qualitatively some of the basic reasons, in Section 4, why this and other structures similar to those that have been tried in this country are inherently limited. It is interesting to note that the results closely approximate Cover's estimate (see references) of expected performance of such networks. His estimate is based upon averages taken over all possible classification problems, and the 75 % figure arises in two-class cases. This leads one to suspect that the training procedure employed here must possess some equivalence to a two-class dichotomization—for example, this class versus all other classes—even though the problem is posed in four-class terms.

—Editor.]

Figure 38. Forms of the letter *A* used in training.

In general, several aspects of the program could be improved to increase the percentage of letter recognition. However, this was not done in view of the following critical analysis of the principal possibilities of the program, discussed in detail in sections below.

4. Merits and shortcomings of the program Geometry

The total number of possible states of the program *Geometry*, each corresponding to a different network structure, is very great. For example, each connection of the ganglion cell can enter 256 different cells. Therefore, connections can be organized in about 10^{20} ways. This does not even consider the fact that connections could be either inhibiting or excitatory, and that the ganglion cell could have different thresholds. Furthermore, the subcortex selects one function from 117 possible (13 functions, 9 thresholds for each function) for each layer of ganglion cells. This results in 10^{90} different possible functions for all layers. And finally, the cortex selects the combination of columns in Table 18 from a total number of about 14,000 combinations.

It is clear from this that a complete consideration of all sets of characteristics, which is possible in principle, would take inconceivable time. The selection is, of course, limited, first, by selecting components (see Chapter 3, Section 5). For example, the subcortex performs only 117×45 selections instead of 10^{90}. The second method for limiting selection is the use of "multistage" instructions. That is, the cortex seeks a combination of columns not for all possible variations of the subcortex, nor even for 117 variants, but only for one, which is selected during training of the subcortex. The subcortex seeks a transformation in a similar way, not for 10^{20} ganglion cells, but only for the selected 45.

The multistage structure of the program *Geometry* is one of its merits. The basic idea is that the results of training different stages possess different degrees of universality (bipolars are not instructed; ganglion cells learn for the totality of problems; the cortex and subcortex are instructed for only the given problem). Using such an approach it would be possible to design programs that would retrain the upper stages (less stable) each time a new problem is encountered. If retraining does not produce the desired results ("the world changed sharply") retraining of the earlier stages starts. In nature, no doubt, this principle is widespread.

[This idea is inherent in principle in Widrow's Adaline structure,[5] and other multistage adaptive networks. However, to the editor's knowledge, there has been no demonstration or proof that a multistage network will converge to a better result when more than one stage is allowed to adapt. That is, adaptation of a single stage in a multistage network appears so far to produce performance results comparable to or better than adaptation of two or more stages—whether the two are adapted simultaneously or in succession. The destructive effect of changing one stage upon the functions previously learned by another appears to produce as much backward as forward progress. Thus, while the author's conjecture is intuitively appealing, a theoretical hurdle still remains to be overcome.

—Editor.]

Consider now the shortcomings of the program *Geometry*. Why does it recognize letters only fairly well, despite its complexity and multistaged training? Let us start with the most evident circumstance. Each layer of ganglion cells sends only one number (from 0 to 1,152) to the subcortex, indicating how many cells of the layer were excited. But information regarding the location of these cells is lost during this process. This information cannot be restored later, either by the subcortex, or by the cortex. Furthermore, information regarding the location of the excited ganglion cells in different layers with respect to each other does not reach the cortex at all. Because of this, the program *Geometry* cannot solve, for example, the problem shown in Fig. 39a if the distance between vertical and horizontal lines is more than 8 squares of the raster.

The program *Geometry* can solve neither the problem shown in Fig. 39a, nor the one shown in Fig. 39b because, among the many states accessible to it, those are absent that are needed for these problems. This is not on account of a poor training process. A large number of states does not guarantee by itself the availability of those needed for certain problems. The number of different possible pictures that may appear on the raster is $2^{1,152}$. They can be divided into two classes in $2^{2^{1,152}} > 10^{10^{340}}$ different ways. The number of states of the program constitute only a small fraction of this number. Therefore, there is little hope that a needed state will be found at

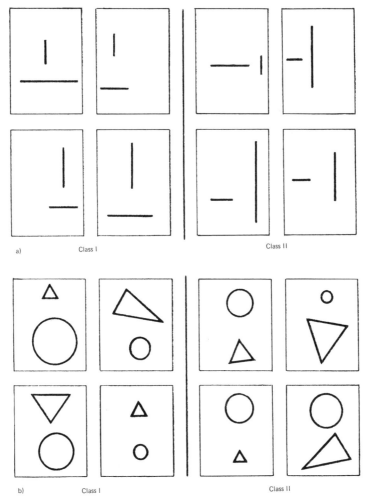

a)   Class I   Class II

b)   Class I   Class II

Figure 39. Pattern classification problems not soluble by the program, *Geometry*.

random for some problem. As a result of the oversight of programmers, the program *Geometry* language cannot express such concepts as *at the right-hand side, above, fraction, distance, equality* (angles, distances), *convex, area* (of *contour* figure), *inside*, and *diameter*.

[The editor cannot help applauding this comment. The relationships among parts of a figure are the very things that enable us to classify it. Yet many approaches to pattern recognition have deliberately or inadvertently destroyed this information.

—EDITOR.]

Therefore, the program solves poorly problems that are easy for man. It has no common language with man. It cannot imitate a man because of the differences in blocks (see Chapter 4, Section 2).

It was noticed that much information is lost because each layer of ganglion cells communicates to the subcortex only its "average excitement." Is it possible to improve performance by changing this particular aspect of the program? What would happen if instead of counting the number of excited ganglion cells, a second stage of ganglion cells is designed to make connections with the first stage of ganglion cells analogous to those existing between the bipolars and the first-stage cells (see Fig. 35)? Then the excitement of each cell of the second stage would be influenced by the location of the excited cells of the first stage. It is possible, evidently, to design third, fourth, etc., stages. In addition, if the number of cells in each succeeding stage is smaller than in the preceding stage a "pyramid" will be obtained, the excitement of the "apex" being a complex function of the excitement at the "base." Will such a multistage pyramid have a "common language" with man?

Generally speaking, if the structure of a pyramid is not subject to any limitations, it can perform any division of pictures into classes. For example, the following "universal" system can be imagined. There are 2^m (where m is the number of raster elements) ganglion cells (A elements). Each cell is excited if one particular picture appears on the raster. The cell for this purpose is connected with all m receptors; the exciting connections lead to illuminated points (ON), and the inhibiting connections to non-illuminated points (OFF). It is easy to see that if the threshold for each cell is equal to the number of exciting connections, then it will be excited by a given picture, and will not be excited by any other. Thus, a set of 2^m cells can be selected in such a way that only one cell responds to each possible picture. If these cells are connected now with the cells of the second stage, an arbitrary subset of pictures can be distinguished. A corresponding number of cells in the second stage can divide the pictures into any number of classes.

However, in practice it is absolutely impossible to design such a system (or even one resembling it in some respects). Some $2^{1,152} > 10^{340}$ ganglion cells are needed even in the case of the very small raster of *Geometry*. This number far exceeds the number of electrons in the entire visible Universe. Can the task be made easier if instead of a two-stage cascade a multistage cascade is designed? Evidently not, because we still would need about 2^m degrees of freedom for designing a "universal" system. Even if it were possible to design such a universal system, it would be of no interest to us because showing all pictures to be encountered during test is required during training. Such a system cannot produce brief descriptions of classes (generalized ideas). It simply remembers everything shown to it during training.

Thus, any actual system will have a relatively small number of states. Among them there will not be, almost certainly, states corresponding to such "human" concepts as *circle, inside, symmetry, related*, etc., if special steps are not taken to design the system in such a way that these concepts are accessible. A plan for a system that has a "common language" with man is discussed in the next chapter. Below, a very widespread misconception is discussed.

5. Self-organizing nerve networks

One can often hear such conversations as the following: "There is no need, of course, to design a universal (solving all problems) system. However, it is possible to impose some limitation on the capability of the system. For example, the restriction may include the number and design of the components that constitute the system. Therefore, if we design a system consisting of elements resembling animal nerve cells, then the capabilities of the system will resemble, probably, the capabilities of the brain. The properties of nerve cells are satisfactorily modeled by threshold elements to a first approximation. This means that if we design a system containing a large number of threshold elements, then it will imitate brain functions. If it turns out that a large combination of threshold elements only poorly imitates the brain, then a system will be needed consisting of different elements that are able to imitate nerve cells more precisely."

Where lies the error in this thinking? The fact is that the nature of the elements does not impose limitations on system capabilities in most cases. For example, an arbitrary division of pictures into classes can be accomplished, in principle, with the use of logic elements "AND" and "NOT." The same is true of threshold elements, "Sheffer strokes," and elements "OR" and "NOT," or, in general, any logically complete set of elements. The number of elements needed for realization of a given classification depends little on the type of element. (It is easy to prove that the number of necessary elements will be increased not more than by $K_{\alpha,\beta}$ times, where $K_{\alpha,\beta}$ is a constant that depends only on α and β, on going from the α set of elements to the β set of elements. Thus, the limitations originate not in the selection of the type of elements, but in the relation existing between them. Precisely, the organization of the relations determines if the system will have a "common language" with man. Evidently, the organization of relations is the basic and more difficult part in designing a recognition system.)

But advocates of self-organizing nerve systems say: "We also accept the fact that relations between elements are of great importance. But is it necessary for a man to design a new system of relations? Let the relations establish themselves in the course of preliminary learning (as in the case of ganglion cells in the program *Geometry*). At first only arbitrary relations can be formed. A system will possess "human" concepts after preliminary learning, and later on it will be able to learn those problems generated by man."

Let us assume that this plan can be put into practice. Let us compute now how many pictures should be shown to the system during preliminary and final learning. If no limitations are imposed on relations between elements during the design of the system, then the system will solve any problem after training (preliminary and final). Using the *Geometry* raster, it means that the system will select some state from $2^{10^{340}}$ possible. This means an initial indeterminacy of 10^{340} bits. Each picture shown during learning (in the case of the most optimal decoding) carries useful information of about 10^3 bits. More than 10^{330} pictures will therefore be needed during learning! The situation cannot even be rescued by the fact that many states are satisfactory for the solution of each problem. Even $2^{10^{339}}$ states that could satisfactorily solve the problem are above all imaginable possibilities.

It is evident from this that a system that is capable of learning from a reasonable number of demonstrations must possess a high initial organization. But this kind of organization cannot be achieved in the course of preliminary learning. It should be integrated from outside by the designer.

In actual experiments with learning systems, a man, in spite of his intentions, imposes very strong limitations on the number of possible states. If these facts escape the attention of the designer (as was the case with the Perceptron, and many other "nerve systems"), the systems cannot achieve states that are needed for the imitation of man. As a rule, the baby is thrown out with the bath water.

The only way to avoid this problem is to design a system that has relatively few states (10^3 or 10^5 times) more than those able to imitate man. The chances that such a system will organize itself are about as good as those of getting a working watch from pieces put into a box and shaken.

When a good performing algorithm is found and a good specialized recognition system designed, there will still be a question as to what kind of elements should be used. However, this is a technological problem, and answers will surely be found for different machines and individual blocks. In any case, until we have good recognizing algorithms, the problem of elements is premature.

REFERENCES

1. R. C. Minnick, "Linear-Input Logic," (*IRE Trans. on Electronic Computers*, Vol. EC-10, No. 1, March, 1961), pp. 6–16.

2. R. A. Stafford, "A List of Weights for Six Variable Threshold Functions," (CSFTI report AD 264 227, September, 1961).
3. F. Rosenblatt, "Principles of Neurodynamics," (Cornell Aeronautical Lab. Report No. VG-1196-G-8, March, 1961).
4. L. Uhr, *Pattern Recognition*, (New York: John Wiley & Sons, 1966).
5. B. Widrow, "Generalization and Information Storage in Networks of Adaline Neurons," *Self-Organizing Systems—1962*, Yovits, Jacobi, and Goldstein, Eds., (New York: Spartan Books, 1962).
6. T. M. Cover, "Geometrical and Statistical Properties of Systems of Linear Inequalities with Applications in Pattern Recognition," (*IEEE Trans.*, Vol. EC-14, No. 3, June, 1965), pp. 326–333.

CHAPTER 9

Language of the Recognition Program

1. The Perceptron language and the language of man

LET US RECALL how the Perceptron describes classes of pictures. Each resolution element of the Perceptron may or may not be stimulated by a given picture. With respect to a given picture, the Perceptron can tell which A elements are stimulated by it, and which are not. The Perceptron describes the difference between classes in this way: "The first A element is stimulated more often by pictures of the 2nd class; the second A element is stimulated equally often by both classes of pictures; the third A element is stimulated only by pictures of the 1st class, etc." No matter what the problem, the Perceptron uses the same language all the time. Furthermore, it tries to describe all pictures using this language. It does not possess any notion about irrelevant objects.

[Literally translated, "trash." This is a fairly fitting term, and is retained wherever appropriate in the text.

—EDITOR.]

At best, it can show uncertainty in the determination of the class to which a picture belongs. But the Perceptron is never at a loss to describe any new picture in its own language.

A man does not behave in this way at all when asked to describe the difference between two classes of pictures. Examining Fig. 20a, a man would say that triangles constitute one class, and circles another. Classes in Fig. 20b he would characterize as solid and outline; and in Fig. 20c as small and large. In all these cases a man gives a short description of classes, but this is not achieved using any universal terminology. In fact, in order

132

to distinguish a triangle from a circle, the pictures are subjected to completely different treatment, as in the case of small and large, or solid and outline pictures. At the same time, the terminology used in different cases is not necessarily so complex, the same terms being applicable in a number of ways, in principle, for various pictures. Take, for example, Fig. 40. It is easy to see that pictures containing *different* figures form the first class of pictures, and *identical* figures form the second class. Can the pictures shown in Fig. 41 be described using the same terms? Evidently not, because the description of classes in Fig. 40 is applicable only for those figures divided distinctly into individual figures, as opposed to the pictures in Fig. 41 that do not possess this property.

Class I   Class II

Figure 40.

Note that the conceptual problem does not lie in the fact that pictures can occur that are "intermediate" between classes, and we encounter difficulty in their classification. For example, we may encounter a picture containing two "almost identical" figures. Such a difficulty can be eliminated by a more precise definition of the boundary between the given classes. In Fig. 40, it is the degree of similarity needed for classifying figures as identical.

No, we speak here not about this type of measurement accuracy, but about the unacceptability of the whole concept of a given object. Such a situation is the rule rather than the exception. For example, if we have two classes, animals and plants, then to which class do frying pans belong? If the classes are furniture and dishware, then where do we place a horse? If coins and medals, where do a comb or trousers go?

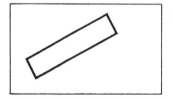 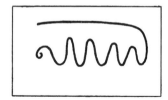

Figure 41.

Thus, as opposed to the Perceptron, a man produces short descriptions of classes by using different terms and different transformations of terms during the solution of different problems. And the terms are very special and they are very nonuniversal.

2. Strong imitation and short descriptions

Assume that we need to solve the problem shown in Fig. 42. Evidently, the system must first classify as "irrelevant" ("trash"), all pictures that do not represent triangles, and must further divide all triangles into acute (Class I) and obtuse (Class II). Let us calculate the percentage elimination

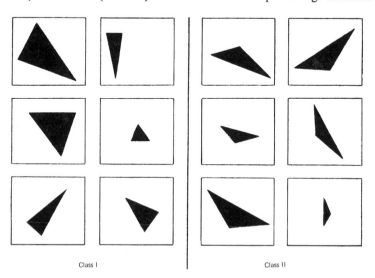

Figure 42.

of pictures by this procedure. Assume that pictures remain on a raster of 100×100 elements. This raster contains altogether $2^{10,000} \cong 10^{3,000}$ black and white pictures. There are $\left(\dfrac{10^4}{3}\right) \cong 10^{11}$ ways to select three points on such a raster. Let us assume that after the selection of triangle vertices, we succeed in many billions of ways to connect each vertex in such a manner that the system is still capable of recognizing a figure as being a triangle. Then there remain only $10^{11} \times (10^{18})^3 = 10^{65}$ pictures that are not classified as "trash," or nontriangles.

[The author here is apparently estimating on the basis of an average triangle side length of 50 elements—half the raster width—leaving $2^{50} \cong 10^{18}$ ways of filling in each of the three connecting lines. This omits a great number of other possibilities such as various ways of filling in the interior and exterior fields. Nevertheless, the point is still valid; the constraint has enormously reduced the possible pattern variety that can occur.

—EDITOR.]

Thus, the final number is 10^{65} out of a total of $10^{3,000}$ pictures. It means that only an insignificant number of all possible pictures are triangles. From this, we clearly see why man succeeds in producing short descriptions of classes. When he speaks about acute and obtuse triangles, the word *triangles* decreases immediately the number of objects that can possibly be encountered. Even more important, it means a still further (relative) decrease in the number of possible problems. That is, the subset formed in this case by triangles contains a far smaller number of problems, compared to the set consisting of all possible pictures. Therefore, if the recognition system can somehow manage to undertake searches only among those states that "strongly imitate" the problem, then uncertainty sharply decreases.

A man does not usually notice that by separating triangles from other figures, he is in fact eliminating "trash." He separates the simply connected figures, then polygons, and finally triangles. Each step decreases the uncertainty of the problem. All these steps are united by the word *triangles*. In an artificial recognition system, it is probably expedient to preserve some memory of the steps in this process without introducing new words such as *triangles* to indicate, for example, simply connected regions bounded by a closed broken line consisting of three sections. That is, we may be able to remove irrelevant objects in a number of ways by using combinations of a smaller number of terms.

Evidently, there is no need to distinguish between terms necessary for the separation of classes, and terms needed to eliminate "trash." The term *simply connected region* in the above example helped to separate out useful figures, but in another example it might not be suitable even to separate classes.

The search for states that can "strongly imitate" the problem may be considered as a search for some *description* of the whole learning material *without consideration of its division into different classes.* In other words, a common feature in all pictures is searched for. However, we must remember that classification may become impossible when, among parameters distinguishing one picture from another, only those are considered that will yield a short description of the difference between classes.

[The author here is again getting into the field of "picture grammars," "picture linguistics," "syntactical descriptions," or "parsing of pictures." As previously mentioned, the parts into which pictures are "parsed" range from directed line segments (note the author's similar ideas), to sequences of direction changes around a boundary (this could also be used for three-sided figures in the present case), to whole-image segments related by some concatenation of parts (for example, a triangle). This concept has been repeatedly promulgated by Narasimhan[1,2,3], recently by Shaw,[4] and in a slightly different form by Ledley.[5,6,7]
—EDITOR.]

In Fig. 42, this is demonstrated by two classes of pictures related by the fact that they are all simply connected. Then it may be noticed that the sides of all figures consist of linear sections. The number of these sections is identical, namely, three. Besides this, there is nothing in common among the figures. They differ from each other by many parameters, for example, by the length of the larger side. However, this feature would not divide them into classes. The same can be said about the value of the smallest angle of the triangle. But when we consider the value of the largest angle, then we see that this characteristic indeed divides one class from another.

As mentioned before, the final search occurs among descriptions that include only a small fraction of all possible pictures. However, can we speak, for example, about the shortest side, or about the largest angle for a picture such as Fig. 43? It is clear that we have idealized the search

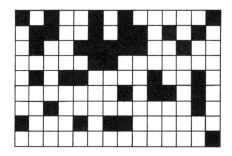

Figure 43.

scheme substantially by dividing it into two parts with respect to time (the search for a common feature, and the search for differences). Evidently, it is expedient to use both parts of the search alternatively. But in any case, descriptions that simply do not fit irrelevant objects will help to reduce the magnitude of the selection problem. It is not necessary, of course, that the elimination of "trash" itself be perfect. Enormous reductions in the difficulty of the problem are gained even when only part of the irrelevant objects are removed from consideration.

3. What makes it possible to produce short descriptions?

Descriptions cannot be short if the language must be adaptable to any picture. If we consider a field of 100×100 points, then to describe it we need 10^4 bits of information. Any less information is not sufficient because each point of the picture can be either black or white, independent of other points. At the same time, any *triangle* can be described by much less information. In a strict geometric sense, the triangle is determined by the locations of its apexes. Each apex may be located at one of the 10,000 field points. Therefore, only 14 bits of information ($2^{14} = 16,000$) are needed for the description of one apex, and 42 for three apexes. Even if we want to describe all possible small indentations on the sides of the triangle (made by random projections), we would need only about another 200 bits of information.

The reason for this large reduction in information is simply that the different points of the picture are not independent. For example, if any two arbitrary points on the field are black and have no white neighbors, then all points between them will also be black. (Note: The term *triangle* has two meanings here: one, a closed line consisting of three sections; and two, an area bounded by such a line. Here, as in Fig. 42, we use the second meaning. The remark about the absence of white neighbors is made only to eliminate boundary points because of possible exceptions due to small perturbations near the boundary.)

The simple presence of a dependence between the values of different points within the field does not exhaust all possible interrelationships for the triangle (the above rule is also true for convex figures), but it illustrates one of the reasons for the presence of redundant information. Using the above relation, we can reestablish the value (black) of the majority of internal points without receiving any further information about it.

The conclusion is clear: Some dependence between the different parts of a picture is the prime reason that a short description of a given picture is possible. There are many types of correlations that help to produce short descriptions. For example, the redundant information in a symmetric figure is the information about one of its halves. For a circle all other data is irrelevant except the location of its center and radius. In a picture of a man, the possible locations of the head are strongly limited by the location of other parts of the body, etc. The types of relationships that the recognizing system is capable of detecting and using determine the capability of the system.

The preceding chapter considered the reasons that the system cannot be "self-organized." Therefore, the problem as to the type of relationships accessible to the system should be solved by the designer. All peculiarities of problems that a system will be dealing with should be accounted for. If a man is going to be the source of the problems, all relationships or dependencies accessible to him should be considered (i.e., all those limitations of a man's memory). If some physical device is the source of problems, all those limitations should be considered that are imposed by natural laws.

Detecting the presence of correlations (relationships) is, evidently, the "sieve" for eliminating "trash." It has been already noted that the use of the same set of terms is expedient for eliminating "trash," and for classification. Therefore, the selection of correlations to be made accessible to the system determines its "mother tongue." The rules required for the construction of classes, which can be concisely described in a language of this type, will be "simple" for the system. This means that it will discover such rules in a short time with a minimum of training material.

[The author is calling for a big order here: to insert all of the rules of human behavior as well as the known natural laws into the recognition system, a priori. Of course, he would be the first to agree that this is an outrageous requirement. Nevertheless, he sees clearly that the *language* (the "mother tongue") of pattern descriptions, is the key to the problem. Again, this is picture-grammar (semantics, if you like), and the notion that how we "see" a problem determines to a large extent whether we are able to solve it, is no doubt a valid concept with ramifications in physiology as well as in machine pattern recognition.

—EDITOR.]

4. Vocabulary for geometric problems

In this and succeeding sections, the objects are binary pictures presented on some field. A man is the generator of the problems. From Chapter 4, Section 2, we know that a man cannot solve most of the problems generated by another man. Therefore, limitations need to be introduced here, namely, that problems should be such that another man could solve them. In other words, we need a system that can imitate man not as a generator of problems, but as a recognizing device.

We exclude, of course, problems for the solution of which a man uses information about objects not present in the pictures. For example, a man will easily combine into one class the objects automobile, ship, and airplane, and into another class the objects mailbox, radio station, and telephone pole. During subsequent testing he will correctly classify the locomotive in the first class, and the telegraph in the second. However, in order to do this he uses information impossible to obtain from the pictures themselves. A man simply knows that a ship, for example, is a means of transportation on water, has an internal combustion engine, many metal parts, etc. Any of these previously known facts can be used by a man for grouping together a steamship and other similar objects. The artificial system, which is deprived of these advantages, cannot solve this problem.

The thing that makes it difficult for an artificial system is the description of classes used by man. If the description is given in terms of geometrical properties, then everything is all right. If the description is in terms such as: *means of communication*, *predatory animals*, or *ridiculous situation*, etc., then pictures, in all probability, will not contain the needed information.

It has been mentioned many times that if the recognizing system must have many different states, then it should be designed in the manner of a child's Tinker Toy. In this case, a few types of basic building blocks can produce many different structures when arranged differently.

[Again, the "Tinker Toy" concept is strongly reminiscent of the picture-grammar viewpoint. In the latter, one of the basic premises is that images can be described ("constructed") out of successively lower-level "primitives" that are the basic building blocks. See the references for further expansion of this concept.

—EDITOR.]

It is also easy to see the analogy between the desired recognition system and descriptions of classes provided by man in human language. Man uses a comparatively limited number of terms for classification. By combining these terms in various phrases, different descriptions of classes are produced.

This is a useful concept to test. Let us compile a sample list of terms that may help to solve complex problems. It may seem at first that we need a great number of such terms. We have used up to now for some simple problems such terms as *circle, ellipse, triangle, rectangle, pentagon, hexagon, large, small, right, left, in the center, on the top, oriented vertically, oriented horizontally*, etc. Is it possible that we need such a cumbersome vocabulary for the solution of complex problems that it would be quite difficult to use?

We do not think so. The fact is that we do not need many terms like *triangle, rectangle, right angle*, etc., as principal terms. This case was encountered in Section 2 when for the word *triangle* we substituted the phrase: *an area, the boundary of which consists of three straight line segments*. It is obvious that a combination of the words *boundary* and *straight line* with the numeral *four* will give us the concept of a rectangle. A set of numerals will also be needed in problems containing a number of figures, as well as in problems dealing with a number of holes in figures, etc.

Thus, the vocabulary should include only very "refined" notions in order that their number be low. At the same time, these notions should be "extensive" enough so that the phrases describing classes are not excessively long. We need to arrive at some compromise here. The following vocabulary, for example, might constitute a good starting point for experiments:

shell	*coordinates*
contour	*distance*
direction	*extremum*
curvature	*part* (of a figure or contour)
area	*end*
length	*neighbor*
center of gravity	*negative*
diameter	*scattering*
axial line	*subset* (possessing some property)
difference	*node*
ratio	*average*
internal	

[The author here gives a good, but only a beginning, list of some of the geometrical relationships that have been considered applicable to pattern recognition problems. Starting from a similar "picture-linguistics" viewpoint, Evans[8] describes the use of several other terms, including *inside, right, left, above, below,* etc., and presents an excellent summary of the bibliography in this field.

—EDITOR.]

An operator (subprogram) should correspond to each of these words. The operator receives input information, and produces its result in a strictly definite form. For example, the operator *area* should have a picture at the input and a number at the output. The operator *contour* should produce a picture containing only the input figure contours. The operator *length* can work if a line is presented at the input, but cannot process a number of arbitrary pictures, etc.

In due time, some combinations of words become "legitimate" and some forbidden. For example, the phrase *the direction of maximum diameter of the uppermost figure in the picture* is legitimate, but the combination, *the area of coordinates of the center of gravity* is illegitimate because the operator area cannot process numbers.

In order to avoid producing illegitimate phrases, the program should contain "grammar rules" in addition to vocabulary. These rules are very simple in a given case. All information that operators exchange among themselves is divided into several types. These include two-dimensional pictures, sets of pictures, unidimensional lines, numbers or sets of numbers, etc. Therefore, it is sufficient to mark every type of information with some symbol, and instruct the operator to see if a given symbol is acceptable. In this way, all grammatical rules are automatically satisfied.

Among the operators present in this vocabulary are two marked by an asterisk that differ from the remaining ones. All other operators treat input information in an identical manner. The result, for example, of the operator *contour* depends only on the picture at the input. Operators that divide a picture into parts or separate a subset of numbers, however, are different. Consider a set of numbers obtained from area measurements of different figures. What principle should be used to divide this set into subsets? Evidently there is no simple answer to this question. If the figures, for example, are triangles and circles (Fig. 44), a separate treatment of the

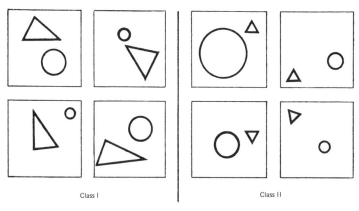

Class I   Class II

Figure 44.

areas of triangles and circles is a logical approach. If these figures had a sharp division into those located at the upper and lower positions, then it would be reasonable to consider the areas of the upper and lower figures. Thus, the result of the operator *subset* should depend not only on its input, but also on the grouping of pictures or their parts during processing by other operators.

The operator *part* should behave similarly. In one case, it will divide pictures into individual figures. In another, it will divide a picture of a man into hands, feet, head, and torso, and in the third case it will separate individual sides of polygons, etc. The method of separation must depend upon peculiarities of the entire set of training material.

It can be said, then, that in the general scheme of the program, special blocks must control the performance of the operators *part* and *subset*. Principles of such control are discussed in Section 6 of Chapter 10.

Note that the properties of the operators *part* and *subset* lead to an approach such that the program does not need to check all of the descriptions of all classes in order to solve a given particular problem, even though, in principle, a great number of different "syntactical constructions" are possible. That is, the decision-tree "branching" problem is reduced, and the descriptions obtained in this manner are, in a given case, *not* suitable for all possible pictures (i.e., they "strongly imitate" the problem).

5. *A short coding without loss of information*

A decrease in the length of the picture description because of correlation between different parts of the description was discussed in Section 3. If we accept a loss of information, of course, the length of the description can always be shortened (without limitation). For example, a lower-resolution field can be designed with fewer elements, or we can sacrifice all information about the location of black and white dots, and limit our information to "average grayness" of the picture by recording only the number of black dots. Many methods can be devised to shorten the description, but all of them lead to loss of information.

However, there is an essential difference in the short description of triangles described previously, and other methods, namely, brevity is achieved without loss of information. Thus, if the coordinates of the triangle apexes are known, all other details can be determined. Of course the *concept* triangle must be stored. But this need be done only once, and with this information many types of triangles can be described.

Now, in fact, in the "world of triangles" everything is significant, but not everything is possible. There are always some rules and laws that impose limitations. There are many limitations in our physical world. Elementary particles can have only a certain charge, not just any charge; it is impossible to lift oneself by the hair; a body at a distance from the observer loses its characteristic details, etc.

Our ability to think about impossible happenings is indeed extraordinary. It exists because of a system of coordinates within which we are accustomed to describe events (this system is predetermined by the structure of our senses). Using these accustomed descriptions, we imagine there are considerably more degrees of freedom that exist in reality. With the progress of science and new discoveries, it becomes clear that some parameters of our initial description are not independent. Then it is said that "a new law of nature" is discovered. Within limits, the scientific process strives to describe the world in a system of coordinates in which all coordinates of events are independent. In such a system, all combinations of coordinates are possible and there are no limitations. Therefore, the aim of science is to find a way to reflect our familiar coordinates onto the coordinates of "the world where everything is possible."

The recognition program is in an analogous situation. The system of coordinates in which we describe a triangle is decided by its "sense organ," i.e., the field. Therefore, the apparent number of degrees of freedom exceeds by far the actual number. The problem for the program is to achieve the "decorrelation" of the description. After this, the description appears (for example, apex coordinates), and it will be short and will not require further limitations. Any set of three apexes produces a triangle. This kind of description does not produce "trash"; the latter is eliminated during decorrelation. We see then that strong imitation, a discovery of internal relations, short decoding without a loss of information are all synonyms. However, the last statement is best suited for use as a formal criterion controlling the behavior of the program. In fact, in order to verify whether "strong imitation" is achieved, the program should permit "reject" pictures. But how can the program decide on these? Also, it is not quite clear how the program will find out whether or not it has actually detected a given internal relation. The answer to these questions is that in some cases it is possible to determine whether short decoding can be accomplished without loss of information. These cases are considered in the next section with the application of the principle: "breakdown into heaps."

[This phrase proved difficult to translate. Sometimes the author appears to be saying the equivalent of "breaking into clusters," or grouping. At other times, a good rendition would be "breaking the problem into manageable size," or "making little problems out of complex, big ones." We have equivocated here, sometimes retaining the original statement and sometimes rendering it in a more appropriate form.

—Editor.]

6. *"Breakdown into heaps," and the program scheme for geometric problems*

How many bits of information are needed to describe the area of a figure? In order to answer this question, it must be known within what limits the area of the figure can fall, and with what accuracy it should be described. Let the figures be given on a field 100×100. Consequently their area can be within the range, 1 to 10^4. A description of the area with an accuracy of one element of the field will take 14 bits of information. If we are satisfied with less accuracy, and agree to label identically all figures that differ in area less than twofold, then four bits is enough.

Further reducing the length of the code used to describe areas, of course, leads to the further loss of accuracy. It may be said, however, that this occurs in the general case, but in any particular case it may not necessarily be so. Consider Fig. 28a, which shows the general case. It gives values of the areas of different figures in the problem illustrated in Figs. 25 and 27. A short coding without loss of information is impossible here. Figure 28b shows the case in which the areas of figures already fall into groups (problem in Figs. 25 and 26). This is the "particular case" when a short coding is possible without loss of information. In fact, the areas of figures in a given group do not differ very much. Therefore, the fact that the left group has an area of 1.5, and the right group an area of 60 makes it possible to say only in which group a given figure is present. If we designate membership in the left group by zero, and in the right one by unity, then the description of area takes only one bit of information. Evidently, such a coding has its limitations.

Thus, whenever a parameter is "broken-down into heaps" the program can find a short code for the value of this parameter without loss of information. Therefore, it is of advantage to pay attention to parameters that divide readily in this way in the search for a short coding of classes.

It should be remembered that the task of the program during adaptation is to find a rule by means of which the classes can be divided. This rule will be a function depending on the values of some parameters. Since our aim is to find short descriptions of classes, restricting consideration to simple functions related to short codes is a distinct advantage. But short codes represent precisely those parameters that are broken into heaps. Therefore, the program should check functions only based upon those parameters that are already strongly separated. It is easy to see that this will lead in many cases to considerable brevity in classification.

Of importance is the following situation. We want to design a system that will imitate man. A man expresses his arguments in terms such as *large–small, right–left, angular–round*, etc. But a man cannot easily handle statements of the type, "the area 7 or 11 or 22, or from 40 to 48, is combined with the length of the largest unit with diameter 10, or from 12 to 17, or 23, or from 32 to 35." That is, a man easily operates with parameters that represent broad categories, but encounters many difficulties in finding a dividing rule in more complex cases. Therefore, a program that only designs functions based upon parameters that produce broad classes will lose only a few rules normally accessible to a man.

There is another method of short coding, but with loss of information, namely, the introduction of a threshold. This type of coding is used in the case of such expressions as *large–small*. Rules of the type "any area smaller than 26 is combined with any diameter larger than 14" can be succinctly coded. However, as opposed to the clustering approach, such methods require multiple sorting. Clearly, the logical thing to do is to arrive at a compromise such that the program passes only parameters that cluster during preliminary selection of arguments for the classification function, and during the last stage checks the classification according to one or more thresholds. The next section describes experiments that compare the difficulty of problems for a man, using the clustering method as well as the threshold approach.

The clustering method should first be applied in an attempt to select those arguments that may be present in the classification function. Only logic functions need be used at this stage, when very short coding of arguments is desired (0 or 1 in the case of two heaps).

The clustering method ("heap" breakdown) should next be applied to control the operators *subset* and *part*. It has been pointed out in Section 4 that the set of numbers can be divided into subsets only when the object to which they relate can be divided into groups according to some other characteristic. For example, the areas of triangles in Fig. 44 can be considered individually, i.e., of figures which differ markedly according to some other parameter (the number of angles). But the "marked difference" is precisely the parameter used to produce clustering, and thereby render the problem tractable.

Let us follow the performance of a hypothetical program. First, the areas of all figures are measured at a certain stage (both triangles and circles). Checking shows that area cannot be grouped into clusters. Then at some later stage the program may happen to find the number of angles in each figure. Now this parameter can be broken down into groups, namely, zero and three. However, membership in this or that group by itself, or in combination with other grouped parameters still does not separate one class from another. Then the cluster program starts to divide into subsets the sets of numbers that did not cluster according to the number of angles in a figure. The same is true of areas. As it turns out, the areas of circles cannot be grouped, but the areas of triangles can. In this case, the membership in a group indicates immediately the class membership. Clearly, of course, more difficult problems than this can be encountered.

The task is more complex with the operator *part*. (Generally speaking, the operator *part* produces subsets of picture points rather than numbers. Therefore, it is more convenient to consider it as a separate subprogram, although from a general point of view this operator strongly resembles a subset.) However, here also clustering techniques can be used to advantage, at least in some cases. For example, by measuring the radius of curvature of the contour of a given figure at all points, it can be seen that some figures break into separate regions markedly. In one case, there may be regions of the contour with zero curvature, and other regions with very large curvature, and the figure naturally divides into sides and angles. In other cases, there will be some points with positive curvature and others with negative curvature, as well as some regions with approximately zero curvature. The whole contour thus divides into convex and concave parts, etc. In each of these cases, separation takes place in a manner appropriate to the world of the particular problem. Sides will be separated out in the case of polygons, but the same program will not even affect the oval.

The general scheme for a program for geometric problems should be evident by now. We have the vocabulary, and a set of operators able to treat pictures, lines, and numbers. Phrases are composed of words that describe pictures in terms of numbers or sets of numbers. These numbers are presented to a filter that selects arguments for separating functions (clustering), and that checks to see whether a given parameter does or does not separate classes (by introduction of a threshold). We also have feedback to control the operators *part* and *subset*. Then there is a logic block that undertakes a final search over the separating function space. The logic block for geometric problems should consist of several stages, and it is described in the next section. It is probably desirable also to establish feedback from the logic block to the operator *subset*, because the function of the logic block will be similar in some respects to the clustering process. Finally, a supervisory program is needed. In particular, it should see that no description of a class (expressible in the system language) is overlooked during checking, except when some description can be disregarded by the program because of the specificity of the training material.

7. *Does a "breakdown into heaps" help?*

When a man is solving some problem, it is often difficult to determine from how many different descriptions of classes he selects the needed classification material. Furthermore, the set of descriptions for different individuals will differ. One and the same individual uses various sets in solving different problems. These complications make it difficult to tell which properties of the training material help in solving recognition problems.

The following method was used to overcome this problem. Experiments described in this section were carried out by L. Dunaevskii. Each picture was a field of standard size. Only one figure was present on each field, either a rectangle or an ellipse (Fig. 45). Figures differed not only by type,

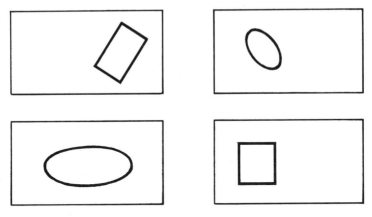

Figure 45.

but also by area (4 gradations), position of the center of gravity (2 coordinates, 5 gradations in each), the extent of elongation (4 gradations), and by the slope angle of the "large axis" relative to vertical (8 gradations). In other words, figures were uniformly described by 6 parameters. The classification of figures in all problems presented during adaptation was a function of only two of these six parameters. For example, in the problem shown in Fig. 46, class membership is determined by the figure area and the height of its center of gravity.

All individuals under test were presented at first with training problems. In the process of solving these problems, the subjects became familiar with the descriptions from which a selection could be made. Basic experiments were carried out with individuals who were aware of the possible complexity of the problems.

The aim of the experiments was to find out if it is natural for a man to try functions based upon those parameters which indeed cluster. If this hypothesis is valid, one would expect a decrease in solution time for those problems in which the "essential" variables do cluster. Therefore, pairs of problems from a large number of problems were selected in which identical variables were essential, and the difference was only that in some of the problems the variables could not be broken into clusters.

The time needed to solve identical problems was different for all subjects. However, each subject more quickly solved those problems that contained variables capable of being grouped, as compared with "paired" problems. A sharp increase in the time needed to solve a particular problem was achieved by the introduction of even one variable that could not be grouped. Let us see the average results. In the case of ten individuals presented with problems in which both essential variables could be clustered ("broken into heaps"), the average time per problem was 54 seconds. Solution of the opposite pairs of these problems, in which neither variable could be clustered, required 142 seconds (the same individuals).

These data relate to the case when the "paired" problems also contained a short description of the classes, but the key to the short coding involved the introduction of a threshold with respect to some variable that did not break into clusters. In other words, there existed a short description but it was not "striking" (an extensive sorting was needed to find it).

In cases where problems required more complex descriptions of classes (e.g., if two thresholds were needed for one essential variable), the solution time increased still further, and in some instances problems were not solved in 5–10 minutes.

A man, evidently, checks first those functions based upon parameters capable of significant grouping ("striking" parameters). Thus, it makes sense to apply similar major-clustering techniques to decrease the amount of sorting required during the solution of geometric problems accessible to man.

[The author has, no doubt not by accident, chosen a reasonably difficult function to illustrate the problem of pattern classification in Fig. 46. It is not surprising that his subjects were unable to "find the rule" when the problem was increased slightly in complexity. We can see this in a somewhat more formal manner, as follows. Let some of the variables represented by the objects in Fig. 46 be defined as follows:

1) x_1 = "altitude" (low = 0, high = 1),
2) x_2 = size (small = 0, large = 1),

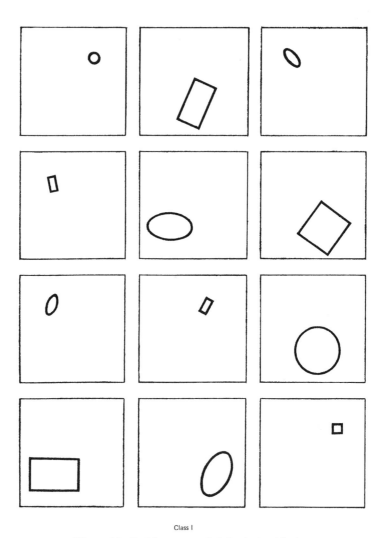

Class I

Figure 46. Problem suggested for test subjects.

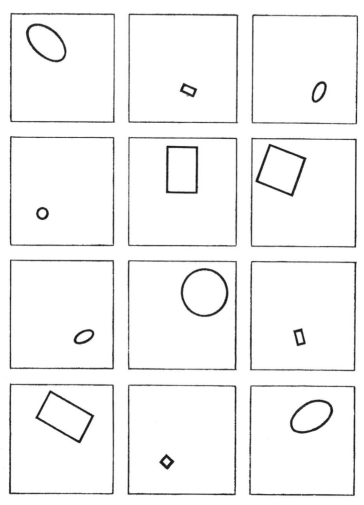

Class II

3) x_3 = cornered (no corners = 0, possessing corners = 1), and
4) x_4 = symmetry (not identical after 90° rotation = 0, identical after 90° rotation = 1).

Then a truth table (Table *D*) of the classification function can be listed as follows. (Class II = 1, Class I = 0).

TABLE *D*

Variable				Class
x_1	x_2	x_3	x_4	Fig. 46
0	0	0	0	1
0	0	0	1	1
0	0	1	0	1
0	0	1	1	1
0	1	0	0	0
0	1	0	1	0
0	1	1	0	0
0	1	1	1	0
1	0	0	0	0
1	0	0	1	0
1	0	1	0	0
1	0	1	1	0
1	1	0	0	1
1	1	0	1	1
1	1	1	0	1
1	1	1	1	1

Of course, we see that the classification function is independent of x_3 and x_4, and is the complement of the Boolean EXCLUSIVE–OR function of x_1 and x_2, or $C = \overline{(x_1 \oplus x_2)}$.

Now, it is hard to make a function of only two variables that is very difficult conceptually. For example, the only "threshold" functions of two variables are listed below in Table *E*.

TABLE *E*

Variables		Functions							
x_1	x_2	1	2	3	4	5	6	7	8
0	0	0	0	0	0	1	1	1	1
0	1	0	0	1	1	0	0	1	1
1	0	0	1	0	1	0	1	0	1
1	1	1	0	0	1	0	1	1	0

All others of the possible 16 are functions of less than two variables, or are not threshold functions (e.g., the EXCLUSIVE–OR). The above table is not very interesting for human classification. For example, Function 7 is the following rule: "If it is high and small, then it is Class I, otherwise it is Class II.

However, increasing the number of variables by only one would probably make the problem nearly intractable even for people. For example, consider Table *F* below.

TABLE *F*

Variables			Function
x_1	x_2	x_3	Class
0	0	0	0
0	0	1	0
0	1	0	0
0	1	1	1
1	0	0	0
1	0	1	1
1	1	0	1
1	1	1	1

This would be the function, "It is either a high rectangular or square (cornered) object, or a large cornered object, or both." Clearly, this becomes more difficult to discern, particularly if one or more of the variables is complemented. It is no surprise, then, that human subjects could find classification problems of this type nearly insoluble.

It may appear that even this problem is not so terribly difficult, but some consideration of the biological evidence shows us how marvelous is man's ability to perform logic processes of this type. For example, a great number of creatures can solve the following recognition problem. Food is presented in a two-dish arrangement. The food is actually under one dish cover (say, the triangular one) and is not under the other (say, the circular one) regardless of whether either appears on the left or right. The truth table for this problem, Table *G*, is as follows (with 0 = circle, 1 = triangle).

TABLE *G*

Dishes		Response	
Left	Right	Left	Right
0	0	x	x
0	1	0	1
1	0	1	0
1	1	x	x

Clearly, this is too simple. The *Left* response simply equals the *Left* input dish. The x's are not allowed to occur; the food must be under one and only one cover.

But the problem is increased in complexity. Now there are three dishes, and the food is to be found under the cover that is different from the other two. The truth table, Table *H*, is below, for the same definition of variables.

TABLE *H*

Dishes			Response		
Left	Center	Right	Left	Center	Right
0	0	0	*x*	*x*	*x*
0	0	1	0	0	1
0	1	0	0	1	0
0	1	1	1	0	0
1	0	0	1	0	0
1	0	1	0	1	0
1	1	0	0	0	1
1	1	1	*x*	*x*	*x*

A much more difficult response function is required—the variables do not easily cluster or break into groups, as the author would have it. Here a number of the lower animals fail the test and drop out of the contest.

Finally, the animal psychologists cleverly devise the four-variable test in which the food is under the *different* cover if the background is one color, and under either of the *similar* covers if the background is another color. Here practically every creature except man drops out of the classification derby (including most but not all apes, and some but not most young children).

We see, then, that the ability to impose complex logic rules on image data is a function of our developed human rule-creating ability, and that the author's attempts to model this are in the proper direction of successively more complex division strategies.

—Editor.]

References

1. R. Narasimhan, "Syntax-directed Interpretation of Classes of Pictures," (*Comm. ACM* 9, 3, March, 1966), pp. 166–173.
2. ———, "Labeling Schemata and Syntactic Description of Pictures," (*Information and Control*, 7, September, 1964), pp. 151–179.
3. ———, "Syntactic Descriptions of Pictures and Gestalt Phenomena of Visual Perception," (Digital Computer Lab. Rept. No. 142, University of Illinois, July, 1963).
4. A. C. Shaw, "The Formal Description and Parsing of Pictures" (Stanford Linear Accelerator Center Rept. No. 84, Stanford University, March, 1968).
5. G. C. Cheng, R. S. Ledley, D. K. Pollock, A. Rosenfeld, (eds.), "The Case of the Touching and Overlapping Chromosomes," *Pictorial Pattern Recognition*, (Washington, D.C.: Thompson Book Co., 1968).

6. R. S. Ledley, "Pattern Recognition Studies in the Biomedical Sciences," (Proc. 1966 Spring Joint Computer Conf., Boston, Massachusetts, New York, Spartan Books, 1966), pp. 411–430.
7. R. S. Ledley and F. H. Ruddle, "Chromosome Analysis by Computer," (*Scientific American*, 212, 4, April, 1966), pp. 40–46.
8. T. G. Evans, "A Program for the Solution of a Class of Geometric Analogy Intelligence-Test Questions" (Data Sciences Lab. Report No. 64, Air Force Cambridge Research Labs., L. G. Hanscom Field, Massachusetts, November, 1964).

CHAPTER 10

Language of the Recognition
Program (Logic)

1. The task of the logic block (cortex)

IT HAS BEEN MENTIONED in the preceding chapter that only those statements should be considered in a given language that produce a concise
code at the output. These can be used as constituent parts of the classification rule. If this requirement is satisfied, then each argument of the
classification rule will be a strict statement of the type *yes* or *no* (if only
one binary unit is at the statement output), or it will consist of a small
number of such statements. Therefore, it is proper to consider the classification rule as some logic function of the statements.

If this approach is used, the final search for the classification rule
should be performed by a block that can construct and check various
logic functions. The kind of functions with which the logic block can
operate determines (together with vocabulary and grammar) the class of
statements expressed in the program language (the class of accessible
classification rules).

Logic blocks were present at the output of the programs *Arithmetic*
and *Geometry*. In the case of *Geometry*, the logic block was called the
cortex. Therefore, the term *cortex* will be used here to denote blocks
searching for classification rules among logic functions.

For the cortex, each object is represented in the form of some binary
code. In fact, it is represented precisely by the code (the number), because
individual bits of the code may not be related to each other.

Recall, for example, the function of the cortex in the program *Arithmetic*.
The vocabulary of *Arithmetic* contained operations of two types: (*a*)
those purely arithmetic (sum, difference, product, quotient), the objects
of which were numbers *A*, *B*, and *C* (in the form of tables), and (*b*) oper-

ators containing some comparison procedure (modulus value, sign, integer-valued). Numbers *A*, *B*, and *C*, as well as the results of operations of the first type, served as objects for operators of the second type. Statements composed of these operators were not longer than two words (for example, the sign of the sum of *A* and *B*). The grammar of the language was thus reduced to enumerating 33 statements. Each statement represented one row of the table by 0 or 1, and all statements together composed a 33 bit code. Because a table could contain several rows, it could be represented by several 33 digit codes at the cortex input (Table 19).

TABLE 19

				33 Bits										
1st Table	1 0 1 1 0 1 0 0	. . . .	0 0 1 1 0
	1 1 0 1 0 1 1 0	. . . .	1 0 1 0 1
	. . . .	. . . .	. . . . .
	1 0 0 1 0 1 0 1	. . . .	1 0 0 1 0
2nd Table	0 0 0 1 1 0 1 0	. . . .	1 1 0 0 0
	0 1 0 1 1 1 0 0	. . . .	1 1 1 0 1
	. . . .	. . . .	. . . . .
	0 0 1 1 0 0 1 0	. . . .	1 0 0 0 1
	. . . .	. . . .	. . . . .
	. . . .	. . . .	. . . . .
	. . . .	. . . .	. . . . .
24th Table	1 0 1 0 1 0 1 0	. . . .	0 1 1 1 0
	1 1 1 0 1 0 1 0	. . . .	0 0 1 1 0
	. . . .	. . . .	. . . . .
	1 0 1 0 0 0 0 1	. . . .	0 1 1 1 1

Each line in Table 19 has its definite content. For example, the 8th column may represent whether or not *C* is integer-valued, and the 18th column may represent the modulus value of $B \times C$. However, the cortex does not receive content information. It deals only with the code itself. Therefore, the cortex treats the input material very formally. It searches for logic functions of pairs of columns, and pays no attention at all to the content of these functions. The separation produced by a function with respect to a set of tables (the useful information carried by a feature with respect to the problem) is the only search criterion.

This can be considered the weakness of the cortex. It checks all logic functions of all pairs of columns, even though it could reduce the amount of checking if it "understood" the content of the columns. But the fact is that different columns may not be independent from each other. Therefore, a function produced by one pair of columns may be identical with another function produced by a different pair. A device knowing the arithmetic rules (in the sense that it is able to perform deduction) could eliminate from consideration the second pair of columns producing the same function. But for the cortex, as it stands, it is another function, and may be repeated time and again.

On the other hand, this formal approach is also the source of considerable universality. The cortex processing algorithm does not depend on the meaning of any column. Therefore, it is possible to introduce any concisely coded information in place of the processed numerical tables. Precisely this was done in the program *Geometry*, but the principle applies to any program.

Thus, the task of the cortex is to find the classification rule after operators that produce concisely coded descriptions of objects or their constituent parts are determined. The structure of the operators and the method by which they are determined are of no importance.

As in the case of other programs (or parts of them), the cortex may not be suited for all problems. However, there is little point in speaking about the cortex's ability to recognize geometric figures, diseases, or language sounds. That is a property of the program's vocabulary. The specificity of each cortex lies in the class of logic functions it is able to consider, in the selection criteria, and in the method of applying selected functions during test. It is also possible that one and the same cortex could cope with medical diagnostics, language sounds, and numerical tables, but that different sets of geometric problems would require different cortex systems.

Several modifications of the cortex are discussed in this chapter, as well as their application to some sets of problems.

2. Search for logic functions by individual parts

The programs *Arithmetic* and *Geometry* both used logic functions, but differed somewhat in structure.

Features for *Arithmetic* were functions of two variables. Stability of the characteristic within each class was required. Features were eliminated if they attached different characteristics to the working and control tables (even for one rule). Since there are not too many logic functions of two variables, *Arithmetic* checked them all. This did not take much time, and because of the small number of functions, the logic product with respect to rows was also checked for all functions.

However, it is questionable whether the search for a function could be done similarly in the case of a greater number of variables. Suppose we need to search for functions of s variables selected from L candidates (in *Arithmetic* $s = 2$, $L = 33$). There are 2^{2^s} different logic functions for s arguments. Furthermore, it is possible to select s arguments from L candidates in C_L^s different ways. The number of functions to be checked is $T = 2^{2^s} C_L^s$. If $L \approx 40 - 50$, then $T \approx 10^4$ for $s = 2$, $10^{6.5}$ for $s = 3$, 10^{10} for $s = 4$, and $10^{15.5}$ for $s = 5$. In the case of machines performing

$10^4 - 10^5$ operations a second, it is already difficult to search for functions of three variables, and is completely impossible for four variables.

The idea that helped to decrease the number of evaluations belongs to M. N. Vaintsvaig, in his book, *Problems of Information Transmission*.

It is known that any logic function can be represented in the form of a logic sum (disjunction) consisting of no more than 2^s terms, each of which is the logic product (conjunction) of arguments or their negation (contains s cofactors). If a function is unity for some value of its arguments, then at least one term of the sum is equal to unity for the same value. Therefore, it was suggested that search be conducted by checking only 2^s conjunctions each of s cofactors, instead of 2^{2^s} functions.

Each conjunction in this case cannot represent a feature able to attach a stable characteristic to objects of a given class (or a given group of classes, as in *Arithmetic*). In fact, a function can be 1 with respect to all objects of a class, while a conjunction present in it can be 0 for many objects (other conjunctions become 1 for the same objects). Thus, if features of the program *Arithmetic* operate on the principle *yes–no* (they are necessary and sufficient features for a group of classes), then individual conjunctions are features of the type *yes–unknown* (i.e., they are sufficient features). In some cases, this interferes, while in others it is very convenient. The Vaintsvaig method is advantageous for problems in which the classification function is the logic sum of conjunctions containing various variables as cofactors.

The number of evaluations decreases by $10^{1.5}$ for $s = 3$, $10^{3.5}$ for $s = 4$, and 10^8 for $s = 5$. It should be added that a realization of one conjunction requires only a few operations, as compared with the realization of an arbitrary function.

It was seen in Chapter 8 that the logic block of the program *Geometry* checks, in fact, individual conjunctions of two and three variables.

3. Selection criteria for conjunctions

Suppose we construct a cortex that searches for features in the form of individual conjunctions. What criteria should it use during the selection of features, and how should features be used during test?

For simplicity, assume that all patterns in a given problem are divided into two classes, and each pattern is represented in the cortex by a row of ones and zeros (as in *Geometry*, but not as in *Arithmetic*). During training, N objects of each class are presented. The input cortex material in this case is in the form shown in Table 20. Features here are logic products of the type $x_{i1} \wedge \bar{x}_{i2} \wedge , \ldots , \wedge x_{is}$ where each cofactor can serve as a variable or its complement. Substituting the actual characteristic of some object into the conjunction transforms it into a 1 or 0. The logic sum of several conjunctions should serve as the description of a class.

Previously, we have assumed that a program should search for short descriptions of the classes. In particular, only concisely coded parameters should enter the cortex.

TABLE 20

Class I N	$\begin{bmatrix} x_1x_2x_3x_4x_5x_6 \; . \; . \; x_{L-1}x_L \\ 1\ 0\ 1\ 1\ 1\ 0\ .\ .\ 1 \quad 0 \\ 1\ 0\ 0\ 1\ 0\ 1\ .\ .\ 1 \quad 1 \\ .\ .\ .\ .\ .\ .\ .\ .\ .\ .\ . \\ 1\ 1\ 0\ 1\ 0\ 0\ .\ .\ 0 \quad 0 \end{bmatrix}$
Class II N	$\begin{bmatrix} 0\ 1\ 0\ 0\ 1\ 1\ .\ .\ 0 \quad 1 \\ 0\ 1\ 1\ 0\ 1\ 0\ .\ .\ 0 \quad 0 \\ .\ .\ .\ .\ .\ .\ .\ .\ .\ .\ . \\ 1\ 1\ 0\ 0\ 0\ 1\ .\ .\ 0 \quad 1 \end{bmatrix}$

Similar constraints should be imposed on the cortex here, too. Brevity, as applied to a cortex of this type, means that a description contains a small number of conjunctions (assuming at the same time that conjunctions are not very long). In other words, the description of a class should consist of a small number of statements connected by "or."

The above reasoning suggests one of the selection criteria, namely, the conjunction to be remembered as a feature should be valid for a sufficiently large number of the training patterns for some class.

Assume that we need to find a description for Class I. For this description to classify all objects shown during training as Class I, at least one conjunction should be true for each pattern. The pattern for which a given conjunction is true is called the pattern characterized by this conjunction. Denote by k_1 the number of patterns characterized by the first conjunction selected, by k_2 the number of patterns characterized by the second conjunction, . . . and by k_n the number of patterns characterized by the last conjunction. Let X be the number of patterns characterized by at least one conjunction. Then $X \leqslant k_1 + k_2 + \ldots + k_n$. It follows that if all k_i are small, many conjunctions will be needed to describe the entire training material.

It is desirable to introduce some limitation, k_0, during selection of the conjunctions, and to remember only those for which the number of characterized patterns exceeds k_0. Clearly, different problems require different limitations. How should we proceed, then, in dealing with different problems? We may start training with large k_0. If a successful description of classes is readily found, we may proceed further. On the other hand, if not all patterns of the training set have been characterized, we decrease k_0, etc. (This means that longer descriptions may also be accepted.)

It could happen, however, that the selected conjunctions do not characterize a sufficient number of patterns, even though all k are large enough. This could happen, for example, if all conjunctions characterize the same patterns (or almost the same). Therefore, a second selection criterion is needed to check the degree of independence of various features. This criterion could be realized in various ways in a program, but the classification produced by a candidate feature should, in any case, be compared to the classification produced by already selected features.

According to the definition given in Chapter 4, we consider classes as being nonintersecting. There is a way for each pattern (automata K_1) to state positively to which class it belongs. The transformation produced by operators that convert the input to 0 and 1 for the cortex is degenerate, generally speaking. Nevertheless, we attempt to design systems such that operators selected for the given problem do not lose the information necessary for classification. Let us assume that this requirement is fulfilled. (It was not fulfilled in the program *Geometry*.)

Under these circumstances, the cortex will attempt to find not only short but also errorless descriptions.

We thus see a third criterion for selecting conjunctions, namely, those that characterize patterns of one class should not characterize any patterns of another class. This is true only when the requirements mentioned above are followed. In actual problems classes can intersect, or some essential part of the information can be lost during transformation. As a result, a concise errorless description may not exist at all.

The requirement that each conjunction be able to characterize many patterns coincides with the requirement that a generalized description of classes be devised, as opposed to simply remembering patterns from the training set. If this requirement is removed, a logic function whose value is 1 for all training objects of Class I can be easily constructed. Each conjunction of this function is the product of all L variables $x_1, x_2, \ldots, x_i,$ $\ldots, x_L$ or their negations. The first conjunction is chosen to be 1 for the first pattern of Class I, and 0 for any other pattern. To do this, an AND function of all the variables and their complements for the first pattern is constructed. In Table 20, it is $F_1 = x_1 \wedge \bar{x}_2 \wedge x_3 \wedge x_4 \wedge x_5 \wedge \bar{x}_6 \wedge \ldots$ $\wedge \ x_{L-1} \wedge \bar{x}_L$. The second conjunction characterizing only the second pattern is constructed in an analogous way: $F_2 = x_1 \wedge \bar{x}_2 \wedge \bar{x}_3 \wedge x_4 \wedge$ $\bar{x}_5 \wedge x_6 \wedge \ldots \wedge x_{L-1} \wedge x_L$, etc.

Clearly, the function $F_1 \vee F_2 \vee \ldots \vee F_N$ characterizes all patterns of Class I in the training set. The function for Class II is obtained in a similar way. However, these functions do not produce "extrapolation" during test. They will characterize a pattern only when it resembles another from the training set. All other patterns are classified as "trash." As a result, each conjunction is excessively "adjusted" to some particular pattern, and represents an excessively detailed description of it.

Suppose we search for conjunctions of fewer variables (as opposed to L), each able to characterize many patterns from the training set. In the course of such a search, we find those combinations of variables that indicate class membership in the presence of different values of the other variables. It is hoped that such conjunctions will characterize patterns despite new (not encountered during training) values of the remaining variables during test.

[This is a pretty fond hope. There is, in fact, no basis for prediction other than some knowledge of the problem. Furthermore, it is hard to believe that the author is seriously proposing any of the above methods for constructing decision functions. The component functions (conjunctions) cover much too small a volume of feature space, namely, a point. And searching through all combinations of various numbers of variables (less than the total number) is much too tedious. While the general synthesis problem remains unsolved, the author is more likely simply stating at least one approach that is rigorous and well-defined, though impractical.

—EDITOR.]

4. Reliability of features—Prejudices

In the preceding section, we considered the search for conjunctions that can serve as sufficient features, i.e., can be encountered in one class but not the other. Remember, however, that only patterns from the training material can be used to check for lack of contradictory examples. Therefore, the possibility always exists that although a conjunction is never encountered in the training set of the second class, it is not a sufficient feature for the first class.

Let us clarify this with an example. A man who knows neither Spanish nor Italian is shown one stack of Italian and one stack of Spanish books. He is told that these books represent objects of Classes I and II, respectively. This man, who knows nothing about the class criterion, will check the format of the books, the number of pages, type size, printing quality, binding hardness, binding color, etc., in order to find some sufficient features. In the case of a small number of books in the training set of each class, he will probably select false features (he will use "prejudices"). If, for example, all Italian books are hardbound, and two of the Spanish books are softbound, the man may use "prejudice," and conclude that softbound books belong to Class II.

The cortex may have identical "prejudices." Some conjunctions may be found several times in one class and not a single time in another. (Features are classified in this section into "useful" and "pure prejudices." Intermediate cases are considered in the next chapter.) If the threshold k_0 is less than the number of patterns characterized by this conjunction, the feature will be erroneously selected as being useful.

With an increase in N (the number of examples during training) and k_0 (selection limitation), the possibility of prejudice decreases.

Another situation, less obvious, needs further elucidation. We were brought to consider individual conjunctions instead of necessary and sufficient features by the desire to make a large number of logic variables accessible to the cortex. If we want the program to discover complex rules, several parameters simultaneously should be considered. The impression has thus been created that a program capable of checking very complex functions is best suited for solving different problems. However, this is not always so.

Let us examine again the example of the Italian and Spanish books. Assume that a large number of books of each class is shown to a man during training, and he decides to select only those features that characterize a large number of books. In this case the probability that the property of binding, for example, will be selected as a useful feature is small. The same can be said about any other prejudice (book thickness, format, etc.). Let us see what happens when a man starts to select complex features instead of simple ones. He may check the difference between the number of words on odd and even pages, or the difference in the number of words found on the twenty-second and twelfth pages. Or he may check the product of the average paragraph length multiplied by the number of pages that begin with a new paragraph; or the quotient of the number of periods by the height of the print, etc. The possibility that each prejudice passes checking is small. But there exist many complex features. Therefore, it may happen that the mathematical expectation for the number of selected prejudices will be large, despite the small possibility of selection for each of them. This means that the memory can begin to clog up with prejudices. Thus, "rich selection" increases not only the range of possibilities of the cortex, but also bears the appearance of prejudices.

Suppose circumstances completely irrelevant to a given problem are selected for the description of patterns. For example, codes describing patterns of both classes (Table 20) may be selected randomly with equal probability for all codes. Such a problem is insoluble in principle. Each feature selected under these circumstances will be a pure prejudice. It is desirable, therefore, that the range of selection for features be small in this case. This imposes limitations on the allowable length of the code L. In fact, for any N, k_0, and s (the number of conjunction terms) there is an L such that the mathematical expectation M for the number of selected prejudices will be larger than M_0, where M_0 is any arbitrary number.

Thus, the cortex should not be overloaded with excessively long descriptions of patterns. The allowable length of the description depends, clearly, on the number of objects presented during training.

The mathematical expectation of the appearance of a prejudice depends on s, all other conditions being equal. The number M for small k_0 can increase with s due to an increase in the number of conjunctions considered. Therefore, the complexity of the functions checked by the cortex should be commensurate with the number of patterns used in training, as well as with the degree of their homogeneity (uniformity), or heterogeneity (the value of k_0 at which training is possible depends on the latter).

Is it possible to determine the percentage of prejudices among features selected by the cortex for a given problem? On the basis of the algorithm for selecting conjunctions, it is possible to estimate the presence of pure prejudice. Consider the process of choosing samples of conjunctions at random, testing, and accepting or rejecting them. Depending upon the number of samples tested (and upon the given values of N, k_0, s, and L), one can expect that on the average the number accepted will be M. Almost all of these will be pure prejudice (dependent upon chance peculiarities of the data). If the number of actually selected feature B is close to M, the cortex has probably not discovered a good classification rule, but has mostly created only prejudices. On the other hand, if $B \gg M$, we have reason to hope that the features reflect the classification rule. That is, because the acceptance of a number of features larger than M is less probable a priori, the fact that a large number has been found means that some structure has been discovered in the problem.

On the basis of this, we can state that the shorter the rule, the stricter the selection criterion needed to decrease the probability of appearance of prejudices. On the other hand, in problems with lengthy descriptions of classes and many features selected during training, it is possible to perform a "soft" selection, and allow more chance for the "penetration of a prejudice."

Our discussion has concentrated on the polar notions of "pure prejudice" and "useful feature." The next chapter considers evaluation methods when each feature can occupy an intermediate position between these poles. In this case, it is useless to discuss the appearance of prejudices, but we can estimate the probability that a selected feature will make an error during test. This estimate is also based on comparing the number of selected features with some a priori value that is a function of the selected algorithm.

5. Test algorithm

During the consideration of individual conjunctions, it was assumed that the classification function is a logic sum of the features. In this case, the program classifies a pattern during test as Class I if only one of the features characterizing patterns of Class I assumes the value 1. Analogously, patterns are classified as Class II when only one of their features assumes the value 1.

If there is not a single prejudice among features, such a procedure cannot lead to contradictions. The pattern may be classified as Class I or II, or as any other class, and there cannot be any error if the pattern is at least assigned to some class.

Unfortunately, this nice picture falls apart if a certain percentage of prejudice is present among selected features. In this case, it is possible that a pattern will be assigned to two classes during test. Also, the program may produce no answer, and the number of such refusals to supply an answer will be too great.

Suppose the cortex has selected many features during training. Each of them characterizes several (not less than k_0) patterns. Therefore, each pattern in the training set is characterized on the average by many features. Assuming independence of features, the number of features characterizing each pattern differs little from the average, i.e., is also large. If the training set accurately represents the problem, patterns will also be characterized by many features during test. Thus the following situation prevails during test: a pattern of Class I is characterized by many Class I features, and in addition by some prejudices considered by the program to be features of Class II. However, if prejudices constitute only a small fraction of selected features, the number of Class I features characterizing a given pattern will exceed the number of Class II features (in fact, prejudices) characterizing the same pattern.

Thus, it may be a good idea to consider "voting" during test when a large number of features has been selected. This makes it advantageous to use the arithmetic rather than the logic sum of conjunctions as the classification function.

Would it not also be advantageous to attach different weight to different conjunctions (proportional, for example, to their k)? It is difficult to establish a theoretical basis for any weight system unless the precise statistical characteristics of the problem are known. Experiments with actual problems have not shown any preference for such weighting systems, compared with "democratic voting."

Consider now the case when only a few features have been selected during training, but they nevertheless characterize the entire training set. Suppose M is also small, and we think that there is no prejudice. Voting is useless under these circumstances. In case of contradictory statements, the pattern should either be classified as "trash," or should be described completely according to its Class I or Class II features.

Figure 47 shows such a problem. The program finds the following features for Class I during training: (a) the figure is located on the right side of the field, (b) the figure is a triangle, (c) the figure is solid dark. Features of Class II are, respectively: (a) the figure is located on the left side of the field, (b) the figure is a circle, (c) the figure is outlined.

Suppose Fig. 48 is shown to the program during test. Two features will claim that this pattern belongs to Class II, and one feature will claim that it belongs to Class I. In this case, clearly, there is no reason to settle the question by majority vote. Rather, the program should be designed to classify Fig. 48 as "trash," or simply to convey the features important to the problem. In the latter case, the program should state that at the left side of Fig. 48 there is an outlined triangle. Then this description, together with the description of classes established during training, should be passed to the system that produced the problem. This may be a man or some super program; the super system in this case should produce a final decision.

6. Logic for geometric problems (multistage cortex)

It is more convenient to see by an example the cortex properties suitable for accomplishing this task.

Assume that a program must solve the problem shown in Fig. 49. All large vertically oriented and small horizontally oriented rectangles belong to Class I, all large horizontally oriented and small vertically oriented rectangles belong to Class II.

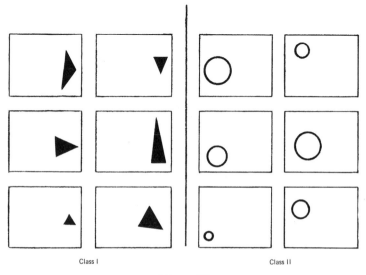

Figure 47.

The program starts with a general survey of figures, i.e., with the application of operators describing the whole figure without dividing it into parts. The values of the horizontal coordinates of the center of gravity of the figures cannot be separated into groups, and therefore cannot be

Figure 48.

allowed to enter the cortex. The same is true of the vertical coordinates. Now comes the turn for the operator *area*. The areas of figures can be

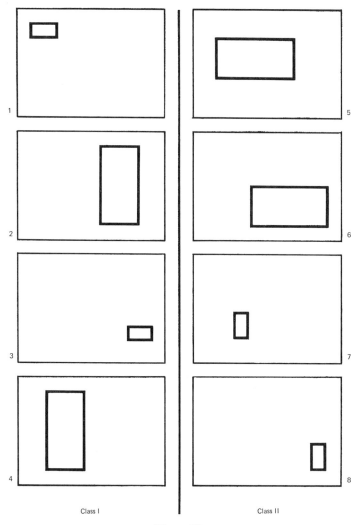

1

2

3

4

5

6

7

8

Class I

Class II

Figure 49.

divided into groups. The area values are then concisely coded (small, large), and enter the cortex in the form of the first column of Table 21.

The cortex will immediately try to use this column for classification. However, the attempt will be unsuccessful. Then the program will try other operators. The perimeters of figures can be also divided into groups. However, if the coded values of perimeters enter the cortex, they will produce a column indistinguishable from the first. But the "novelty filter" will not pass such a column.

Suppose that the dictionary used by the program is such that no new

TABLE 21

	Area	Vacancies		
Class I	0	. . . .		
	1	. . . .		
	0	. . . .		
	1	. . . .		
Class II	1	. . . .		
	1	. . . .		
	0	. . . .		
	0	. . . .		

columns appear in the cortex, although all operators have been exhausted. The classes remained unseparated. Then the program starts to divide figures into parts. The directions taken by the figure outlines can easily be divided into groups (i.e., horizontal, vertical). Using this condition, the operator *part* will divide each rectangle into four parts (the four sides).

Each side has a direction that can be coded in this problem. However, the cortex has no place for designating side directions. Every rectangle has four sides, but there is only one row in the cortex designated for the entire figure.

We may create a "secondary cortex" in which each part of the figure occupies a separate line. Only concisely coded descriptions are allowed to enter the secondary cortex, not of the whole figure but only of its parts. In the example (Table 22), the code for the directions of the sides enters the first column of the secondary cortex. The secondary cortex will try to classify figures by means of this column. However, neither the presence nor the absence of a 1 or a 0 represents a feature capable of separating these figures. The total number of 1's and 0's also leads nowhere.

Therefore, the program starts to use other operators for transforming the parts. At some stage it will arrive at the feature: the ratio of side length to figure perimeter. (For example, is the length of the side greater than or less than one-fourth the perimeter?) This value can be split into groups and be placed in secondary cortex (see Table 23). The second column, by itself, is also useless. But the two columns together make it possible to separate the figures into two groups. For example, the sum of the first two rows in each of these columns, modulus 2, equals 1 for all parts of the 1st, 3rd, 5th, and 6th figures (horizontally oriented rectangles), and equals 0 for all parts of the 2nd, 4th, 7th, and 8th figures (vertically oriented rectangles).

At this stage, the secondary cortex has succeeded in obtaining a short description of the figures. This description is about the orientation of each rectangle. It is of advantage to include this description in the primary

TABLE 22

	Side Direction	Vacancies		Side Direction	Vacancies
1st Figure	0 1 0 1	· ·	**5th Figure**	0 1 0 1	· ·
2nd Figure	0 1 0 1	· ·	**6th Figure**	0 1 0 1	· ·
3rd Figure	0 1 0 1	· ·	**7th Figure**	0 1 0 1	· ·
4th Figure	0 1 0 1	· ·	**8th Figure**	0 1 0 1	· ·

TABLE 23

	Side Direction	Relative Length	Vacancies		Side Direction	Relative Length	Vacancies
1st Figure	0 1 0 1	1 0 1 0	· ·	**5th Figure**	0 1 0 1	1 0 1 0	· ·
2nd Figure	0 1 0 1	0 1 0 1	· ·	**6th Figure**	0 1 0 1	1 0 1 0	· ·
3rd Figure	0 1 0 1	1 0 1 0	· ·	**7th Figure**	0 1 0 1	0 1 0 1	· ·
4th Figure	0 1 0 1	0 1 0 1	· ·	**8th Figure**	0 1 0 1	0 1 0 1	· ·

cortex, which deals only with descriptions of whole figures. As a result, we have the second column in the primary cortex (Table 24).

TABLE 24

	Area	Orientation	Vacancies										
Class I	$\begin{bmatrix} 0 \\ 1 \\ 0 \\ 1 \end{bmatrix}$	$\begin{matrix} 1 \\ 0 \\ 1 \\ 0 \end{matrix}$	.	.	.	.	.	.	.	.	.	.	.
Class II	$\begin{bmatrix} 1 \\ 1 \\ 0 \\ 0 \end{bmatrix}$	$\begin{matrix} 1 \\ 1 \\ 0 \\ 0 \end{matrix}$	.	.	.	.	.	.	.	.	.	.	.

The primary cortex will now discover that the sum, modulus 2, of the first and second columns is equal to 1 for all figures of Class I, and equals 0 for all figures of Class II. This is the rule for classification.

Thus, the presence of operators that divide figures or sets of numbers into parts makes good sense for a multistage cortex. The primary cortex deals with descriptions of objects; its criterion is the separability of classes. It takes material directly from operators or from the secondary cortex.

Short descriptions of parts of figures enter the secondary cortex. Its task is to separate figures. If it succeeds in doing this, the result enters the primary cortex as new material. Note that information about class membership may not even enter the secondary cortex, because its criterion is not the separability of classes but the grouping of figures into two subsets.

If the program's task is to imitate man in the recognition of geometric figures, then there is no point in letting the secondary cortex check functions of many columns simultaneously. But it is of advantage to allow it to produce phrases such as: "occurs for some parts," "takes place for all parts," "does not occur for any part," etc.

It should also be empowered to count the number of figure parts possessing some property. And if these numbers divide into groups, they should be coded and sent to the primary cortex.

Problems may be encountered in which it is necessary to deal with parts of the parts of a figure. For example, the problem shown in Fig. 50 requires separating the pictures into individual figures, and then breaking the figure outlines into parts (sides or angles) in order to count these parts. The task of such encoding can be entrusted to a secondary cortex of the second order. Its task is to supply material to the secondary cortex of the first order, i.e., to produce a description of the picture parts (individual figures in this case). Separation of figure parts is the selection criterion for a secondary cortex of the second order.

If necessary, it is possible, clearly, to design cortexes of the third order, fourth, etc. The results of describing parts of the ith order by the operator *breaking up into groups*, or the output of the $(i + 1)^{st}$ order cortex, will be the input material for a cortex of the ith order. (Here a part of the ith order is called a part of the $[i - 1]^{st}$ part. A whole picture is a part of the zero order.)

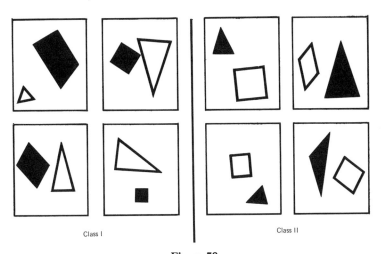

Class I   Class II

Figure 50.

So far, we have considered only one function of a cortex of the $(i + 1)^{st}$ order. This function is to provide a concisely coded description of parts of the ith order for the cortex of the ith order. However, it makes sense to use it also to control the operator *subset*. In fact, what does it mean to transfer a new column from a cortex of the $(i + 1)^{st}$ order to a cortex of the ith order? This is a signal that the cortex of the $(i + 1)^{st}$ order has found a sharp difference between some parts of the ith order. Consequently, it may be beneficial to consider individually the subset of parts of the ith order that have the characteristic 1 in this column, and to consider also separately the subset with the characteristic 0. Therefore, it may be beneficial to include the operator *subset* each time a cortex of the $(i + 1)^{st}$ order transfers a column into a cortex of the ith order.

The need for a multistage cortex originated in programs designed for geometric problems. However, it is clear that such a cortex may be of advantage in other cases as well. When it is logical to consider patterns as consisting of parts, it may be very wise to produce statements based on both the properties of parts and of the whole object simultaneously. Precisely this can be accomplished by a multistage cortex. The need to consider subsets of parts will probably also be encountered in many cases.

CHAPTER 11

The Role of Statistical Criteria

1. Nonintersecting classes

ACCORDING TO THE DEFINITION given in Chapter 6, recognition is a "weak imitation" of the device that generates the problem. From this viewpoint, the actual task of categorizing an object as belonging to some class contains no probabilistic elements. The classification network is simply a terminal automaton. Given that the network is in some definite state, it will "rigidly" divide objects into classes. If an object is classified once in some particular way, it will always be classified in the same way thereafter, regardless of the number of intervening inputs to the network.

This situation corresponds to the case of so-called nonintersecting classes. There are no objects that "with some probability could belong to both Classes I and II." Therefore, it is possible in principle to design a device that could solve problems without errors (it could be an exact copy, for example, of the problem generator).

Nevertheless, it is not possible in practice for the classification network or program, even after training, to correctly recognize all objects, even though all objects, in fact, belong to some definite class. The reason for this is that the program, which selects characteristic features on some basis during training, can only check them against a relatively small number of objects (those in the training set). It is not impossible, therefore, that a feature that performed without error on the training material turned out to be nothing more than a "prejudice."

Every recognition program or network selects characteristic features during training on the basis of some criteria. For example, one criterion may be: "It is encountered frequently in one class, and is never encountered in another." However, checking is necessarily confined to training material. As a result, affirmations only of a *probable* nature are possible during test. There is, therefore, a need to evaluate the degree of *statistical suffi-*

ciency of the criteria used to select characteristic features. It was mentioned in the preceding chapter that a criterion that is sufficiently reliable when an object is described by a short code may produce some degree of prejudice when a long description is used. Thus, statistical evaluations are needed even in the case of nonintersecting classes because of the constraints on the training material. The criterion itself is, in a sense, statistical (for example, the criterion "frequently encountered in one class, and never in another").

Clearly, programs that evaluate the statistical sufficiency of characteristic features are not interchangeable with programs that transform objects into the space of characteristic features. But the presence of some degree of statistical treatment does not obviate the need for special abilities peculiar to the recognition system, namely, the ability to construct many characteristics (selecting as many as the program can manage), and the ability to weed out characteristics during checking in each case. If these special abilities are collectively called "recognition," then it may be said that statistics are needed not in place of recognition, but as a supplement to it.

2. Intersecting classes

This section title may puzzle the reader because we have just finished saying that classes cannot intersect. But consider the following. For the sake of brevity, we have directly or implicitly employed the expression, "the object is presented to the input of the recognition network." However, it is clear that an actual automaton never deals with the real object, which has many characteristics, but only with some description of the object. For example, if we wish to design a system to differentiate one type of star from another, it would be of no value (not to say impossible) to present the object itself to the recognition system. Instead, a certain description of the star is supplied containing such information as its spectrum, brightness, distance, planets around it, etc. Even when the object is actually introduced into the recognition system (print-reading machines, for example), the system is concerned only with some of its characteristic features. Properties accessible to the system are determined by the nature of its "organs of sense." For example, a reading automaton with photoelements as organs of sense can use a description of the location of dark and light points on the object, but it does not have information regarding the odor of printer's ink, paper thickness, etc. Therefore, the expression "the object is presented to the automata input" should be supplemented with some indication of precisely what description of the object is supplied.

Imagine now that two automata have different organs of sense. They would therefore require (and receive) two different descriptions of the same object presented at the input. In particular, one of the automata does not receive precisely the same information used by the other automaton in the process of classification. This could have the effect of rendering the task of error-free recognition unresolvable to one of the automata. In fact, it might appear to one of the automata that the other operated on a statistical basis, classifying the same object sometimes in Class I and sometimes in Class II.

Let us see this in an example. Let personal passports be the classification objects. Suppose one automaton can read all the information written in passports, and the other automaton can read only the surname of the passport bearer. Assume that the first automaton divides passports into two groups, those belonging to men and to women. The second automaton must try to understand the principle of classification by "seeing" only the surnames. It may succeed in principle, providing only such names as *Petrov, Ivanov, Zinov'eva,* and *Sanina* are encountered. But as soon as the names *Boiko* or *Gruzd'* are encountered, errorless recognition becomes impossible in principle.

Thus, the concept arises that the classes intersect, due to the fact that the automaton receives a description of the objects that is insufficient for solution of the problem. Does this mean that recognition in these cases is impossible? The answer depends upon requirements placed upon the accuracy of imitation. Clearly, errorless imitation in the case of intersecting classes is impossible. However, if less than perfect accuracy of imitation is acceptable, the problem is not hopeless. The fact is, among the parameters constituting the description of the objects may be found some that are related to, but are not the same as, the actual classification principle.

Precisely such a situation exists in the above example of passport classification. Suffixes and the endings of personal surnames according to which people are divided into males and females are closely related to the sex of the passport bearer, although they do not represent the characteristic feature. A device with a sufficient knowledge of Russian language rules can divide personal surnames into groups belonging to males, females, and "neutral." It is clear what to do with men's and women's names. But what to do about neutral surnames?

A reasonable answer to this question depends upon the properties of the problem generator, namely, the probability of appearance of passports with neutral surnames. If we take, for example, a small village, the permanent inhabitants will have definite male and female surnames. The neutral surnames among them will belong only to outsiders, among whom there are more men than women. Then it is obvious that the system should classify all passports with neutral surnames into the male class. In this way, the system will commit the minimum number of errors.

It is easy to foresee other situations in which it would be advantageous to employ a different classification algorithm for passports with neutral surnames. For example, the system might refuse to classify, or classify them in the female class.

How then can the system know what classification to use on passports with neutral surnames in each particular case? Probably only by statistics acquired during training. If it turns out that neutral surnames are more frequently encountered among men in a given problem, then during test they should be categorized into this class; if more frequently encountered among women, then categorize them into that class, etc.

It may be thought from the above that statistical processing of the training material in the case of intersecting classes plays a more important role than in the case of nonintersecting classes. Remember, however, that the program can "guess" that the surnames with endings -ov, -ev, and -in must belong to men. That is, the program will subject surnames to different transformations during learning, and will check to see if all these transformations are of any benefit for classifying surnames into males and females. For example, it will check to see if it makes any difference which letter, vowel, or consonant starts the surname. Statistics will indicate that this is of no importance. Other characteristics, such as the number of letters or syllables, etc., will also be eliminated. When separation according to individual endings is tested, however, the statistics will indicate that the ending -ov is encountered sometimes in one class but never in another, i.e., it is a sufficient characteristic for a man's surname. It will also be found that the ending -o is encountered more frequently among men's surnames. Therefore, if the program considers this ending a characteristic feature for men's surnames, it will make fewer errors, as opposed to not using this characteristic feature at all.

Thus, *statistics* occupies an equal place among intersecting and non-intersecting classes. It is true that we can question the expediency of different selection criteria for characteristic features in both these cases. In fact, if there is hope of finding "rules without exception" for noninter-secting classes, then for intersecting classes it is necessary from the beginning to agree on the selection of only "arguments for. . . ." However, checking a large number of "candidates" among useful characteristic features is necessary in both cases. This means that in both cases program blocks are needed to perform a number of transformations on the initial description of the objects.

Thus, statistics does not substitute for, but rather supplements, recognition in the case of intersecting classes.

3. Selection criteria

Let us consider again the question of different criteria used during selection of characteristic features for intersecting and nonintersecting classes. We say that if classes do not intersect, then there is hope of finding adequate characteristic features for the classes. But why do we say "there is hope," and not "they will be found"? The fact is, any actual program can check only a limited number of characteristic features (on account of time limitations). Thus, it can certainly happen that an adequate characteristic feature ("a rule without exception") is not included in the set of features being checked in a given problem. In other words, although an adequate characteristic feature exists in reality, it may be too complex for the program. At the same time, a much simpler characteristic feature might serve as an acceptable approximation to the strict rule, and there is good reason to select it during training.

As an example, consider the sufficient characteristic features of women's surnames. The preceding section considered the endings *-ov*, *-ev*, and *-in* as sufficient characteristic features for men's surnames. In fact, nobody will doubt that *Sidorov*, *Silant'ev*, and *Zimin* are men. On the other hand, if we speak about women, the surnames are *Sidorova*, *Silan'eva*, and *Zimina*. It can be asked, then, if the endings *-ova*, *-eva*, and *-ina* are not sufficient characteristic features for women's surnames? In many cases, it will be true, and we will be completely confident that surnames like *Kuznetsova*, *Kameneva*, and *Vasina* belong to women. However, there are surnames with respect to which it is difficult to say whether they belong to men or to women. For example, the surname *Obnova* is confusing because we do not know if it belongs to a man or to a woman, although it ends in *-a*. It is equally possible to have *Peter Obnova* and *Mary Obnova*. Furthermore, when *Obnova* is a woman, her father or husband may have the name *Obnov* or *Obnova*. The same properties are attributed to such names as *Malina* and *Bicheva*.

What, then, characterizes the surnames having *-ova*, *-eva*, and *-ina* endings that may belong to either men or women? It turns out that all these words are Russian nouns. Therefore, the rule for one sufficient characteristic feature of women's surnames may sound like this: "All words ending with *-ova*, *-eva*, and *-ina*, which are not Russian nouns, belong to women."

Clearly, only a very complex program could develop such a rule, which depends upon a very large vocabulary of Russian words. None of the programs existing today could find such a characteristic feature, although it exists! On the other hand, a comparatively simple program can detect that the endings *-ova*, *-eva*, and *-ina* are encountered more frequently among women's surnames than among men's, i.e., it can find a simplified proximal rule (and therefore not errorless).

Thus, in the case of intersecting classes, and sometimes even in the case of nonintersecting classes, there is reason to select characteristic features of the type *frequently–seldom*. However, if classes are nonintersecting, and a strict characteristic is accessible to the program, then the selection of less authentic characteristic features is difficult to justify. What to do in this case? The situation is further complicated by the fact that it is unknown beforehand, in many cases, whether the classes are intersecting or not.

In view of the above, it is probably impossible to decide beforehand on an intelligent selection criterion for characteristic features. Instead, the selection of criteria for each individual problem is probably more justifiable. It is possible, for example, to start by using the most rigid criterion, such as retaining only those features that occur in a large fraction, k, of patterns in one class, and not at all in the other class. If use of such a criterion produces features that divide the training material, then we can stop at this point. If the training material is representative, this means that the classes are not intersecting.

On the other hand, if features cannot be found in this way, then there is reason to "soften" the criterion. Softening can proceed in two directions: (1) decrease k, and (2) accept some number of contradictions (objects of the other class having the characteristic feature). A purposeful combination of these directions depends, generally speaking, on the problem, i.e., it can be established only by trial and error.

[In the foregoing, the author has, in a rather informal way, dealt with the problem of how best to evaluate candidate features. He approaches some aspects of this problem more formally in Section 5. It should be noted, however, that there exists a formal and intuitively attractive measure for the "value" of a given feature. It is the amount of information added when the feature is used compared to the information present when it is not used. The calculation of this measure can be based upon versions of the entropy measure adapted to this problem. In principle, the measure can be calculated in a straightforward manner. In practice, the calculation is excessively cumbersome because of the large number of terms that must be evaluated. In addition, the problem still remains as to how to search the feature space efficiently. Because this aspect of the search is so crucial and yet so difficult, it is likely that simple feature evaluation criteria are adequate. If a really "good" feature is found, a relatively unsophisticated evaluation function will no doubt notice it. Thus the author's somewhat casual approach to this problem is probably justified.

—Editor.]

The appearance of a distinctly new task for the learning process should be noted here. That is, we have encountered a situation in which the selection criterion itself should be adjusted to fit the problem, and this means that it must be developed (selected from many sets) during learning. In principle, one can imagine a hierarchal system having many levels, with the higher levels selecting criteria for the lower levels. The first level is reevaluated each time a new problem is taken, while the upper levels remain "inertial" to an extent that increases with increase in level. The more levels such a system contains, the less chance there is that the selection of characteristic features is based upon criteria predetermined by man.

4. Supplemental learning

It should not be thought that different "degrees of rigidity" of criteria are useful only for different problems. Cases can be encountered in which it is advantageous to select some characteristic features with "rigid" criteria and some with "soft" criteria for one and the same problem.

Consider once more the example of passport surnames. Assume that we started the learning process with an attempt to select "rules without exception." Several suitable characteristics may be found (for example, features for men's surnames). However, not all objects in the training set will be defined by these features. In the case of a rigid selection criterion, the program will not find characteristic features for neutral surnames (because of intersecting of classes), or for some women's surnames (because of too complex characteristic features).

Let us refer to the objects that cannot be characterized by the selected features as "retarded." The retarded objects in this case are all those passports with neutral surnames.

At this point learning should be continued, but directed now toward a search for the features associated with retarded objects. It is also necessary, at this stage, to soften the selection criterion for features regardless of the reasons for retardation. Of course, features selected on this basis will make more errors during test, but with their help it is possible to arrive at some judgment regarding the majority of objects. If this judgment is more often correct than incorrect, then the program using these features will be preferred.

Repeated training with decreased requirements placed upon features can be undertaken, evidently, many times. The approach described is a particular case of "the adjustment of selection criteria for features to the problem" because a separation of retarded objects takes place prior to each stage of supplemental learning. Of course, if classes do not intersect, and adequate features are accessible to the program despite their complexity, then there will be no retarded objects immediately after the first selection stage, and learning will stop. On the other hand, if these conditions are not satisfied, then some objects (and maybe all) become retarded. The program then begins to lower requirements upon the quality of features until some compromise is found between error probability during test and percentage of retarded objects.

[The author does not claim, and there is no guarantee, that this procedure will converge to acceptable classification results. It is easy to find examples, in fact, in which successive lowering of the acceptance threshold never does any good, but the selection of new features solves the problem. Consider objects involving three sensed variables with the classification rule being that the object is of Class 2 if two or more of the variables are present, and of Class 1 otherwise. Labeling the variables x_1, x_2, and x_3, the problem is:

Note that the first three features individually separate the objects into two equal classes, but that the error rate in each case is 50%. Even combinations of those features do not help since the same combination sometimes occurs for Class 1, and sometimes for Class 2. The next three features do better, each one individually providing 75% accuracy. These are the author's "sufficient" features: whenever the feature is present (1) it is *certainly* Class 2, when absent (0) we

TABLE *I*

Variables				Features							
Object	x_1	x_2	x_3	Class	1	2	3	4	5	6	7
1	0	0	0	1	0	0	0	0	0	0	0
2	0	0	1	1	0	1	1	0	0	0	0
3	0	1	0	1	1	0	1	0	0	0	0
4	0	1	1	2	1	1	0	0	0	1	1
5	1	0	0	1	1	1	0	0	0	0	0
6	1	0	1	2	1	0	1	0	1	0	1
7	1	1	0	2	0	1	1	1	0	0	1
8	1	1	1	2	0	0	0	1	1	1	1

can only say it is *probably* Class 1. But a "residue" (retarded objects) process would work here. For example, given that Feature 4 has correctly classified Objects 7 and 8, we go to work on the remainder with Feature 5, and find that it correctly adds Object 6 to Class 2. Now applying Feature 6 to Objects 1 through 5, we find that it correctly adds Object 4 to Class 2. The critical nature of "sufficient" features, as the author clearly recognizes, is apparent.

—EDITOR.]

In order to stop at the right time and not retain in memory a large number of characteristics that will produce errors during test, the program should be capable of evaluating prior to test the extent to which the selection criteria for features correspond to a given problem. The next section is devoted to this problem.

5. Evaluation of feature selection criteria

What we would like to do is predict the expected quality of the test results based on observations obtained during training. For this purpose, we need to make some assumptions about the relationships between the statistical properties of the training material and the test material. We choose to assume that the selection of objects m from a set M takes place during training, and test with one and the same probability distribution, $s(m)$. In addition, we assume that the probability distributions are such that objects of Classes I and II will be chosen with equal frequency. Because of this assumption, the percentage of errors during test will be related to the case when equal numbers of objects of Classes I and II are presented. The division of objects into classes is considered fixed in the following discussion.

Assume we have some feature a. Let $\phi_1 = \phi_1(a)$ be the probability that this feature characterizes objects of Class I. Since

$$\sum_{m \,\epsilon\, C_1} s\,(m) = 1/2\,,$$

then

$$\phi_1\,(a) = \frac{\displaystyle\sum_{m \,\epsilon\, C_1} s\,(m)\,\delta\,(m,\,a)}{\displaystyle\sum_{m \,\epsilon\, C_1} s\,(m)}$$

$$= 2 \sum_{m \,\epsilon\, C_1} s\,(m)\,\delta\,(m,\,a)\,,$$

in which

$$\delta\,(m,\,a) = 1,\ \text{if } a \text{ occurs with } m,$$
$$= 0,\ \text{if } a \text{ does not occur with } m\,.$$

Similarly, let $\phi_2 = \phi_2\,(a)$ be the probability that the feature characterizes Class II objects. Assume that this feature will be selected during training, and will "vote" for membership in Class I or II. The feature will be encountered during test with the frequency $n\,(a) = (\phi_1 + \phi_2)\,/2$. Let the fraction of encounters of the feature in conjunction with Class I be $p_1\,(a) = \phi_1/\,(\phi_1 + \phi_2)$, and similarly for $p_2\,(a)$ in conjunction with Class II. The quantity p characterizes, clearly, the degree of reliability of the feature, a. If p is 1, the feature never makes an error on the corresponding class; if p is 1/2, the feature is hopeless.

Thus two numbers $n\,(a)$ and $p\,(a)$ for each feature indicate how often it will be encountered, and how often it will make errors during test.

Now, consider the entire set of all features checked by the program during training. Let us think in terms of some distribution function $R\,(n,\,p)$, that describes the probability density function for features possessing the measures n and p. (Strictly speaking, because of the finite size of the feature set, there is some *fraction* of features with measures n and p. However, if we consider programs that may evaluate perhaps 10^6 to 10^7 features, and do not examine regions of the function R that are too small, then it is not illogical to regard $R\,[n,\,p]$ as a probability density function. There is little reason to examine very small regions of R anyway, because of probable inaccuracies in determining n and p.)

[Notice that the author has here defined a function $R\,(n,\,p)$ that is capable of grossly describing the behavior of all possible features. The problem is thus reduced to one of estimating our chances of picking a feature with desirable behavior, namely, $n = 1/2$, and $p = 1$.

—EDITOR.]

To formalize $R\,(n,\,p)$ as a probability density function, let

$$\iint R\,(n,\,p)\,dndp = 1\,. \tag{25}$$

What we now need is a more detailed description of R. The somewhat unusual domain of this function is illustrated in Fig. 51. The domain is unusual because completely arbitrary values of n are possible when $p = 0.5$; that is, $0 \leqslant n \leqslant 1$. However, when p is unity (the feature is encountered in only one class), then n cannot exceed 0.5.

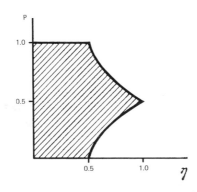

Figure 51. Range of values for n and p.

Consider now some selection criterion for features based solely upon n and p as measured during training. It might appear to be very desirable, of course, if the criterion only accepted features possessing values of n and p within selected regions. For example, we might be quite sure that by accepting only those features whose parameters n and p lie within the shaded region of Fig. 52, the mathematical expectation of errors during test should not amount to more than 10%.

Unfortunately, this is not possible to do because the criterion can only be formulated in terms of the training material, and its properties are related only statistically with the parameters n and p. For given values of n and p, different selections of features will produce differences both in the number of objects so characterized (during test), and in the fraction of objects belonging to a given class (again, during test). Therefore, selecting a feature on the basis of n and p measured during training can only be done on the basis of some probability distribution $W(n, p)$ that describes the probability of selecting features with the particular properties n and p (or ϕ_1 and ϕ_2), in the general case.

The function $W(n, p)$ does not depend on the problem. It is determined by the selection criterion, and may be calculated beforehand, as opposed to $R(n, p)$.

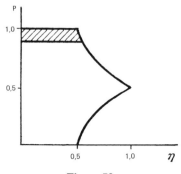

Figure 52.

[For example, from Table I in the preceding section, there exist precisely $256 = 2^{2^3}$ possible "features," that is, all possible binary functions of three variables. Many of these functions will produce identical values of n and p, thus leading to the "probability distribution" $R(n, p)$. This function is completely determined by the problem, namely, the probability of occurrence of patterns, and the classification function. However, given some procedure for selecting features based upon n and p (or ϕ_1 and ϕ_2), the distribution function $W(n, p)$ is determined independently of the classification function. That is, we can calculate all of the possible ways that the given procedure could be satisfied during test by a given feature. This gives the "probability" $W(n, p)$ that features possessing given parameters will in fact be selected. The author illustrates this in the following.

—EDITOR.]

For example, if the system selects features that occur with no less than k_0 of the objects of Class I (out of N), and not a single object of Class II (also out of N), then

$$W_1(n, p) = \sum_{k=k_0}^{N} \phi_1^k (1 - \phi_1)^{N-k} (1 - \phi_2)^N$$

$$= \sum_{k=k_0}^{N} (2 p_1 n)^k (1 - 2 p_1 n)^{N-k} (1 - 2 n + 2 p_2 n)^N,$$

because $\phi_1 = 2 p_1 n$, and $\phi_2 = 2 n (1 - p_2)$. Similarly for W_2, by reversing the roles of ϕ_1 and ϕ_2.

[The terms in the above expression of course correspond to the probability that, given two buckets (classes) with black and white balls (features) in which the black balls (1's) occur with relative frequencies ϕ_1 and ϕ_2, we will pick exactly k black and $(N - k)$ white from the first bucket, and N white from the second bucket. Thus $W(n, p)$ is the probability that, given buckets with ϕ_1 and ϕ_2, we will in fact make an observation in $2N$ trials that produces k_0, or more black balls from one bucket and none from the other. The properties of the two functions R and W can be illustrated by again referring to the Table I example of the previous section. Assume that the possible functions are not 256 but only 7 (those listed in Table I). Then $n = 1/2$, $p_2 = 1/2$ occurs three times (Features 1, 2, and 3), $n = 1/4$, $p_2 = 1$ occurs three times (Features 4, 5, and 6) and $n = 1/2$, $p_2 = 1$ occurs once (Feature 7). A plot of $R(n, p)$ for this case is shown in Fig. B. For simplicity in calculation, let $N = 4$. Then it can be verified

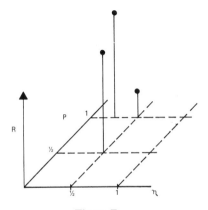

Figure B.

that the probability of the features producing an observation of, say, $k_0 = 3$ (three times or more it so happens that we pick objects from Class 2 with the feature present, and four times we pick objects from Class 1 with the feature absent) is $W(1/2, 1/2) = 1/128$, $W(1/4, 1) = 1/8$, and $W(1/2, 1) = 1$. This is shown in Fig. C.

—EDITOR.]

The function $W(n, p)$ is shown approximately in Fig. 53. It reaches a maximum of unity at point $p = 1$, and $n = 0.5$ at any k_0 ($k_0 \leqslant N$). The sharpness of curvature increases with an increase in k_0.

Let training be carried out with a criterion that produces the feature selection probability $W(n, p)$. Then the mathematical expectation for the probability that the found features will work correctly in this case is

$$M = \frac{\iint pnW(n, p) R(n, p)\, dndp}{\iint nW(n, p) R(n, p)\, dndp} \tag{26}$$

Clearly, the larger the value of M, the more reliable the features will be during test. The difficulty of evaluating this function is related to the fact that the function $R(n, p)$ must be known for a given problem before formula (26) can be used. What kind of information can be derived from the results of learning in regard to this function?

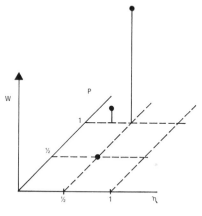

Figure C.

Some information is provided by the number of selected features. Let a total of G features be checked during training, and g features be selected from among them. The mathematical expectation for the number of selected features is

$$g = G \iint W(n, p) \, R(n, p) \, dndp \, . \tag{27}$$

The correlation (27) together with (25) imposes some limitations on $R(n, p)$. For example, it is improbable that $R(n, p)$ will be small in an

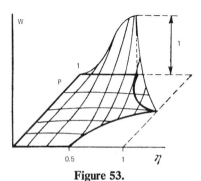

Figure 53.

area of large p and large g. The fact is, if all features in a given problem have small p then the probability of the selection of them by $W(n, p)$ will also be small, and a small number of features will be selected. Therefore, if many features are selected, $R(n, p)$ must be large in the region of large p and consequently M is also large.

This situation is analogous to one mentioned in Chapter 10, Section 4, in regard to "pure prejudices." Namely, that a large number of selected features indicates that the percentage of prejudice among them is small. If we consider M as a measure of the "average degree of prejudice" of features, then a large number of selected features indicates their "high quality."

It is unfortunate that the words *small* and *large*, encountered frequently in the previous paragraphs, are based upon difficult correlations to calculate from a practical point of view. In order to evaluate M, we need to find the minimum value of the expression (26), provided expressions (25) and (27) are satisfied. The ensuing calculation is very cumbersome.

In addition, this approach may sometimes lead to an unnecessarily low evaluation of M. Assume that all G conjunctions have $p = 1$ and very small n. In this case, a very small number of features will be selected, but an evaluation of M will indicate high performance.

[In fact, $M = 1$ in this case.

—EDITOR.]

(In order to make a good evaluation, it would be necessary in this case to conduct training with very large N and relatively small k_0. Then $W(n, p)$ would be decreasing slowly in the region of small n and large p. As a result, the number of selected features would be increased, and the quality of their evaluation would be improved.)

We have considered until now only one type of information obtained in the course of learning, namely, the number of selected features. The result was an overly cumbersome calculation and unnecessarily low evaluation. However, it is possible to obtain more direct information about $R(n, p)$ during training with modest effort. When checking features, we can calculate each time how many objects of the first and second classes each feature characterizes. Let these numbers be t_1 and t_2. Assume that $\frac{t_1}{N} \cong \phi_1$, and $\frac{t_2}{N} \cong \phi_2$. In this case, $n \cong \frac{t_1 + t_2}{2N}$ and $p_1 \cong \frac{t_1}{t_1 + t_2}$. The frequency of occurrence of the features with different combinations of n and p should be recorded (regardless of their selection as useful features). At the end of training, we obtain the distribution $R(n, p)$. Generally speaking the ratio $\frac{t_1}{N}$ is not equal to ϕ_1, and $\frac{t_2}{N}$ is not equal to ϕ_2 because t_1 and t_2 were calculated from only a few selections of N objects.

[The author is distinguishing here between the estimators t/N, and the underlying distributions ϕ. In the previous example, it was implicitly assumed or defined so that these were identical.

—EDITOR.]

However, the probability is low that this estimate will lead to serious error. If we consider that the training material is sufficiently representative, then we can reasonably accept it for the measurement of $R\ (n, p)$. Some contemporary programs can check hundreds of thousands of features. The effective regions of $R\ (n, p)$ will be covered (on the average) sufficiently densely, and accidental deviations will not influence very much the general picture. (Strictly speaking the distribution obtained in such a way will have systematically a "softer landscape" than the actual $R\ (n, p)$. A corresponding correction can be introduced in principle. However, there is no need for it from the practical point of view.) After $R\ (n, p)$ is found, the calculation using formula (26) presents no difficulties.

It is easy to imagine further a program which, after determining $R\ (n, p)$, evaluates M for different selection criteria (different $W\ [n, p]$), and selects the best one for use in the subsequent search for features.

6. Independence of the characteristic features

We have discussed so far the probability of error of the individual characteristic feature, and how to decrease this probability. The question is: Should we worry about the decrease in probability of individual errors? Can we instead simply increase the number of selected characteristic features? If one characteristic feature makes errors in 10% of the cases, then perhaps three such features will produce only 3% errors, and five characteristic features, only 2% (provided the decision is reached by voting). This would be precisely the case if characteristic features were mutually independent. However, ostensibly different characteristic features are, in many cases, strongly correlated. Due to this, the probability of error of combined characteristic features will not be much less than the error probability of individual characteristic features.

For example, if we want to make a distinction between men and women, then tall stature serves as evidence that we are probably dealing with a man. Low-heeled shoes are also a characteristic feature of men, because there are fewer women wearing low-heeled shoes compared to men. It may appear that the second characteristic feature is taken from an entirely independent area. However, it is clear that the number of women whom we mistake for men, when we use these two characteristic features, is the same as when we use only the first characteristic feature. The truth lies in the fact that characteristic features are interdependent, namely, tall women seldom wear high-heeled shoes.

Clearly, the combination of characteristic features will work better if there is less dependence among them. Therefore, it is desirable to introduce the degree of independence of characteristic features as an additional selection criterion during adaptation. The program can compare the set of responses produced on the training material by the candidate characteristic feature with responses produced by already selected characteristic features. If an identity to an existing set of responses is detected, the candidate is eliminated.

Checking of characteristic features by comparing response patterns has been used in the program *Arithmetic*. In the case of the program *Geometry*, "stock exchanges" in the subcortex and cortex program blocks were responsible for independence of the characteristic features. (See Chapter 8, Sections 2–4.) The largest number of experiments was carried out with the program *Arithmetic*, because it provided for changing the allowable degree of noncoincidence of responses (the degree of independence of characteristic features). These experiments showed that requiring a high degree of independence among characteristic features considerably influences the performance of the program. First, the number of selected characteristic features sharply decreases. Second, there is a strong dependence between the characteristic features selected, and the sequence in which candidates are checked. As a result, recognition during test worsened. The test results given in Chapter 3 are based upon cases where only weak requirements were placed upon the degree of independence of characteristic features (the program eliminated candidates only in case of complete coincidence). This should always be remembered, and more rigid independence criteria introduced only with caution.

It is impossible to predict beforehand the degree of independence of characteristic features. This depends on the problem, and it has still another aspect. The programmer designing a system may reason in this manner: "I know nothing about independence among the variables my program will treat. This depends on the problem and upon the blocks that supply its inputs. Since I can do nothing here, my aim is to insure that features checked by the program will be independent if initial inputs are independent. In other words, the program does not have to add interrelations to initial conditions."

Regrettably, the program that checks conjunctions of several variables also constructs nonindependent characteristics. If we know, for example, that functions $x_1 \wedge x_2$ and $\bar{x}_1 \wedge x_3$ are sufficient characteristics of Class I, then we know that function $x_2 \wedge x_3$ is also a characteristic of Class I.

In principle, it is possible to design a program such that if input variables are independent, then it constructs only entirely independent characteristics.

[It is not entirely clear what the author is getting at in the above three paragraphs. He seems to be suggesting that all features should ideally be orthogonal (independent), but that the construction of "conjunctions" leads to nonorthogonality. He then seems to point out that construction of complete sets of orthogonal functions is possible, without noting that if this is done, the problem is automatically solved. This can be seen by means of an example using Table *J*.

TABLE *J*

Object	Variables			Features							Classification	
	x_1	x_2	x_3	1	2	3	4	5	6	7	C_1	C_2
1	0	0	0	0	0	0	0	0	0	0	0	0
2	0	0	1	0	0	1	0	1	1	1	0	1
3	0	1	0	0	1	0	1	0	1	1	0	1
4	0	1	1	0	1	1	1	1	0	0	1	1
5	1	0	0	1	0	0	1	1	0	1	0	1
6	1	0	1	1	0	1	1	0	1	0	1	0
7	1	1	0	1	1	0	0	1	1	0	1	0
8	1	1	1	1	1	1	0	0	0	1	0	0

These features represent a complete orthogonal set over the input objects, and *any* classification function can be represented by a linear combination of them. For example,

$$C_1 = 1/4 \, (f_1 + f_2 + f_3 + f_4 + f_5 + f_6 - 3f_7) \,,$$

or

$$C_2 = 1/2 \, (-f_1 + f_4 + f_5 + f_7) \,.$$

It may be that the author is restricting the use of the term "conjunction" to the particular logic function AND (features in Table *J* are the variables themselves and EXCLUSIVE–OR functions of them), and has omitted any mention of complete orthogonal sets on the basis that such a feature space would be far too large to accommodate in any practical problem involving a reasonable number of variables.

—EDITOR.]

7. *"Statistics instead of recognition"*

When a new area of interest appears in science there is no such thing as a complete break with the past. Any new area of study uses methods and results that were developed before. For example, from any story you tell to someone else, only that part is understood that was known to him before.

Combinations of these peculiarities create a situation in which scientists can say that there is nothing new at all in a new subject, and that everything in it was known for a long time.

The recognition problem did not escape a similar criticism. We have seen that the program block for selecting characteristic features always (even in the case of nonintersecting classes) uses statistical criteria. Furthermore, since training is carried out with a comparatively small set of selections, it is only possible to indicate the probability of characteristic features being selected. It is no wonder, then, that some scientists thought that there was no separate problem of recognition, and everything was reduced to the theory of statistical techniques.

Presently, computers are used for diagnostic purposes in medicine, for oil prospecting, for the differentiation of radiolocation signals reflected from various objects, and for many other purposes. How are these tasks accomplished in the majority of cases? The aim of each such task, naturally, is not the study of the recognition problem in general, but a successful application in each actual case. Therefore (and quite logically) areas for which there is no effective program in existence are dealt with manually. The authors of these manual tasks select the most reliable and useful characteristics from experience accumulated during many years of work. At the same time, empirical observations and theories (as in radiolocation or geophysics) are also utilized.

As a result of this work, a comparatively small set of parameters is created, by the use of which the objects are described for the recognizing program. Because of the selection of "good parameters" (and they are not too numerous), the program is not required to construct complex functions on the basis of raw descriptions of the objects, nor to sort out characteristics. As verification characteristic features, the program can use parameters introduced into it, or sometimes combinations of two, three, or more parameters in sophisticated programs.

It can be said then that a noticeable part of the specific recognition work is accomplished by a man. The machine carries out the statistical evaluation of characteristics, or searches for a dividing boundary among parameters formulated by a man. It is no wonder that many people, upon becoming familiar with the recognition problem in actual applications, conclude that the performance of recognition programs is reduced to pure statistics.

In dealing with the majority of actual problems, designers assign to the computer only the less intellectual tasks. Therefore, even in cases where tasks are formulated in terms of a recognition problem, the systems used presently have few specific "recognition" characteristics. Therefore, this book did not consider in detail the performance of many machines in medicine, oil prospecting, and in other areas, although some definite progress has been achieved in these areas.

However, it should not be concluded that an actual application does not need "highly intellectual" programs. Development of such programs should be carried out, evidently, on model problems.

Regarding the role of statistics, it can be said that the statistical treatment constitutes only a part of the operations carried out by a recognition system. Since this part is best developed, it is the most simple today for programming. While selecting a method to deal with an actual problem, a system designer programs the easy part for the machine (statistical part), and people carry out the description of objects to suit the problem.

CHAPTER 12

Conclusion

1. *Parents and teachers*

DIGITAL COMPUTERS are often called *universal* machines. The reason is clear, because many problems from different fields of knowledge can be solved on these machines. Computing integrals, compiling the railroad schedules, playing tick-tack-toe—all these problems can be treated by computers. How could you help but call them universal! Remember, however, that this universality is very expensive for those who use computers. A new computer, just from the factory, cannot solve any of these problems. The efforts of a very qualified programmer are needed to "breathe life into the lifeless body."

It is sometimes said that the programmer trains the machine to solve a definite problem. What is the training? It is the transfer of some information to the computer. The programmer relates to the machine some information about the method for solving a given problem. He thereby "trains" the computer.

It seems to me that the term *training* is not very suitable in this case because not every method of information transfer is called training.

What does a teacher want when he teaches a child to solve, for example, arithmetic problems? The aim of the teacher is to change in some definite direction the state of some cells in the child's brain. A simple way to achieve this aim would be to influence directly (by passing an electric current, for example, or using some chemical substances) precisely those cells the state of which we want to change. However, the teacher cannot do this. Instead of influencing brain cells that participate in the process of solving the arithmetic problems, the teacher affects the child's receptors (vision and hearing). He changes the light distribution on the retina of the child, and vibrates the air in front of the tympanic membrane, and in these indirect ways causes changes in the brain cells.

Such a training method requires a much more complex brain structure compared to the method of directly influencing the needed cells. Different combinations of stimuli on the same receptors (for example, the cochlea) can cause changes in completely different sections of the brain. This means that a special mechanism is needed to decide in each individual case the state changes of the nerve cells. Such a mechanism would not be needed in the case of direct influence.

Why did nature not reject the indirect method of information gathering by animals? The truth is that this method requires much less knowledge on the part of the teacher, while setting up much stricter requirements on the pupil. In fact, in order to use the first method the teacher must know how the brain is built. His knowledge must be very detailed, including knowledge about which cells and with what algorithms this or that function is carried out. Furthermore, the teacher must know what actions on the cell change its state in the required direction, and must be prepared to affect physically millions (maybe billions) of cells. Not a single teacher possesses such knowledge or such ability. Therefore, nature decreased the requirements imposed on teachers because of the complexity of the brain.

It should not be thought that nature does not use the first method of information transfer on young animals. The method is widespread, but in this case we deal not with teachers but with parents. The parents know exactly in which brain cells and with what algorithms such processes as breathing, pupil reflexes, sucking, etc., are realized. This knowledge is stored not in a certain state of the brain cells, but in the genetic code of the chromosomes. Because of this, the knowledge of the parents cannot be expressed in words, but the child can be organized according to the plan stored in the chromosomes.

Let us go back to the work of the programmer. He informs the machine by directly depositing information in those areas of memory where it should be stored. He knows precisely which subprogram carried which algorithms, and where they are stored. The programmer does not use, or *almost* does not use, any indirect action on the subprogram. According to his knowledge and abilities he rather resembles a parent than a teacher.

In this lies both the strength and the weakness of the programmer. His strength comes from the fact that he can input any information into any cell of the machine memory. He can make the machine perform any treatment of the material, provided he knows what operations are needed for the treatment. However, in order to design a machine able to solve certain problems, the programmer must first have a model of his future machine in his head. And this is his weakness. Just as parents cannot transmit by means of heredity those properties that are absent in the genetic code, the programmer also cannot create a system if its model is not in his head.

Therefore, many people have concluded that it is impossible to design a machine able to solve problems that cannot be solved by its creators.

The error of such thinking is obvious. A child of illiterate parents can become a great scientist. He inherited from his parents not knowledge, which they lacked, but the brain structure capable of learning. He receives knowledge from other people, or from his experiments with objects of nature. His teachers (people and nature) may not have any information about the structure of his brain. Rather, on the contrary, he creates in his brain models of the phenomena he studies.

All these ideas are applicable completely to learning programs. They obtain information not only from "parents" (engineers, scientists, programmers) but also from "teachers" (those who select training sets). It is of interest to note that those who teach computers, just as those who teach children, do not interfere directly with the given part of the memory. They influence only the receptors, a small designated subset of cells where the codes for objects are introduced (for example, figures, numerical tables, etc.). The program changes by itself the states of many other cells in the course of training, for example, those where the selected features are stored. At the time of test the state of the machine does not coincide with a state intended initially by the programmer. In particular, it depends on which objects were shown during training. Figuratively speaking, the machine creates within itself a model of a given problem. This means a model which was nonexistent in the programmer's brain.

The programmer bestows upon his creation the ability to learn (just as in the case of child and parents). He created to some extent a universal program. But this universality is costly, just as in the case of universal digital computers, because the machine cannot solve a single problem immediately after its birth. It needs specialized programming, namely, training.

Thus, the program may "know" more about some things than the programmer who designed it. After successful training it knows the state of block k_1 of the problem generator because it has designed for itself a model of this state. Could the program know more than its teacher? Evidently yes, because a man who is shown the training material for a machine may not know the classification principle (be unable to recognize).

This does not mean that both talented and poor teachers will train the machine with equal success. Selection of the training material will depend upon an understanding by the teacher of the meaning of the problem, and the nature of its difficulties. The talent of a teacher is of special importance in the case of multistage programs in which the early stages are trained not on principal problems but on auxiliary problems (for example, *Geometry* and other programs, which are discussed in the last section of this chapter). The selection of auxiliary problems ("guiding questions") by a teacher can predetermine the success or failure of the entire training. It is not necessary for a teacher to be able to solve auxiliary problems. He need understand only that an ability to solve them may be useful during the solution of the principal problem. The teacher of a machine, just as the teacher of a child, may not know the design of the program. He only needs information about the receptors: where to present patterns and in what code. This information is also useful, evidently, for a child's teacher (for example, completely blind children need a different teaching approach).

A question may be raised: From where does the machine get information that could not be obtained either from the programmer or from the teacher? The answer is that the program learns by trial and error during training; in essence it carries out experiments. No wonder that experimental results can be new both for the programmer and the teacher. (Another description is also valid, namely, the program possesses a much stronger method of decoding the training material and, therefore, it derives more useful information from it.)

2. Goals, points, seconds

Two things are always mentioned in any type of athletic competition: First, the conditions that must be obeyed for the results to be valid, and second, the parameter for a win (time for runners and swimmers, points in basketball, etc.). It would sound funny for the man who came last in a running competition to claim first place because he ran with a load. The load is not included in this type of competition.

There is a need presently to establish some standards for the comparison of different recognition programs. Programs may differ from one another in the number of commands, training time, testing time, testing quality, total set of problems, memory volume, etc.

With regard to a new program, it is sometimes difficult to say to what kind of "sport" its achievements belong. Therefore, some agreement should be reached on evaluation criteria in the pattern recognition area in order that achievements not be mixed with those obtained in economy of machine time, machine memory, or the work of the programmer.

Let us start with essential conditions. As has been mentioned before, it is of little interest if a system is tested on patterns with which it was trained. Therefore, the first requirement is that new patterns be used during test. Those pairs of patterns should be considered as different that occur in different classes at least in one problem. The second requirement is that the percentage of errors during test be small.

The system's merit is not too great if highly predigested material enters its input, for example, if the field of useful features is already designed, or if parameters are found that can be used in statistical approaches, etc. Therefore, the third requirement is that decision surfaces in receptor space should be sufficiently complex for the majority of problems. (There should be no short description of these surfaces in terms of their geometric properties.) There should also be no common space of useful features for a significant fraction of problems in which the dividing surfaces become simple. Of particular interest is the case in which a system itself finds the space suitable for a given problem.

The initial indeterminacy of feature space characterizes the property that is primary for a recognition system, namely, its universality. The greater the initial indeterminacy of feature space selection, the more interesting is the problem.

We should mention here a confusion that could exist. The essential conditions mentioned at the beginning also allow quantitative evaluation. For example, there may be 0.5% errors during test, but the percentage of errors could also reach 6%. Would it not be right to evaluate a program according to this parameter?

It seems that the approach used in athletics is also applicable in our case. It is true that even a weak wind behind a runner helps him, but this is not considered up to a certain point. A similar approach could be applied to the evaluation of program performance. We should decide beforehand what percentage of errors is acceptable to us, and after this make no differentiation between programs performing within the acceptable error range.

The parameter *training time* occupies a special place. We can, of course, require that the time be within the limits of some allowable range (for example, 1/10 of the average time between machine malfunctions). However, if we look ahead, we see that the set of problems to be solved can increase with time indefinitely without introducing into the program any new ideas. Therefore, this parameter is extremely important.

Therefore, recognizing programs should be valued mainly for their universality, although recognition accuracy may suffer. This approach agrees with the aim of recognition, namely, to model difficult functions of the brain such as intuition, reasoning by analogy, etc. Man's brain strikes us mainly by its universality, and not at all by its accuracy (to err is human).

The fact that inaccuracy distinguishes man from other animals was noted by K. Marx when he wrote: "A bee by its wax cells shames some architects. But even the poorest architect differs from the bee by having a model of the cell in his head before he builds it."

The majority of actual problems, which seem at first to belong to the recognition problem (medical diagnostics, radiolocation signals, etc.), does not satisfy this third requirement for universality at the present time. Therefore, the design of programs to solve these problems does not signify that great success has been achieved on difficult tasks in pattern recognition.

What types of problems can serve at present as a touchstone for recognizing programs? We do not have good methods for formally describing large sets of problems that would satisfy the universality requirement. Maybe in the future we will learn to describe sets of problems by means of automata structure (the problem generator). Maybe it could be achieved by indicating the reactions among problems of certain sets, just as properties of a signal can be described by the reactions of a set of harmonic oscillators. However, this is all in the future. For the moment we must continue, therefore, to describe sets of problems by using a large number of examples and words ("etc. problems"), and by using the ability of man to extrapolate and generalize.

In Appendix 3, several sets of geometric problems are presented in this way. The design of a system capable of solving these problems (or even part of them) will have to overcome many difficulties. Solving these and similar sets of problems will move us closer to the mechanization of many thought processes, as opposed to the recognition of oil-bearing layers, scarlet fever, submarines, etc., according to parameters specially selected by man for the given case.

3. Accumulation of experience

So far we have discussed in this book systems that start the solution of each problem from the same initial state. While attempting to solve a new problem, the system forgets everything it has learned before. At the same time it is clear that if a system is in a relatively stable state, the use of previous experience would be a logical forward step.

The simplest way to design a system that would accumulate experience is to make the program remember how often it needs to use the same features. While solving a new problem, the program would check features in decreasing order of these frequencies.

Such a program shortens the search during training only when problems requiring the application of different features with unequal frequency are encountered. In essence, it minimizes the initial indeterminacy with regard to features that it needs.

A system that could use accumulated experience, even when all features are needed with equal frequency, is of great interest. In principle, it can be designed in the following manner: after solving a certain number of problems, the program by itself collects into one group those problems requiring the application of certain features, and into another group those that do not require certain features. As a result, a new problem appears (let us call it a problem of the second order) in which problems of the first order represent patterns. While solving this problem, the program finds features (of the second order) indicating the right way to try a given group of features of the first order. (A good teacher could be of great help at this stage. By a careful selection of "guiding questions" [problems of the first order], he could decrease sharply the training time, and protect the program from prejudices.)

During training on a new problem of the first order, such a system decides by the use of features of the second order which features of the first order are worthwhile checking. In other words, the system first recognizes to which group a given problem belongs, and only then starts the search for features, as applicable to the given set of problems. As opposed to other systems, this program preserves its experience not in the form of a probability distribution of features, but in the form of "features of features" (features of the second order).

Assume now that the system's environment changes sharply (it encounters a new set of problems). It could also happen that the selected features of the second order ceased being of help, or even started to interfere. The signal that precisely this had happened would be a sharp increase in search time during training on problems of the first order.

Then it would be necessary to use a substantial sorting-out in order to avoid accumulating many solved problems from the new set. At this time, training on second-order problems can be conducted using the selection of new features of the second order. If sets have changed many times, problems of the third order may be designed in which objects are represented by sets of problems. Features of the third order will decrease the search for features of the second order on going to a new set of problems.

A system can be imagined with features of the fourth, etc., orders. To be successful, such a system should possess a large memory because patterns corresponding to problems of the second and all other orders will be very large. However, the essence of the system operation is not the mechanical storing of material, but the development of analysis algorithms that lead to decreased search.

The design of a multistage system for a wide range of problems will encounter many difficulties, for example, selecting dictionaries for problems of the second and higher orders; automatic division of groups of patterns into problems of the second, etc., orders; organization of a flexible interaction of all stages, etc. Remember, however, that a considerable part of generating new problems would not be completely new. We have encountered this in previous discussion, for example, in the program for recognizing geometric objects. This makes us hope that success in the design of a reliable geometric program will serve as a first step toward creating systems capable of flexibly and skillfully using accumulated experience.

The behavior of multistage systems during the solution of problems of the first order will be, evidently, very amusing. An observer will see that only a negligible portion of the features accessible to the program are checked. Furthermore, even features that proved unsuitable would be, in general, "logical" ones to try. They would be difficult to discard on the basis of "common logic."

Suppose that someone observes program performance only superficially. For example, he sees only the end result (test quality), training time, and the diversity of problems submitted to the program. He will see first of all the discrepancy between the variety of problems and the training time. More often than not he will say that the system possesses an unusual intuition. When told that the system was trained on large amounts of material he may state: "It makes no difference that the system memory is filled with all kinds of information. Searching through all information would take too much time, and the ability to find the needed answer in memory without long deliberations means that the system has a highly developed network of associations, and this is strongly related to intuition."

Thus, functions that are called *associative memory* and *intuition* break into the recognition chain at different levels. Therefore, the multistage recognition system will possess intuition in exactly the same sense as man, although at the beginning to a much lesser degree. We should add here that for a superficial observer the program will exhibit all the features of indeterminate behavior ("free will"). It will use an "informal approach" during the solution of a problem, again in the same sense as man.

Therefore, all research in the field of recognition should be considered part of the creation of thinking machines.

It should be noted that some scientists do not agree with the above ideas. They say that the brain of contemporary man is the result of evolution that took many millions of years. It is impossible to train a machine for such a long time, and therefore there will be no thinking machines.

Despite some truth in this reasoning, it contains, nevertheless, an error. Following this same line of reasoning, we could argue that it is impossible to create an airplane. In fact, the organism of the bird was created in the course of long evolution. Millions of years passed before strong muscles were built, light bones, and perfect feathers. The error of such thinking lies in the assumption that the machine will carry out the function (thinking, flight, etc.) by copying both the method and the course of evolution of nature.

It took hundreds of thousands of years for man to learn multiplication and division of large numbers. It takes only several days to teach this art to the great collection of resistors, condensers, and transistors of which computing machines are assembled. People, of course, used knowledge accumulated by mankind over thousands of years to create airplanes or computing machines. Accumulated experience will be used in the same way to create thinking machines. And if we include the evolution of man's ancestors (mammals, amphibians, reptiles, etc.) in the evolution time of mankind, then the "evolution record" of thinking machines should likewise include the time of evolution of man. Machines will start to learn on the basis of an already high level of initial organization contributed by man. And training will be conducted by man. Talk about millions of years of evolution is not very convincing in this case.

Another type of objection concerns man as a "social being," the thinking process of which results from the collective activity of people (social life). The machine, on the other hand, is a separate entity, and consequently it cannot think. Some say that a child will never become a human being if left alone after birth; thinking is the function of mankind and not a single man.

These considerations contain the same error, namely, the hypothesis that there is only one way to think. No doubt, social interaction helped greatly in the development of man's thinking. However, this does not mean that a machine with a high level of initial organization cannot progress individually in the process of solving more and more difficult problems. Furthermore, it is certainly possible that several machines (a collective of machines) could solve a variety of different problems to satisfy the requirements of mankind, or the requirements of the same machine collective. (The name *machine collective* is, of course, questionable because it is impossible to distinguish a collective from one large machine. There are cases when the exchange of information within one part of a system exceeds the exchange of information between individual parts. We have reason then to speak about a "collective" consisting of separate "individuals." In the animal world, it is difficult sometimes to distinguish an organism from a collective. What is, for example, a beehive in which worker bees cannot reproduce, the queen bee cannot feed herself, and drones have only one half the standard number of chromosomes?)

Thus, the notion that social processes played a great role in the development of thinking in mankind and in separate individuals proves little. As stated before, we have no reason to believe that it is impossible in principle to create thinking machines.

However, knowing that it is possible in principle to build such machines is a long way from actually building them. Mankind at present is only at the very beginning of this road. It is difficult to foretell how much time it will take. It is equally difficult to foresee the consequences to which an ability to create thinking machines will lead. Most probably they will be as real as the consequences of electric generators, or uranium reactors. One thing is clear. We should spare no effort on our part to move forward in this area because the game is worth playing.

APPENDIX 1

Hypotheses Containing the Truth, and the Optimal Hypothesis

We often describe different situations by statements such as, "the truth, but not the whole truth," or "not only the truth," etc. To what formal relationships do these statements correspond? Let us start with the simplest case.

Assume that someone, Z, wants to find out the location of a particular reference in a book containing 100 pages. Let the reference be on page 45. Suppose that Z thinks this reference is in the first half of the book. Z's hypothesis in this case is the truth. However, the hypothesis is not very strong. A hypothesis indicating that the reference is located between pages 40 and 50 would be much stronger. Furthermore, a hypothesis that the reference is located between pages 47 and 50 is stronger yet, but it is false.

In these examples, it is easy to determine whether the hypothesis is true or false. We need only check to see if the answer is within the region limited by the hypothesis.

There are, however, more complex situations. Suppose the book in question was printed twice, 10,000 copies the first time, and 30,000 copies the second time. The reference is located on page 45 in the first edition, and on page 48 in the second edition. We do not know which edition we have at hand. Under these conditions what can be said about a hypothesis that the reference is between pages 30 and 46 with a probability of 0.3, and that it is located between pages 47 and 50 with a probability of 0.7? Evidently, we cannot say whether the hypothesis is true or false. In order to describe the relation between the hypothesis and the problem, we need in this case some new approach. This approach should not contradict the usual notion of truth and falsity in simple situations.

Notice that problem indeterminacy cannot serve as a measure of the truth of the hypothesis. Consider two hypotheses in the example of the book.

a) The reference is between pages 35 and 50, and the probability of finding it between pages 35 and 42 is lower than that of finding it between pages 43 and 50.

b) The reference is between pages 1 and 100.

The problem indeterminacy in case (*a*) is lower than in case (*b*). We feel intuitively that hypothesis (*a*) is more risky, but possibly contains more information about (not only) the truth. Hypothesis (*b*) we accept as the truth, although it leads to much greater problem indeterminacy. Why is this so? Evidently, significance lies not only in what truth the hypothesis gives, but also in what it promises (the hypothesis power). Hypothesis (*b*) gives little, and it promises nothing. Therefore, we do not feel that we are deceived.

How, then, to measure the power of a hypothesis? In the case of the book, the stronger hypothesis was the one defining the smaller search area. When the hypothesis is about the distribution of probabilities $q_1, q_2, \ldots, q_n$ that the object belongs to Class I, II, $\ldots$, n, the entropy of this probability distribution $H(q)$ can serve as its measurement. (It is easy to see that the hypothesis q promises an indeterminacy equal to $H[q]$. In fact, if the hypothesis is absolutely accurate, then $p_i = q_i [i = 1, 2, \ldots, n]$, and therefore, $N[p/q] = H[q]$.) Accordingly, we will consider that the hypothesis q' is stronger than the hypothesis q'', provided $H(q') < H(q'')$.

Now we can compare what the hypothesis promises, and what it actually gives. Consider the general case, when the solution algorithm deals not with one problem but with a set of problems. In this case, we do not have any definite distribution of answer probabilities p, but only some relationships of the type

$$\left.\begin{array}{l} f_1(p_1, p_2, \ldots, p_n) \geqslant 0, \\ f_2(p_1, p_2, \ldots, p_n) \geqslant 0, \\ \cdots\cdots\cdots\cdots\cdots\cdots \\ f_k(p_1, p_2, \ldots, p_n) \geqslant 0, \end{array}\right\} \qquad (28)$$

that limit the range of possible values of p. In addition, there always exists the constraint,

$$p_i \geqslant 0,$$

and

$$\sum_{i=1}^{n} p_i = 1.$$

Let the system of limitations be such that there is at least one distribution p that satisfies all inequalities (the set contains at least one problem).

Call the distribution of probabilities $\tilde{q}$ a hypothesis containing only the truth with respect to limitations (28), if

$$max_p\, N\,(p/\tilde{q}) \leqslant H\,(\tilde{q}) \qquad (29)$$

where max_p is the upper boundary with respect to all distributions p that satisfy limitations (28).

In other words, a hypothesis containing only the truth is one that in fact produces no higher indeterminacy than it promises for all problems in a set.

Hypotheses that do not satisfy (29) are those stronger and more risky ones that possibly contain more information about (not only) the truth. Notice that there is at least one hypothesis $\tilde{q}_i = 1/n\,(i = 1, 2, \ldots, n)$ containing only the truth regardless of the system of limitations. In fact, in this case

$$max_p\, N\,(p/\tilde{q}) = \log\,(n) = H\,(\tilde{q})\,.$$

The hypothesis $\tilde{q}^0$ is called the strongest hypothesis containing only the truth, if $\tilde{q}^0$ is a hypothesis containing only the truth, and

$$H\,(\tilde{q}^0) \leqslant H\,(\tilde{q}) \qquad (30)$$

where $\tilde{q}$ is any other hypothesis containing only the truth. It can be shown (we do not give any derivations here) that the number of hypotheses containing only the truth is closed, and $H\,(\tilde{q}^0)$ is the lower bound on the uncertainty, because $H\,(\tilde{q}) \geqslant 0$; consequently there always exists a strongest hypothesis containing only the truth.

We have noted in Chapter 7, Section 3, that if the solution algorithm without feedback deals with a single problem, then the best hypothesis is $q = p$. Let us generalize this idea about the best hypothesis for a set of problems (limitations [28] are valid).

A distribution of probabilities q^0 with respect to (28) we call the optimal hypothesis, provided

$$max_p\, N\,(p/q^0) \leqslant max_p\, N\,(p/q) \qquad (31)$$

where max_p is used in the same sense as in (29), and q is any other arbitrary hypothesis.

It is easy to see that in the case of a single problem (a definite p), the optimal hypothesis is a hypothesis containing only the truth. Is this relation valid in more complex cases? Would it not be advantageous to look for an optimal hypothesis among those containing more information about (not only) the truth in the case of a set of problems? The following theorem will supply the answer to these questions.

Theorem. For any system of limitations imposed on p, there exists a unique optimal hypothesis q^0. The optimal hypothesis q^0 is identical with the strongest hypothesis $\tilde{q}^0$ containing only the truth. In this case,

$$max_p \, N \, (p/q^0) = H \, (q^0) \, .$$

In order to prove this, we will use geometric interpretations of such ideas as "the probability distribution of answers to the problem," "hypothesis," "entropy," and "indeterminacy."

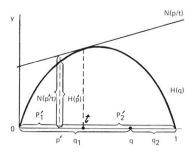

Figure 54. Geometric representation of the concept of "indeterminacy."

Let us start with $n = 2$. Because $q_1 + q_2 = 1$, the possible problems can be regarded as unidimensional. Represent the hypothesis by a point q within the segment $(0, 1)$ on the abscissa (Fig. 54). The point p is also located on the same segment. In order to find the indeterminacy of a problem characterized by p' and the hypothesis $q = t$, we plot a curve $y = H \, (q)$, and draw a line tangent to this curve at a point that corresponds to t. The tangent will be a graph of the function $y = N \, (p, \, t)$.

In fact, $N \, (p/t) = -p_1 \, \log t_1 - p_2 \, \log t_2$ is a linear function of p, $N \, (t/t) = H \, (t)$ and $N \, (p'/t) > H \, (p')$ at $p' \neq t$. Thus, $y = N \, (p/t)$ should be a straight line located above $y = H \, (q)$ at $p \neq t$, and should have a common point with $y = H \, (q)$ at $p = t$. Furthermore, $y = H \, (q)$ is con-

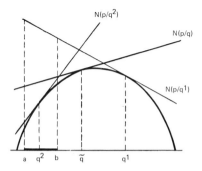

Figure 55.

vex, continuous, and has a continuous derivative at all points, except $q_1 = 0$ and $q_1 = 1$, and thus $y = N(p/t)$ is tangent to $y = H(q)$.

Let the limitations imposed on p be such that p can be located only on segment ab (Fig. 55). The hypothesis $\tilde{q}$ (among all hypotheses shown in this figure) contains only the truth with respect to these limitations, and q^1 and q^2 are hypotheses that contain not only the truth, because

$$max_p \, N(p/q^1) > H(q^1)$$

and

$$max_p \, N(p/q^2) > H(q^2).$$

In this example, $\tilde{q}^0$ coincides with the point b.

[It may help to clarify the author's concepts and terminology if numbers are attached to his previous example of the books. Suppose the problem contains only one distribution, namely, out of 40,000 books the probability of the item being located on page 45 is 0.25, and of being located on page 48 is 0.75. The (uniform) hypothesis that the reference is between pages 1 and 100 leads to $N(p/q) = H(q) = 4.60$ bits. The hypothesis that it is located (uniformly) between pages 30 and 46 with probability 0.3, and between pages 47 and 50 with probability 0.7 leads to $N(p/q) = 2.31 < H(q) = 2.45$ bits. This hypothesis thus contains "only the truth." A much stronger (but wrong) hypothesis that the reference is located on page 40 with probability 0.3, or on page 50 with probability 0.7 produces $N(p/q) = \infty \gg H(q) = 0.61$ bits. This hypothesis does not contain "only the truth." It promises much more than it delivers, and the author refers to this situation as "not only the truth." A strong (but correct) hypothesis, namely, the optimal one that $q = p$ yields $N(p/q) = H(q) = 0.56$ bits. It is the author's theorem that this is the strongest one containing "only the truth."

—EDITOR.]

If n is arbitrary, then p and q are points on an $(n-1)$–dimensional tetrahedron (simplex). Denote by K the $(n-1)$–dimensional hyperplane containing this tetrahedron. In the n-dimensional case, $y = H(q)$ is an $(n-1)$–dimensional convex surface. Place an $(n-1)$–dimensional hyperplane so that it is tangent to the surface $y = H(q)$ at a point corresponding to $q = t$. The equation of this hyperplane is $y = N(p/t)$. Let us see what properties it possesses. First, construct the $(n-2)$–dimensional intersection of hyperplanes $y = N(p/t)$ and $y = H(t) =$ a constant. Project this intersection onto K. The resulting projection F is also an $(n-2)$–dimensional plane. If $p \,\epsilon\, F$, then $N(p/t) = H(t)$. F divides K into two parts. For points p located on one side of F, $N(p/t) < H(t)$; for those located on the other side of F, $N(p/t) > H(t)$. The point h with coordinates $h_i = 1/n \, (i = 1, 2, \ldots, n)$ always occurs in the region of large indeterminacy. In fact, $N(h/t) \geqslant H(h) \geqslant H(t)$. Strict inequality prevails when $t \neq h$. The plane $y = N(p/t)$ coincides with $y = H(t)$ when $t = h$ and F completely fills the whole tetrahedron.

Now project the region formed by the intersection of the surface $y = H(q)$ and plane $y = H(t)$ onto K. Designate this projection G. Evidently, $t \epsilon F$, $t \epsilon G$, and F is tangent to G at point t.

Designate by L the set of all points of the tetrahedron that satisfy limitations (28), including boundary points. The intersection of L and F is designated by M. Figure 56 shows the plane K for $n = 3$.

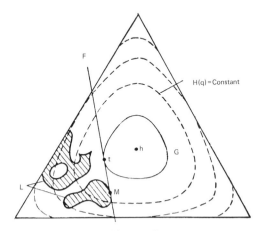

Figure 56.

In order to find out if t is a hypothesis containing "only the truth" with respect to (28), or with respect to region L, we need to draw the surface of constant entropy through t, and to construct the hyperplane F tangent to it at point t. If F separates L and h (L may have points on F), then t is a hypothesis containing only the truth. (Evidently, F divides L and G at the same time.)

It follows from this that if region L is such that there is no $(n - 2)$-dimensional hyperplane dividing L and h, then the hypothesis $q = h$ is the only one that contains only the truth. Figure 57 shows an example.

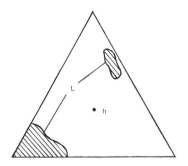

Figure 57.

We can now state the following lemma.

Lemma. If $\tilde{q}^0$ is the strongest hypothesis containing only the truth, then points $m^1, m^2, \ldots, m^j, \ldots, m^s, m^j \epsilon M$ ($s \leqslant n - 1$) and numbers $\alpha^j > 0$ can be found such that

$$\sum_{j=1}^{s} \alpha^j = 1$$

and

$$\sum_{j=1}^{s} \alpha^j m^j = \tilde{q}^0,$$

in which the m^j are $(n - 1)$–dimensional vectors.

Let B be the convex shell stretched over the region L. Consider the relationship between B and the surface G that passes through $\tilde{q}^0$. In principle, the following four situations are possible: (1) B and G intersect each other; (2) B and G do not have common points; (3) B and G are tangent to each other but not at point $\tilde{q}^0$; (4) B and G are tangent at point $\tilde{q}^0$.

The first case cannot occur because there is no hyperplane that separates B (and therefore L) and G.

The realization of the second case would contradict the assumption that $\tilde{q}^0$ is the strongest hypothesis containing only the truth. That is, we could design another surface G' that includes G and does not intersect B. There will always be some point t on G' such that the hyperplane tangent at this point to G', separates G' from B. This means that t would represent a hypothesis containing only the truth. But $H(t) < H(\tilde{q}^0)$, showing the contradictory nature of this assumption.

The third case, just as the first, is incompatible with the assumption that $\tilde{q}^0$ contains only the truth. In fact, G is a convex surface and does not have any plane parts. Therefore, the hyperplanes tangent to it at two points cannot coincide. Since B and G are tangent to each other, the only hyperplane that separates them is tangent to G at the same point. This means that the hyperplane tangent to G at $\tilde{q}^0$ does not separate B from G.

Thus, only the fourth case is left. It follows that $\tilde{q}^0$ necessarily belongs to B. Since B is the convex shell of the region L, then $\tilde{q}^0$ must be capable of being expressed as the positively weighted center of gravity of several points $m^1, m^2, \ldots, m^j, \ldots, m^s$ of the region L.

The last statement means that there can be found numbers α^j and points $m^j \epsilon L$ such that

$$\sum_{j=1}^{s} \alpha^j = 1 \qquad (32)$$

and

$$\sum_{j=1}^{s} \alpha^j m^j = \tilde{q}^0, \qquad (33)$$

with the constraint

$$\alpha^j > 0 \, (j = 1, 2, \ldots, s) \, . \tag{34}$$

Since $\tilde{q}^0$ belongs to the hyperplane F, and L is located on one side of F, then $m^j \in F$; and consequently $m^j \in M$. Thus, the lemma is proved.

Consequence: If $t = \tilde{q}^0$, then M is not empty. This means that

$$max_p \, N \, (p/\tilde{q}^0) = H \, (\tilde{q}^0) \, . \tag{35}$$

Now we attempt to prove the theorem. From (33) it follows that

$$N \, (\tilde{q}^0/q) = \sum_{i=1}^{s} \alpha^j \, N \, (m^j/q) \, . \tag{36}$$

Considering (32) and (34), we obtain $N \, (\tilde{q}^0/q) \leqslant max_j \, N \, (m^j/q)$, where max_j is the maximum taken with respect to s along points m^j. Since $m^j \in L$, we then have

$$N \, (\tilde{q}^0/q) \leqslant max_p \, N \, (p/q) \, , \tag{37}$$

when $q \neq \tilde{q}^0$

$$H \, (\tilde{q}^0) < N \, (\tilde{q}^0/q) \, . \tag{38}$$

Comparing (35) and (38) with (37) we get

$$max_p \, N \, (p/\tilde{q}^0) < max_p \, N \, (p/q) \, . \tag{39}$$

This means that $\tilde{q}^0$ is an optimal hypothesis and at the same time unique.

Consequence: a) It follows from (35) that

$$max_p \, N \, (p/q^0) = H \, (q^0) \, . \tag{40}$$

b) The unique strong hypothesis containing only the truth follows from the unique optimal hypothesis.

c) If the region L is such that there is no $(n - 2)$–dimensional hyperplane separating it from point h, then $q^0 = h$ is the optimal hypothesis. For example, if no limitations are imposed on p (with the exception of $\Sigma \, p_i = 1$) then $q_i^0 = 1/n$ is the optimal hypothesis.

The consequence (c) explains how best to apply the widely used approach that states that "since we do not have information about the probability of some events, consider them as being equally probable."

Consider a case in which the system of limitations (28) is of the type

$p_{j_1} + p_{j_2} + \ldots + p_{j_s} + \ldots + p_{j_k} = 0$. This means that the answer can have only $n - k$ values, not n values. Since nothing is said about the remaining coordinates of the vector p, the optimal hypothesis will be $p_i = 0$ when $i = j_s$ and $p_i = \dfrac{1}{n - k}$ when $i \neq j_s$. In our first hypothesis about the book with a reference located in the first half, we subconsciously assumed that this hypothesis indicated equiprobably the location of the reference on all pages in the first half of the book. In other words, we subconsciously optimized the hypothesis within the limits allowed by certain stipulations. As a result of optimization, the hypothesis contained "only the truth." If freedom of selection is narrowed, the hypothesis that the reference is located in the first half of the book could contain "not only the truth." For example, the hypothesis that the reference is located between pages 1 and 10 with a probability of 0.99, and that it is located between pages 11 and 50 with a probability of 0.01 contains "not only the truth," although it states that the reference is located in the first half of the book.

Thus, while evaluating the truth of the hypothesis we try different approaches to optimize it. If, after this, the resulting hypothesis contains "only the truth," then we are inclined to think that the initial statement was also true. It can be said that we have "the presumption of truth." Until proved otherwise, we assume that someone tells the truth.

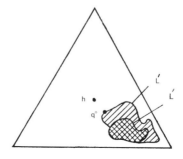

Figure 58.

In conclusion, consider one additional situation that explains why a hypothesis satisfying (29) is referred to as containing "only the truth." Let the inequalities (28) determine some region L (Fig. 58) within which p could be located. Assume that not all inequalities are given to us. In other words, we are told "only the truth," but "not the whole truth." The limitations given us determine some region L'. Evidently $L' \supset L$. If our aim is to find the optimal hypothesis, we will choose the hypothesis q^0 on the basis of information in our possession, which is optimal with respect to region L'. It will not necessarily be optimal with respect to region L, but it will always contain "only the truth."

APPENDIX 2

Optimal Solution Algorithms for Value Functions That Differ from the Logarithmic

Why have we selected the logarithm of the average number of trials in Chapter 7 to characterize problem difficulty for a given solution algorithm? Why not the number of trials or the square of the number of trials? It is quite clear that the "price" for the use of the W algorithm should be different for different actual cases. For example, if the realization of the W algorithm is the most time-consuming part of the computer program (and we price machine time), then it is logical to consider difficulty as being proportional to the number of trials. In another case, when much time is spent constructing an experimental unit, but the experiments cost little to run, a reasonable evaluation of difficulty will be based upon some function that rises rapidly at the beginning, but slows down with an increasing number of trials.

There is no universal method for evaluating difficulty. Why, then, have we devoted so much time in Chapter 7 to the logarithmic function of value?

The theory of information is not the only subject dealing with such problems. For example, which is better—a source of 12 volts d.c. that produces 15 amperes, or 120 volts a.c. with a current of only 1 ampere? It is impossible to answer this question if we do not know for what purpose the current source is used. Assume that we can use different current-transforming devices. This means that we can include rectifiers, transformers, etc., in the network. If no limitations are imposed on this apparatus, then we can compare current sources. If the 120 volts a.c. is transformed into 12 volts d.c. with a step-down transformer, then the maximum d.c. current cannot exceed 10 amperes. This limitation follows from the law of energy conservation. On the other hand, if d.c. from the original source is transformed into 120 volts a.c., then current greater than 1 ampere can be obtained in principle (the theoretical limit is 1.5 amperes).

Actually we have just compared two current sources. The first has 180 watts, and the second, 120 watts. If we do not have transformers, then the amount of current is not the decisive factor in the selection of a source. For example, for a 120-volt 40-watt light bulb the second current source is suitable, and the first is unsuitable. When current transformers can be used, power serves as a common equivalent because the energy conservation law can be applied to it regardless of the current, voltage, frequency, type of pulse, etc. Thus the energy conservation law separates values that are equivalent.

In Chapter 7, we have also required the concept of problem indeterminacy. To solve some problems the system conducts experiments and "knows" that one of the A_i is the answer, but it lacks information as to which of the A_i is the right answer. The missing information is established by experiments carried out by the solution algorithm. There is still another method for obtaining information regarding the right answer for a given problem. Namely, the use of information coming along the communication channel. Our aim is to find the "coefficient of equivalence" between these two methods. In what units can we measure the experiments necessary for problem solution in order to be able to predict changes that could occur in this value after the arrival of a given signal?

Formula (11) shows that the relationship between the quantity of necessary experiment and the properties of the communication channel is established if the quantity of necessary experiment is measured by problem indeterminacy (in logarithmic units).

This relationship resembles the energy conservation law: problem indeterminacy cannot be diminished by more than the transmission capacity of the communication channel.

We know, however, that it is not enough just to have the equivalent of a conservation law applicable to different problems, channels, or signals. We need transformers to relate the communication channel and the signal to the solution algorithm. It happens that there is such a transformer. Formula (13) indicates that if a decoding algorithm matrix is constructed according to formula (12), then the solution algorithm will be able to use the full transmission capacity of the communication channel. These ideas explain in what sense the logarithmic function of value for difficulty is advantageous.

Consider the following situation. We have a problem for the solution of which the algorithm (based on the hypothesis that answers are distributed uniformly) requires on the average of 10^9 trials. Furthermore, we have two systems trying to solve this problem. The first system has the following properties: in 99% of the cases, it solves the problem in 1,000 trials; in 1% of the cases, in 10^9 trials. The second system in 99% of the cases finds the solution in 10 trials, and in 1% of the cases in 10^9 trials.

Which of these two systems is the best? Anyone will say that the second system is.

Compare the performance of the systems using the average number of trials. For the first system this number is $0.99 \times 1{,}000 + 0.01 \times 10^9 \cong 10^7 \times 1.0001$; for the second system it is $0.99 \times 10 + 0.01 \times 10^9 \cong 10^7 \times 1.000001$. The relative difference is negligibly small. Using the average number of trials as a criterion, both systems can be accepted as being of virtually identical value for the solution of this problem.

Compare now both systems using problem indeterminacy. For the first system the indeterminacy is $0.99 \log 1{,}000 + 0.01 \log 10^9 = 3.06$; for the second system, $0.99 \log 10 + 0.01 \log 10^9 = 1.08$. The resulting difference is very noticeable and corresponds well to the intuitive feeling that the second system solves the problem almost always 100 times faster than the first one; and in 1% of the cases neither system can solve the problem.

Thus, there are cases when indeterminacy is closer to the intuitive evaluation, as opposed to the average number of trials.

All arguments in favor of the logarithmic function of value beg the question that in each actual case we could be interested in a peculiar (and not the logarithmic) value function. We can thus raise the question: Are not the optimal solving and decoding algorithms (Chapter 7, Sections 3, 5, 6) optimal only for indeterminacy? Would not each different value function require its own solving and decoding algorithms? This would be, evidently, very inconvenient.

If the class of solution algorithms is limited to those without feedback, then different probability distributions would be the best, actually, for different difficulty value functions. For example, for algorithms without feedback and problems with $n = 2$, the lowest average number of applications of the W algorithm is achieved when

$$q_1 = \frac{p_1 - \sqrt{p_1 - p_1^2}}{2p_1 - 1}, \quad q_2 = \frac{p_2 - \sqrt{p_2 - p_2^2}}{2p_2 - 1},$$

and not at $q_1 = p_1$ and $q_2 = p_2$, which secure the lowest indeterminacy.

Remember, however, that algorithms with constant probability distributions (algorithms without feedback) are not absolutely optimal. When the algorithm can use information about the results of previous tests to change the probability distribution for subsequent tests then the same solution algorithm will be optimal for quite a large class of value functions. We will attempt to prove this below.

Let $F(x)$ be a nondecreasing function determined on $x \leqslant 1$. Call F the difficulty value function, and let $T(m_k) = F(\bar{K}_k)$ be the problem difficulty with respect to pattern m_k for a given solution algorithm, where $\bar{K}_k$ is the average number of W algorithm applications required to solve the problem with respect to pattern m_k.

The difficulty of the entire problem A is then

$$T(A) = \sum_k p(m_k) T(m_k) = \sum_k p(m_k) F(\bar{K}_k).$$

It is easy to see that indeterminacy corresponds to a difficulty function with logarithmic form. Let $F(x)$ be convex if for

$$\left. \begin{array}{c} \alpha_1 \geqslant 0, \quad \alpha_2 \geqslant 0, \quad \text{and} \quad \alpha_1 + \alpha_2 = 1, \\[2mm] \alpha_1 F(x_1) + \alpha_2 F(x_2) \leqslant F(\alpha_1 x_1 + \alpha_2 x_2). \end{array} \right\} \tag{41}$$

Theorem. Problem difficulty for a solution algorithm that checks the A_i in order of decreasing probabilities p_i will be lowest for any convex value function.

Repeated testing of the same A_i can only increase the average number of trials, and thus the difficulty. Therefore, only algorithms with feedback are considered. Indexes on A_i are arranged in such a way that

$$p_1 \geqslant p_2 \geqslant \ldots \geqslant p_n.$$

Designated by $\pi_{i,j}$ the probability that if the answer is A_i, then it will be found on the jth test. Evidently,

$$\sum_{j=1}^{n} \pi_{i,j} = 1, \tag{42}$$

because the answer will be found for sure in not more than n tests.
It can be shown that

$$\sum_{i=1}^{n} \pi_{i,j} = 1. \tag{43}$$

The relationship (43) occurs because $\pi_{i,j}$ is the conditional probability of checking A_i on the jth test, if the first $j-1$ tests did not find the answer.

The difficulty of the problem A for the solution algorithm, which is characterized by the matrix $\|\pi_{i,j}\|$, is

$$T(A) = \sum_i p_i F(\sum_j j \pi_{i,j}). \tag{44}$$

Designate $T(A)$ by $f(\boldsymbol{p}, \|\pi_{i,j}\|)$.
Introduce the function f' in the following manner

$$f'(\boldsymbol{p}, \|\pi_{i,j}\|) = \sum_i p_i \sum_j \pi_{i,j} F(j). \tag{45}$$

Due to the convex nature of F and the equality (42)

$$f(\boldsymbol{p}, ||\pi_{i,j}||) \geqslant f'(\boldsymbol{p}, ||\pi_{i,j}||). \tag{46}$$

Consider the matrix

$$||\pi'_{i,j}|| = \begin{Vmatrix} \pi_{11} \cdots \pi_{1,j_1} & \cdots \pi_{1,j_2} & \cdots \pi_{1,n} \\ \cdots\cdots\cdots\cdots\cdots\cdots\cdots\cdots\cdots\cdots\cdots \\ \pi_{i_1,1} \cdots \pi_{i_1,j_1} + \alpha \cdots \pi_{i_1,j_2} - \alpha \cdots \pi_{i_1,n} \\ \cdots\cdots\cdots\cdots\cdots\cdots\cdots\cdots\cdots\cdots\cdots \\ \pi_{i_2,1} \cdots \pi_{i_2,j_1} - \alpha \cdots \pi_{i_2,j_2} + \alpha \cdots \pi_{i_2,n} \\ \cdots\cdots\cdots\cdots\cdots\cdots\cdots\cdots\cdots\cdots\cdots \\ \pi_{n,1} \cdots \pi_{n,j_1} & \cdots \pi_{n,j_2} & \cdots \pi_{n,n} \end{Vmatrix} \tag{47}$$

that was obtained from $||\pi_{i,j}||$ by changing four elements, where $\alpha > 0$, $j_2 > j_1$, and $i_2 > i_1$.

It can be seen that

$$f'(\boldsymbol{p}, ||\pi_{i,j}||) - f'(\boldsymbol{p}, ||\pi'_{i,j}||) = a(p_{i_1} - p_{i_2})[F(j_2) - F(j_1)] \geqslant 0. \tag{48}$$

Properties of (42) are preserved after the transformation (47). Let $\pi_{1,t}$ be the first number in the first row of the matrix $||\pi_{i,j}||$ that differs from $\pi_{1,1}$ and is not zero; and let $\pi_{s,1}$ be the first number in the first column that differs from $\pi_{1,1}$ and is not zero. Perform transformation (47) with $i_1 = 1$; $i_2 = s$; $j_1 = 1$; $j_2 = t$, and take the smaller of $\pi_{1,t}$ and $\pi_{s,1}$ as α. If the element $\pi_{1,1}$ was not equal to unity in the initial matrix $||\pi_{i,j}||$, then after the transformation, matrix $||\pi'_{i,j}||$ has one more zero in either the first row or the first column.

Repeat this operation until a matrix of the following type is obtained

$$||\pi^2_{i,j}|| = \begin{Vmatrix} 1 & 0 & 0 & \ldots & 0 \\ 0 & \pi^2_{2,2} & \pi^2_{2,3} & \ldots & \pi^2_{2,n} \\ 0 & \pi^2_{2,3} & \pi^2_{3,3} & \ldots & \pi^2_{3,n} \\ \cdots\cdots\cdots\cdots\cdots \\ 0 & \pi^2_{n,2} & \pi^2_{n,3} & \ldots & \pi^2_{n,n} \end{Vmatrix}$$

No more than $2n$ to 3 operations will be needed to accomplish this. Since the relationship (48) is obeyed during each transformation,

$$f'(\boldsymbol{p}, ||\pi_{i,j}||) \geqslant f'(\boldsymbol{p}, ||\pi^2_{i,j}||).$$

Repeat the same operation with the second row and column, etc., until the unique matrix $||\pi^n_{i,j}||$ is obtained. Evidently,

$$f'(\boldsymbol{p}, ||\pi_{i,j}||) \geqslant f'(\boldsymbol{p}, ||\pi^n_{i,j}||). \tag{49}$$

But $f'(p, ||\pi_{i,j}^n||)$ coincides with the problem A difficulty function $f(p, ||\pi_{i,j}^n||)$, which corresponds to an algorithm that tries answer A_i with probability one on the first step, answer A_2 with probability one on the second step, etc. (Note that $p_i \geqslant p_2 \geqslant, \ldots, \geqslant p_n$.) Comparing (49), (46), and (44) we obtain

$$T(A) \geqslant f(p, ||\pi_{i,j}^n||) = \sum_i p_i F(i), \tag{50}$$

and the theorem is proved.

Since the logarithm is a convex function, this theorem is valid for it. From this follows the optimal property of the logarithmic function with a rigid sorting rule used in Chapter 7, Section 6.

The above theorem has one important consequence, namely, for all convex value functions of difficulty, one and the same decoding algorithm is optimal, and it is identical with the decoding algorithm optimal for indeterminacy. Therefore, if, for example, the value of difficulty is represented by the number of trials (not the logarithm of the number of trials), then violation of inequality (21) still signifies that the decoding algorithm selected on the basis of that value could be improved (because the linear function is convex).

In Appendix 1, the concept of an optimal hypothesis for a set of problems was discussed (for algorithms without feedback). It could also be applied to nonlogarithmic functions of difficulty value. The problem is more complex due to the concept of a hypothesis containing only the truth. In expression (29), there is also the entropy of the hypothesis distribution, in addition to indeterminacy. What is the analog of entropy in the case of other value functions of difficulty?

Let $F(x)$ be the value function of difficulty. Designate by $H^F(p)$ the minimum difficulty of the problem A for a solution algorithm without feedback. It is self-evident that the function H^F, with respect to the difficulty function at hand, plays the same role as entropy with respect to indeterminacy. In particular, the hyperplane tangent at point t to the surface with equation $y = H^F(q)$ expresses the problem difficulty in the case of hypothesis t (see Fig. 54).

Therefore, substituting $H^F(q)$ for $H(q)$ in (29) and (30) does not invalidate the theorem regarding the identity of the optimal hypothesis with the strongest hypothesis containing "only the truth."

For example, N. D. Newberg succeeded in proving that $H^F(p) = \left(\sum_i \sqrt{p_i}\right)^2$ for the linear value function of difficulty.

Using this expression instead of entropy, we can still speak about hypotheses containing "only the truth" when evaluation is made according to the average number of trials, and not according to indeterminacy.

APPENDIX 3

Problems for the Recognition Program

Several times in this book we have considered interesting and non-interesting sets of problems. Presented below are some sets of geometric problems of current interest for pattern recognition. The reader himself will be the recognition system in dealing with these problems. Instead of formal definitions, the reader is given 100 examples of problems making up the sets. The author hopes that readers will be able to design similar sets after training on these problems.

Each problem is represented by 12 patterns (6 figures in each class). Answers to these problems are given at the end of the book, i.e., a definition of classes for all 100 problems.

The reader will no doubt notice that some words (for example, *triangle*, *angle*, *part*, *inside*, *line*, etc.) assume different meanings in the answers to various problems. Here lies a serious difficulty for any recognition program designed for a given set of problems. The program should be very flexible, and while adapting to numerous situations should use its dictionary (its set of elementary operators) nonmechanically.

This set of problems can be used to test those recognition programs designed to imitate more complex thinking processes.

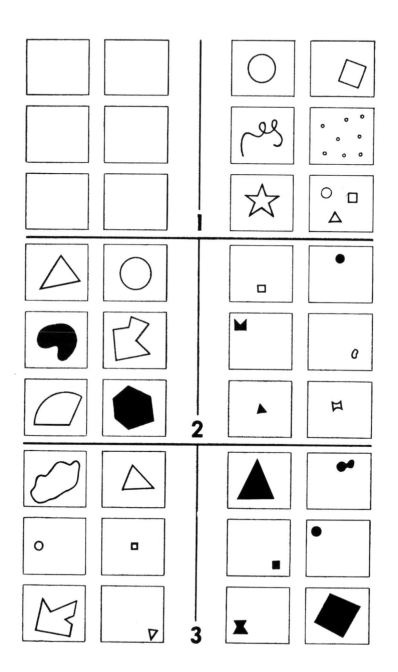

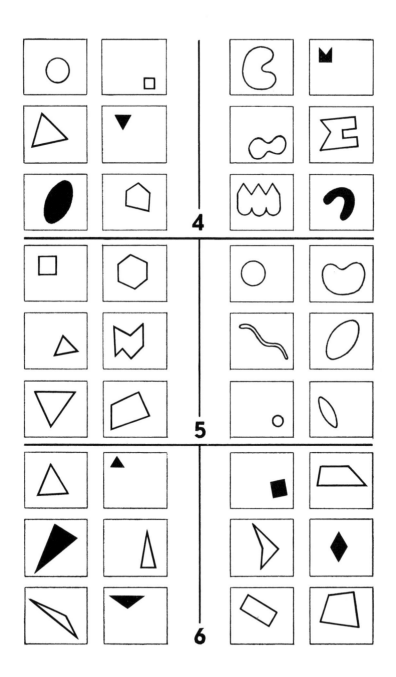

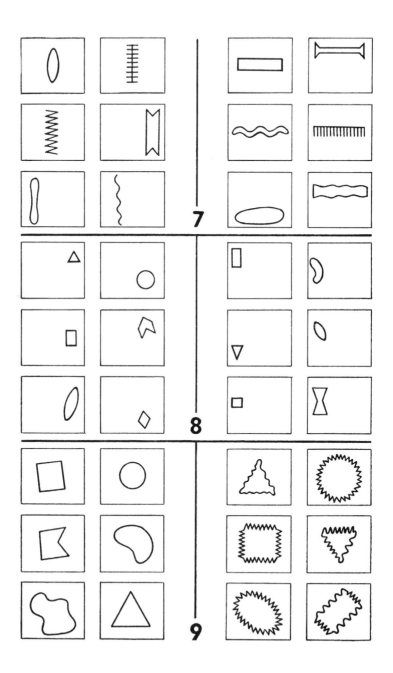

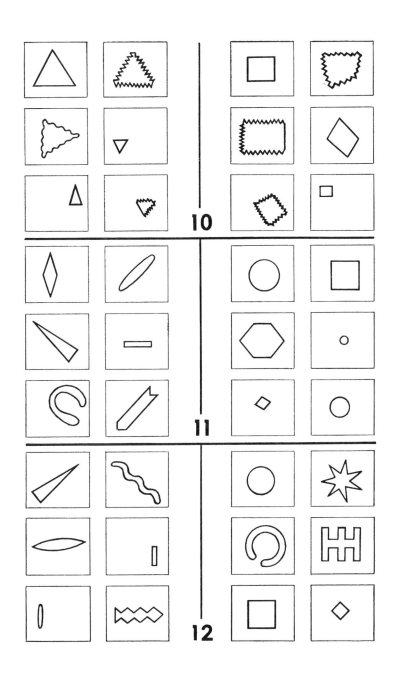

10

11

12

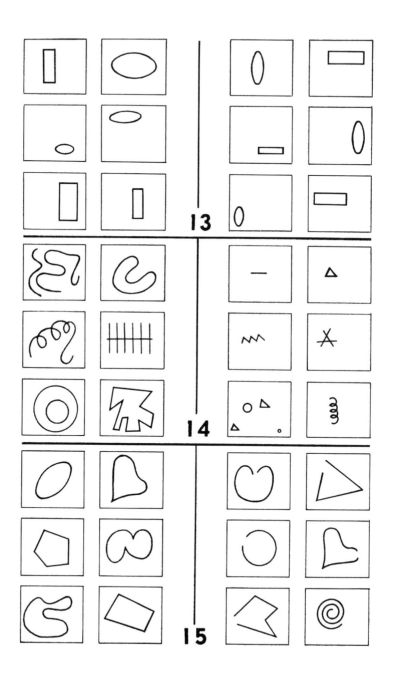

13

14

15

16

17

18

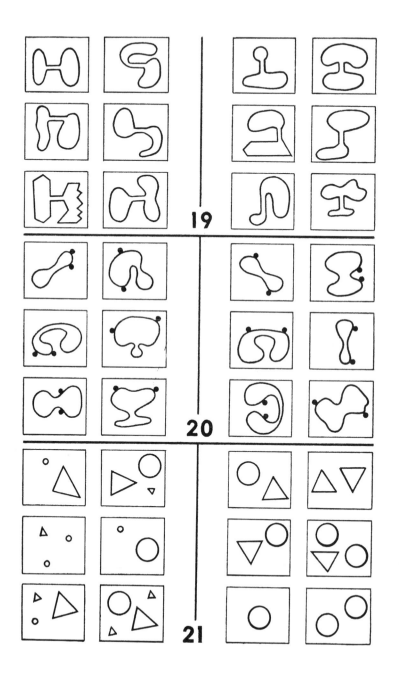

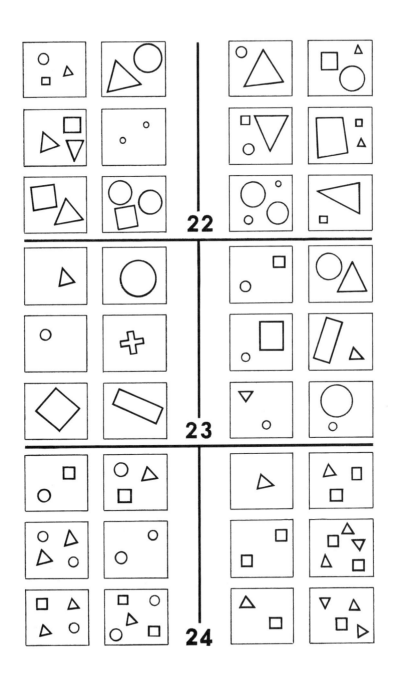

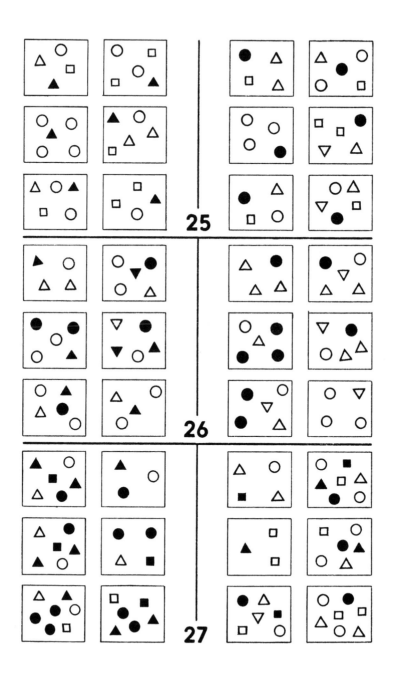

25

26

27

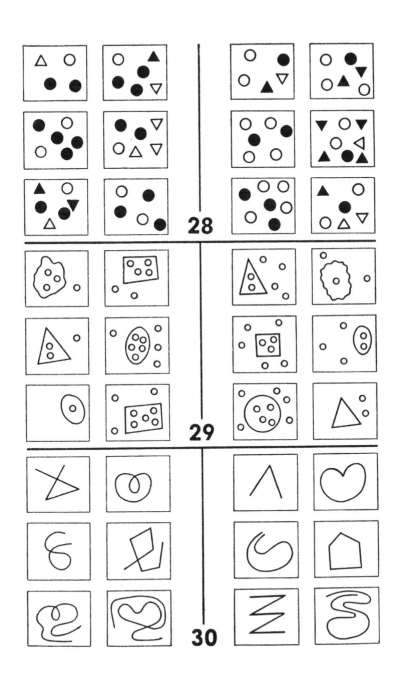

28

29

30

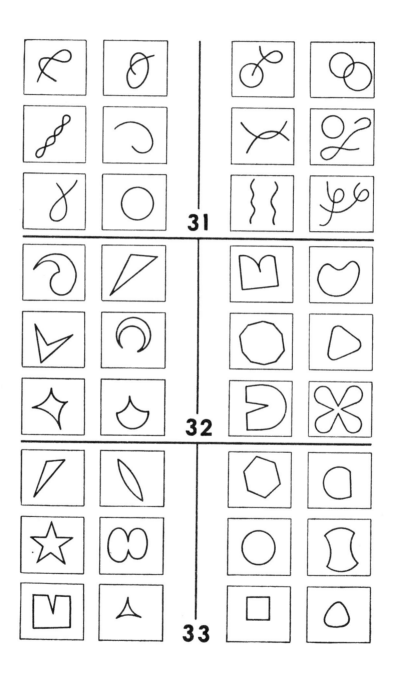

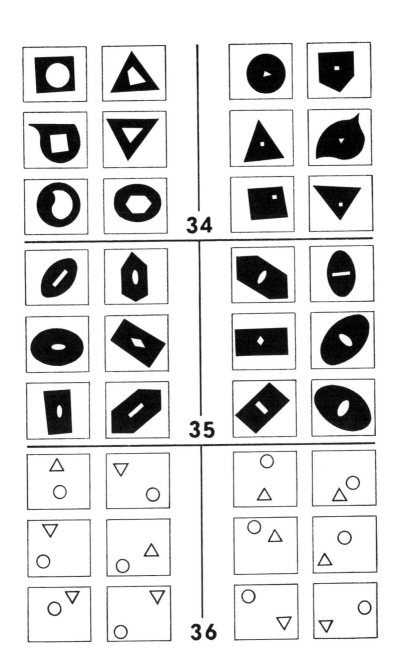

34

35

36

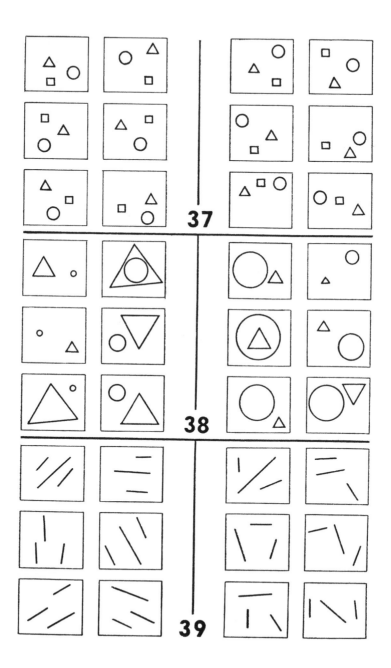

37

38

39

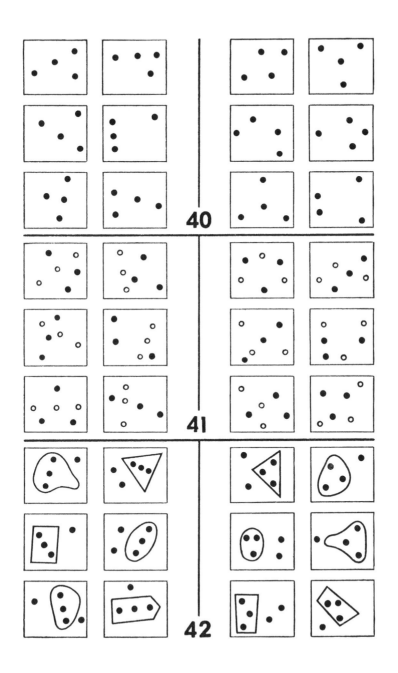

40

41

42

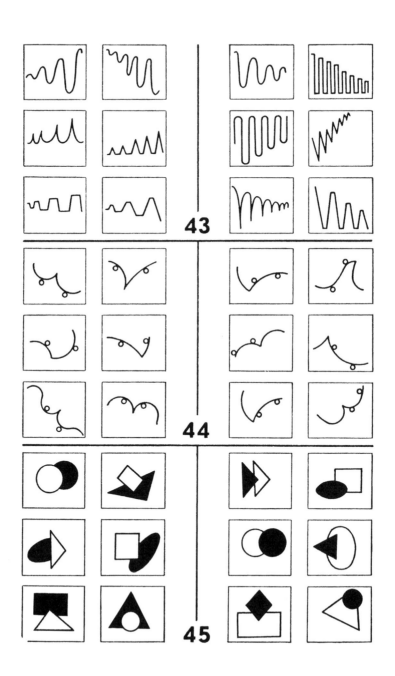

43

44

45

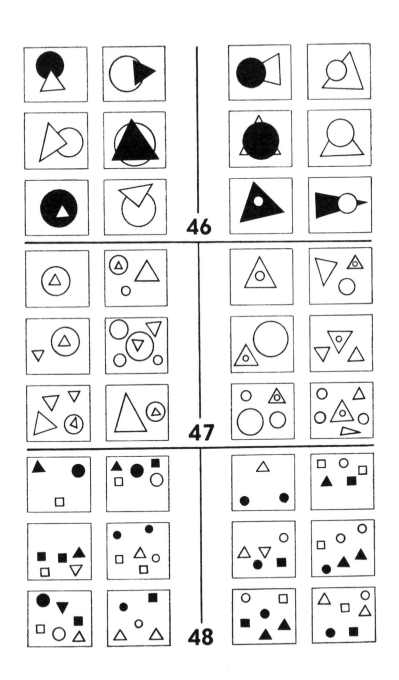

46

47

48

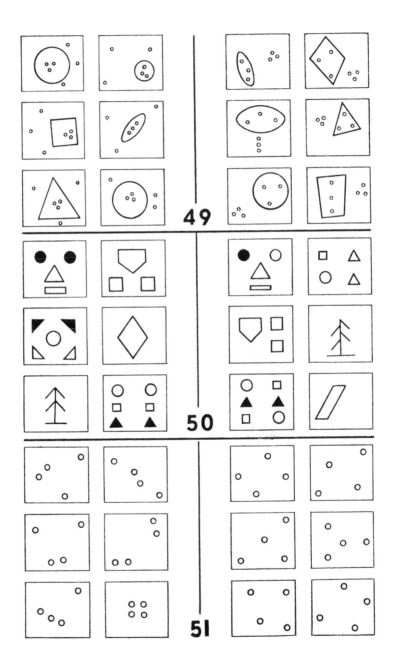

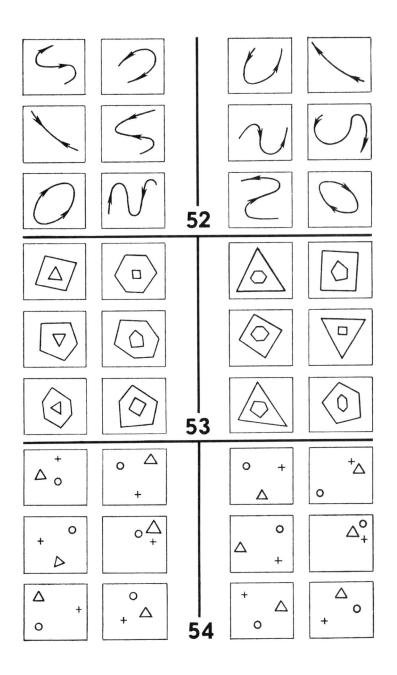

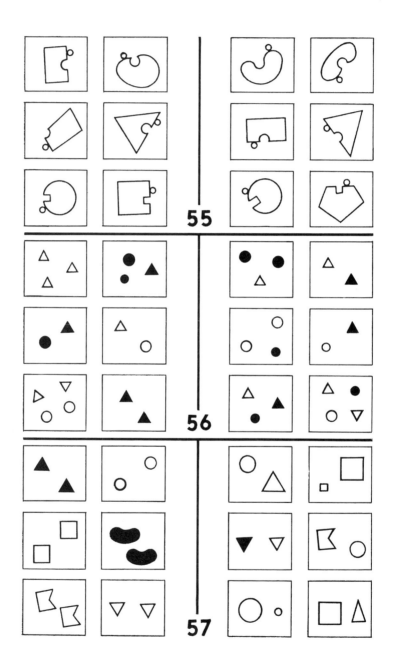

55

56

57

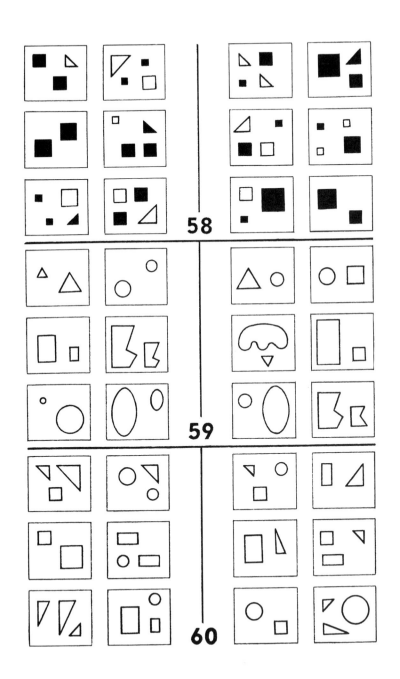

58

59

60

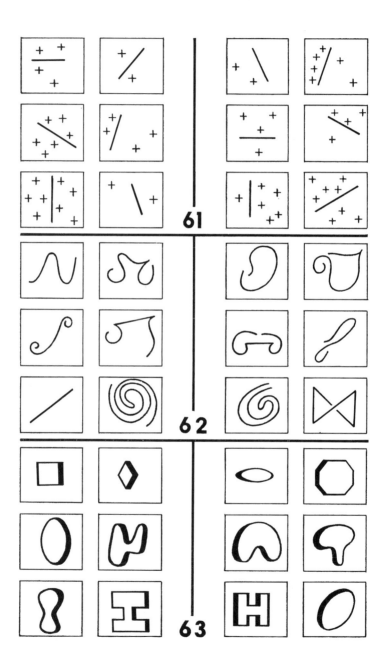

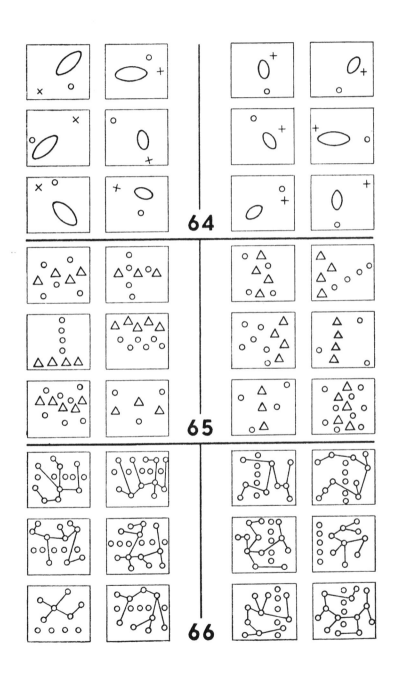

64

65

66

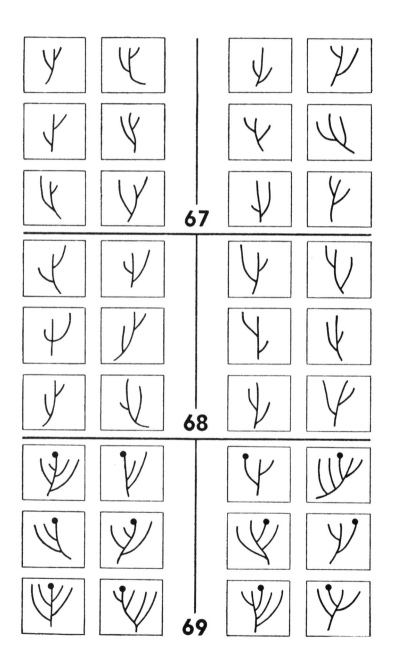

67

68

69

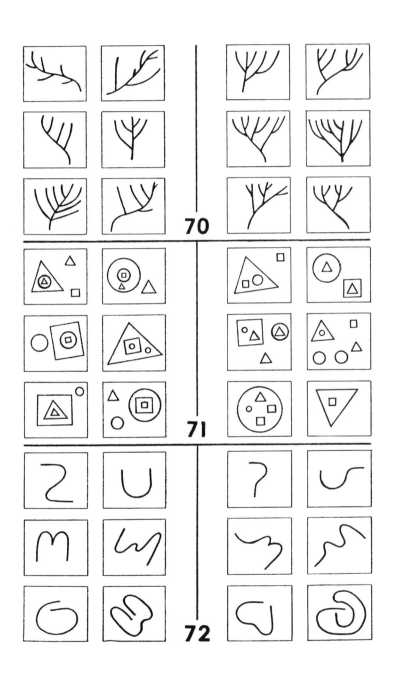

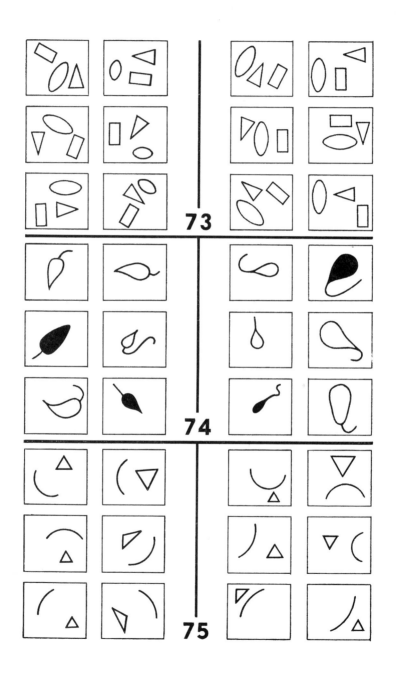

73

74

75

76

77

78

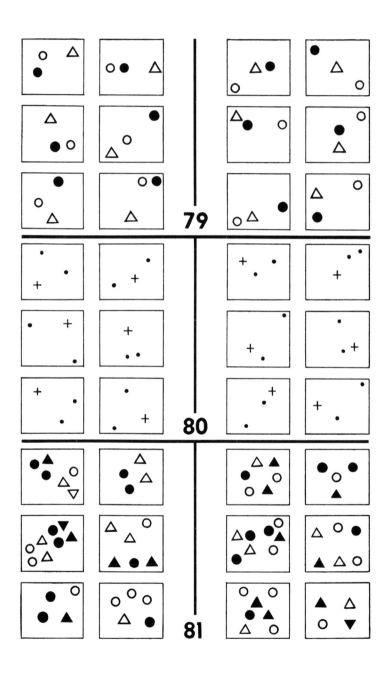

79

80

81

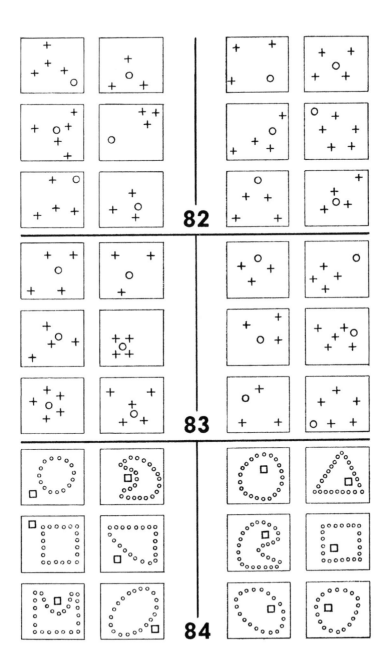

82

83

84

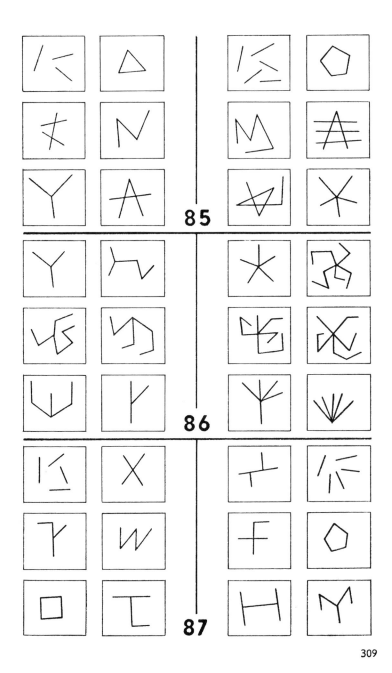

85

86

87

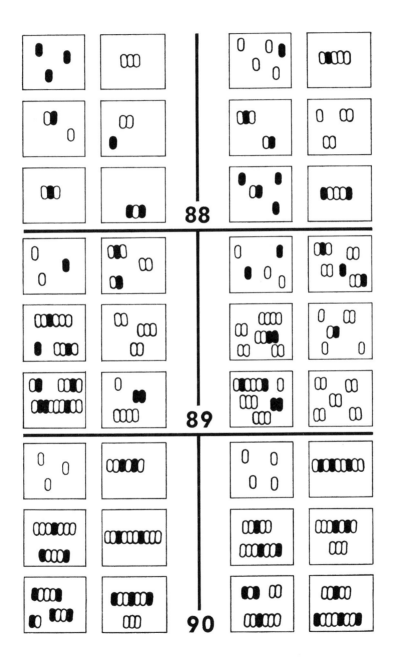

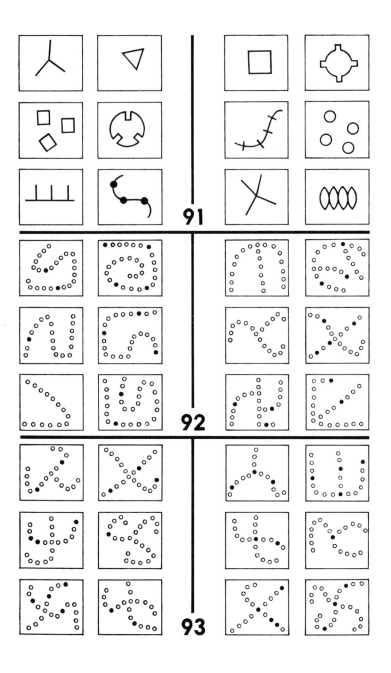

91

92

93

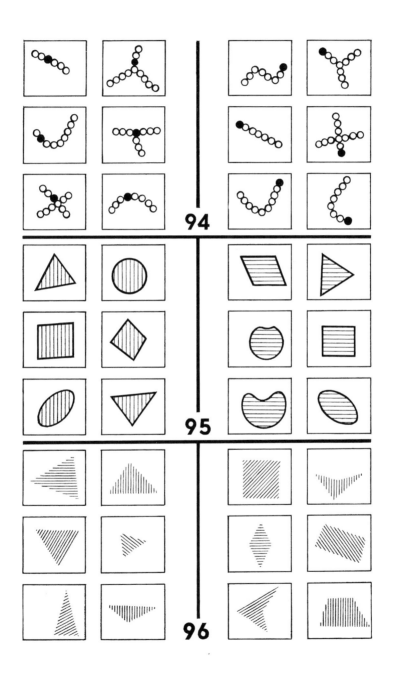

94

95

96

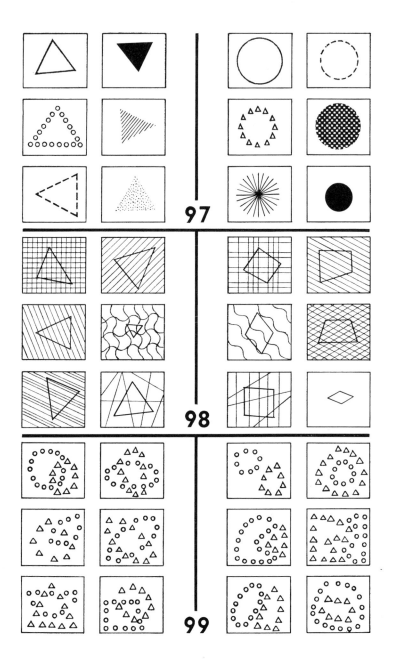

97

98

99

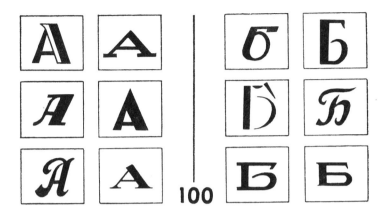

ANSWERS

1. Empty picture	Not empty picture
2. Large figures	Small figures
3. Outline figures	Solid figures
4. Convex figures	Nonconvex figures
5. Polygons	Curvilinear figures
6. Triangles	Quadrangles
7. Figures elongated vertically	Figures elongated horizontally
8. Figures on the right side	Figures on the left side
9. Smooth contour figures	Twisting contour figures
10. Triangles	Quadrangles
11. Elongated figures	Compact figures
12. Convex figure shell elongated	Convex figure shell compact
13. Vertical rectangles and horizontal ellipses	Vertical ellipses and horizontal rectangles
14. Large total line length	Small total line length
15. Closed lines	Nonclosed lines
16. Spiral curls left	Spiral curls right
17. An acute angle directed inward	No angle directed inward
18. A neck	No neck
19. Neck horizontal	Neck vertical
20. Points located on one side of the neck	Points located on both sides of the neck
21. Small figure present	No small figure present
22. Areas of figures approximately equal	Areas of figures differ greatly
23. One figure	Two figures
24. A circle	No circle
25. Black figure is a triangle	Black figure is a circle
26. Solid black triangle	No solid black triangle
27. More solid black figures	More outline figures
28. More solid black circles	More outline circles
29. There are more small circles inside the figure outline than outside	There are fewer small circles inside the figure outline than outside
30. A line with a self-crossing	A line without a self-crossing
31. One line	Two lines
32. A sharp projection	No sharp projection
33. Acute angle	No acute angle
34. A large hole	A small hole
35. The axis of the hole is parallel to the figure axis	The axis of the hole is perpendicular to the figure axis

36. Triangle above circle | Circle above triangle
37. Triangle above circle | Circle above triangle
38. Triangle larger than circle | Triangle smaller than circle
39. Segments almost parallel to each other | Large angles between segments
40. Three points on a straight line | No three points on a straight line
41. Outline circles on one straight line | Outline circles not on one straight line
42. Points inside the figure outline are on a straight line | Points inside the figure outline are not on a straight line
43. The vibration amplitude increases from left to right | The vibration amplitude decreases from left to right
44. Small circles on different arcs | Small circles on one arc
45. Outline figure on top of solid black figure | Black figure on top of outline figure
46. Triangle on top of the circle | Circle on top of the triangle
47. Triangle inside of the circle | Circle inside of the triangle
48. Solid dark figures above the outline figures | Outline figures above the solid dark figures
49. Points inside the figure outline are grouped more densely than outside the contour | Points outside the figure contour are grouped more densely than inside the contour
50. Axes of symmetry | No axes of symmetry
51. Two circles close to each other | No two circles close to each other
52. Arrows pointing in different directions | Arrows pointing in the same direction
53. Inside figure has fewer angles than outside figure | Inside figure has more angles than outside figure
54. A cross, circle, and triangle arranged clockwise | Arrangement counterclockwise
55. A circle is at the left of the cavity if you look from inside the figure | A circle is at the right of the cavity if you look from inside the figure
56. All figures of the same color | Figures of different colors
57. Identical figures | Figures not identical
58. Solid dark quadrangles are identical | Solid dark quadrangles are different
59. Figures are similar | Figures are not similar
60. Some similar figures | No similar figures
61. A line separates the crosses in half | A line does not separate the crosses in half

62. Ends of the curve are far apart | Ends of the curve are close together
63. Shading thicker on the right side | Shading thicker on the left side
64. A cross is located on the extension of the ellipse axis | A circle is located on the extension of the ellipse axis
65. A set of triangles elongated horizontally | A set of triangles elongated vertically
66. Unconnected circles on a horizontal line | Unconnected circles on a vertical line
67. The right branch begins at a higher point than the left branch | The right branch begins at a lower point than the left branch
68. The end of the right branch is higher than that of the left branch | The end of the right branch is lower than that of the left branch
69. Large black dot on the main branch | Large black dot on a side branch
70. There are no side branches of the second order | There are side branches of the second order
71. There are inside figures of the second order | There are no inside figures of the second order
72. Ends of the curve are parallel | Ends of the curve are perpendicular
73. The long axes of the ellipse and rectangle are perpendicular | The long axes of the ellipse and rectangle are parallel
74. A tail grows from the obtuse end | A tail grows from the acute end
75. Triangle located at the concave side of an arc | Triangle located at the convex side of an arc
76. Long sides concave | Long sides convex
77. Angle divided in half | Angle not divided in half
78. Extensions of segments cross at one point | Extensions of segments do not cross at one point
79. A dark circle is closer to the outline circle than to the triangle | A dark circle is closer to the triangle than to the outline circle

80. Points located at the same distances from a cross

Points located at different distances from a cross

81. Dark figures can be divided from outline figures by a straight line

Dark figures are impossible to separate from outline figures by a straight line

82. A shell stretched around the crosses forms an equilateral triangle

A shell stretched around the crosses does not form an equilateral triangle

83. A circle is inside of a figure made by crosses

A circle is outside of a figure made by crosses

84. A quadrangle is outside of a figure made by circles

A quadrangle is inside of a figure made by circles

85. Three parts

Five parts

86. Three parts

Five parts

87. Four parts

Five parts

88. Three parts

Five parts

89. Three parts

Five parts

90. Three parts

Four parts

91. Three identical elements

Four identical elements

92. The chain does not branch

The chain branches

93. Branches at outline circle

Branches at solid dark circle

94. Solid dark circle at center

Solid dark circle at end

95. Vertical hatched lines

Horizontal hatched lines

96. Triangles

Quadrangles

97. Triangles

Circles

98. Triangles

Quadrangles

99. Outlines made by triangles and circles intersect

Outlines made by triangles and circles do not intersect

100. The letter *a*

The letter *b*

INDEX